THE AMERICAN BAR

GUIDE
TO
CREDIT
AND
BANKRUPTCY

Everything You Need to Know About
Credit Repair, Staying or **Getting Out of Debt,**
and **Personal Bankruptcy**

RANDOM HOUSE REFERENCE
NEW YORK   TORONTO   LONDON   SYDNEY   AUCKLAND

Copyright © 2009 by the American Bar Association

All rights reserved. Published in the United States by Random House Reference, an imprint of The Random House Information Group, a division of Random House, Inc., New York, and in Canada by Random House of Canada Limited, Toronto.

RANDOM HOUSE is a registered trademark of Random House, Inc.

This is a revised and updated work based on The American Bar Association Guide to Credit & Bankruptcy, published by Random House in trade paperback in 2006.

Please address inquiries about electronic licensing of any products for use on a network, in software, or on CD-ROM to the Subsidiary Rights Department, Random House Information Group, fax 212–572–6003.

This book is available at special discounts for bulk purchases for sales promotions or premiums. Special editions, including personalized covers, excerpts of existing books, and corporate imprints, can be created in large quantities for special needs. For more information, write to Random House, Inc., Special Markets/Premium Sales, 1745 Broadway, MD 6–2, New York, NY, 10019 or e-mail specialmarkets@randomhouse.com.

Visit the Random House Reference Web site: www.randomwords.com

Library of Congress Cataloging-in-Publication Data

The American Bar Association guide to credit & bankruptcy : everything you need to know about credit repair, staying or getting out of debt, and personal bankruptcy.—2nd ed.
p. cm.
Includes index.
1. Consumer credit—Law and legislation—United States—Popular works.
2. Credit cards—Law and legislation—United States—Popular works. 3. Bankruptcy—United States—Popular works. 4. Debt relief—Popular works. I. Title: Guide to credit and bankruptcy. II. Title: Credit and bankruptcy.
KF1524.85.A46 2009
346.7307'7—dc22
2009016760

ISBN: 978-0-375-72300-1

Printed in the United States of America

10 9 8 7 6 5 4 3 2 1

Second Edition

AMERICAN BAR ASSOCIATION

Gregory S. Mager
Port Washington, Wisconsin

Marc S. Stern
Seattle, Washington

Bruce Menkes
Chicago, Illinois

Michael C. Tomkies
Columbus, Ohio

Frederick H. Miller
Oklahoma City, Oklahoma

Lorraine E. Waller
Silver Spring, Maryland

Robert Sohns
Houston, Texas

Robin K. Warren
Charlotte, North Carolina

Shayna M. Steinfeld
Atlanta, Georgia

Elizabeth Yen
New Haven, Connecticut

TABLE OF CONTENTS

FOREWORD

Henry F. White, Jr., *Executive Director*
American Bar Association

As more Americans face increasingly tough financial times, understanding money and credit has never been more important. More and more of us have credit card debt, car loans, home equity loans, and other forms of consumer debt—and this debt load has grown dramatically. Meanwhile, consumer bankruptcies are also surging. The number of personal bankruptcies is approaching two million per year—about six times as many as in 1980, and twice as many as in 1995.

Americans are deeply concerned about their credit scores, their credit reports, their privacy in credit transactions, their ability to obtain credit, and dozens of other credit-related issues. U.S. laws are rapidly evolving to address these and other credit-related issues, such as identity theft and predatory lending. At the same time, bankruptcy law is also undergoing major changes as state legislatures and Congress struggle to find the appropriate balance between creditors and debtors. The Bankruptcy Abuse Prevention and Consumer Protection Act of 2005 alone represents the greatest change in bankruptcy law in almost 30 years.

Now, with the help of American Bar Association experts from all over the country, the ABA Legal Guide to Credit and Bankruptcy is here to provide reliable, unbiased information about the new legal regime and how it affects you. Thanks to all the lawyers who worked on this book, as well as the ABA's Standing Committee on Public Education and its excellent staff, you can be sure that the information included in the following pages is:

- accurate,
- helpful,
- even-handed,
- current,

- written in a reader-friendly style that you can understand easily, and
- reflects a national picture, since ABA members practice in all jurisdictions.

Public education and public service are two important goals of the American Bar Association. The American Bar Association is the largest voluntary association in the world. Besides its commitment to public education, the ABA provides programs to assist lawyers and judges in their work, and initiatives to improve the legal system for the public, including promoting fast, affordable alternatives to lawsuits, such as mediation, arbitration, conciliation, and small claims courts. Through ABA support for lawyer referral programs and pro bono services (where lawyers donate their time), people like you can find the best lawyer for their particular case and receive quality legal help within their budgets.

Henry F. White, Jr., a retired Rear Admiral in the U.S. Navy Reserve, is the Executive Director of the American Bar Association. He practiced law for over thirty years in the private, corporate, and public sectors and served as an arbitrator for maritime disputes.

INTRODUCTION

Dwight L. Smith, *Chair*
ABA *Standing Committee on Public Education*

"**W**e've never had so many who owed so much," declares an economist with Standard & Poor's. About 150 million Americans have credit cards, including many college and high school students. This is nearly an 80 percent increase in just 15 years. And, in that same period, the amount of money charged to credit cards increased by almost 350 percent. Monthly credit card balances are now about three times greater than they were in 1990—and that doesn't take into account mortgage debt, student loans, and automobile loans.

Instances of foreclosures and vehicle repossessions are up, as are credit card delinquencies and missed payments. And the number of bankruptcies continues to soar. In these constantly shifting economic times, many families are facing financial realities they never imagined possible.

The book you are about to read walks you through your rights and responsibilities under current bankruptcy and credit laws and explains the many options they provide. For example, this book shows how legal protections can help you:

- Apply for credit;
- Select the best credit card for your needs;
- Find the best interest rates;
- Check your credit score and credit records—and make corrections if there are errors;
- Avoid identity theft;
- Evaluate home equity loans;
- Report unfair lending;
- Avoid the dangers of predatory lending;
- Understand auto financing options;
- Deal with debt collectors.

These above-listed situations involve federal and/or state laws, regulatory agencies, courts, and a variety of choices. This book will help you understand the options that are available to you if you're being crushed by a mountain of debt, or if you are afraid that a molehill will soon become a mountain. These can range from reliable debt counseling to debt consolidation, or even bankruptcy. And if you have made the decision to declare bankruptcy, we will tell you how the law affects your bankruptcy options and what steps are required to successfully begin and complete the bankruptcy process. We will help you understand what courses of action might best fit your circumstances—and, importantly, how to recognize when you need to consult an attorney.

You won't find legal jargon or technicalities here—just concise, straightforward discussions, with examples drawn from real life, and lots of answers to practical questions from our panel of legal experts.

The principal author of both the original edition and this updated edition is David Hudson, a lawyer, writer, and teacher who has written on a wide range of subjects for the public. His manuscript was reviewed and approved by experts on credit and bankruptcy from all over the country. The entire project was undertaken with the guidance of the ABA's Standing Committee on Public Education.

Together, we've worked to provide you with easy-to-read information that will help you understand and use the law that guides the whole credit and bankruptcy process. Our goal is to help you spot and address problems before they overtake your financial situation—when they're easiest to handle.

HOW TO USE THIS BOOK

We've structured this book chronologically, from topics that affect us all (such as understanding credit and how to apply for it) to important topics that deal with special circumstances such as Internet credit, identity theft, unfair lending, and home equity loans.

Similarly, we begin our consideration of bankruptcy with problem debt and some options for dealing with it. We go on to take a closer look at bankruptcy, including the pros and cons of each type of consumer bankruptcy.

WRITTEN WITH YOU IN MIND

We've made a special effort to make this book practical, by using situations and problems you are likely to encounter. Each chapter is clearly laid out and opens with a real-life situation that shows the practical ramifications of the subject.

Within chapters, brief sidebars alert you to important points. Sidebars highlight:
- practical tips that could be of benefit to you;
- key additional information;
- warnings about a potential pitfall that you can navigate with the right information and help; and
- clear, plain English definitions to legal terms.

Another feature—ask a lawyer—highlights our experts responding to practical questions, providing information that may help you as you grapple with similar issues within your own family. Each chapter concludes with a special section—"Remember This"—which highlights the most important points that the chapter has covered.

New to this edition is a single appendix, "The World at Your Fingertips," in which we direct you where to go for more information if you'd like to explore a topic further—usually to free or inexpensive materials that will fill your mind without emptying your wallet. This edition compiles all of these resources into one location, making your additional research easier and less time-consuming.

With this book, you'll be able to make informed decisions about a wide range of credit issues and opportunities. Should your situation get to the point where you need legal help, this book will not only help you recognize when you have reached that point, but it will also show you how to find an attorney and how to work with him or her once you have. By understanding the issues and options before turning to your attorney, you will be a better educated client and better able to help your attorney identify the correct path for you. Armed with the knowledge and insights we provide, you can be confident that the decisions you make will be in your best interests.

Dwight L. Smith is chair of the ABA's Standing Committee on Public Education and is an attorney in private practice in Tulsa, Oklahoma. His practice focuses on the areas of general business, commercial litigation, dispute resolution, banking, and probate.

PART I

Consumer Credit

CHAPTER 1

Dealing with Debt

Tips on How to Get Control of Your Finances

Every month, you notice that your bills get larger and your disposable income gets smaller. You send the minimum required payments to your credit card companies, but are not making any headway with your debts. You were late making one payment, and now you think your credit card rate has jumped. You don't really know where your money is going; you just know that it's not in your checkbook.

This type of scenario is all too familiar to millions of Americans. To avoid it, you must learn to budget and come to terms with your financial limits and responsibilities. Many people exacerbate their financial situations by living beyond their means. It is essential that you take control of your finances—or at least accurately assess your financial state.

There are many costs associated with debt, aside from the financial cost of the debt itself. As will be discussed in chapter 7, your creditors will report your credit-related delinquencies to credit bureaus. As a result, you may have trouble getting more credit or maintaining the current lines of credit on your credit cards. Some cards may be canceled, or not renewed on their renewal dates. If you are already overindebted, having fewer credit cards may not be entirely bad. But when you really need a good credit record to rent an apartment, get a home mortgage loan, or get a new job, having a bad or even weak credit report can hurt.

Also, as you will see in chapter 13, debt may make you the target of collection efforts from your creditors and ultimately from professional collection agencies. These institutions naturally want to recover the money that you owe. They'll probably write and telephone you frequently.

Finally, debt raises the ultimate possibility of bankruptcy, which is discussed in Part II of this book. Regardless of what you might have heard, bankruptcy is not a pleasant experience. Bankruptcy stays on your credit record for up to ten years and can handicap your access to various forms of credit for much of that period of time. Moreover, in 2005, Congress passed amendments to the bankruptcy law that are thought to make it more difficult to successfully complete the bankruptcy process.

HOW MUCH DEBT CAN YOU HANDLE?

As a rough guideline, one long-standing rule is that if your monthly payments on debts, excluding your home mortgage payment, exceed 20 percent of your after-tax or take-home income (or 30 percent of your pretax income), you have most likely reached your debt limit. Since less than 3 percent of American families spend 30 percent or more of their gross income on debt payments (excluding home mortgage payments), you can see that relatively few families permit their debt burdens to reach or exceed their debt limits. As a rough guideline, your monthly payments on housing-related expenses, including your home mortgage payment, property taxes, home insurance, flood insurance, homeowner's association dues, and similar housing-related expenses should not exceed 38 percent of your pretax income.

With respect to debt, there are several reliable signs of danger. You might be in more debt than you can handle if you:

• can only afford to make minimum monthly payments on your credit card accounts;

• have to use credit for expenditures for which you once paid cash;

• have used a series of consolidation loans, home equity loans, or other types of loans to pay overdue bills;

• are borrowing from one creditor to pay another—for example, taking a cash advance on your credit card to pay amounts owed to other banks or retailers;

- begin to run a few days late on critical payments, such as your rent or mortgage payment, or are consistently late with all your bill payments so that late fees are piling up; or
- dip into savings for normal living expenses.

RESPONSE TO DEBT DANGER SIGNS

If you recognize that any of these danger signs apply to you and your family, you need to take action. The worst thing you can do is nothing. If you fail to change your spending habits and fall deeper into debt, bill collectors will beset you, and you will find your options limited. You might even be forced into bankruptcy.

The first step toward taking control is slowing down your use of credit. If you are going shopping, take only the one credit card that you will need, or try using cash instead of credit cards. Cut up excess credit cards and return them to your creditors, asking them to notify the credit bureaus that you have closed the accounts; it is important that your credit report reflect that each account was closed at your request, and not at the demand of creditors. You may also try contacting some of your creditors and asking for reduced rates. Some creditors may agree to lower your rates if you make timely payments for six consecutive months. Lower credit limits and account balances may help reduce your overall use of credit. If lower credit limits and account balances are combined with lower interest rates, you may also be able to make payments that are slightly higher than required each month, thereby allowing you to pay down what you owe on your accounts faster.

DEVELOPING A BUDGET

Next, find out where your money is going by keeping track of household purchases for two weeks. Make a note of all your expenditures. This may sound burdensome or even trivial, but it really works. For example, if you start the day with $30 in cash and end it with only $5, make a note of where you spent the missing $25. In addition to recording your cash expenditures, make note of all credit purchases made during the same two-week period. When the two weeks are up, examine your expenditures, and hold a household or family conference to discuss how those expenditures can best be reduced. Now is the time to begin educating teenagers, and even younger children, about the value of money.

Above all, you must learn to live within your means. In other words, you must stop spending more than you can afford. Many people spend money—often through the overuse of credit cards—without really thinking about it; spending comes naturally in our culture of immediate gratification. But, as this book demonstrates, there is a steep price to be paid for living beyond one's means. Developing—and sticking to—a budget can help you stay on track.

There are many different types of budgets, but most people benefit from a monthly budget that carefully lists their income and bills for the month. When keeping a monthly budget, you should keep track of all your expenses, including food, housing, transportation, utilities, insurance, education, taxes, and clothing. Many of these expenses will be fixed, in the sense that you can anticipate the amounts you will owe each month before you actually owe them. For example, your rent or mortgage will likely be the same each month, as will your cable bill (unless you order pay-per-view events that increase the amount of your bill).

Once you have a good understanding of where your money is going, you may find it useful for your household or family to prepare a cash budget indicating the highest monthly payments you can afford to make on each of your debts. Such a budget might look something like this, though it can be as fancy or simple as you want:

Family Budget

A. Monthly Income:
    1. Your and your spouse's
       monthly take-home pay   _____
    2. Other income   _____

                Total monthly income: _____

B. Monthly Expenses:
    1. Food   _____
    2. Rent or mortgage payments   _____
    3. Utilities   _____
    4. Telephone   _____
    5. Transportation (gasoline,
       mass transit costs)   _____
    6. Regular Monthly Savings   _____
    7. Other Major Categories (itemize)   _____

                Total monthly expenses: _____

C. Annual Expenses:
    1. Taxes   _____
    2. Insurance (not paid monthly)   _____
    3. Medical and dental bills   _____
    4. School costs   _____
    5. Entertainment   _____
    6. Clothing   _____
    7. Other Major Categories (itemize)   _____

                Total annual expenses: _____

                Divided by 12:   _____

D. Monthly income available for payments on debts
   that are not listed above (add together B and C and
   then subtract that from A):   _____

E. Committed Income (i.e., income already committed to
   monthly loan payments):
    1. Personal loans   _____
    2. Extensions of credit to
       buy a car or truck   _____

                Total committed income: _____

F. Discretionary Income (D minus E):

Note that the above budget includes an "Annual Expenses" section (section C). It is important to allow for annual expenses in your budget; otherwise, you may be unprepared if a bill that you don't think about on a monthly basis, such as an insurance bill or a bill for real estate taxes, suddenly becomes due. Also, it is generally easier to decide on an annual budget for such categories as clothing and recreation, and then divide that annual total by twelve to determine your acceptable monthly outlays in each category. The trick is not to spend your annual budget in the first few months of the year; calculating acceptable monthly outlays may help you to achieve this. Each month, allot a certain amount of money for each expense—for example, allow yourself a set amount of money for dining out, a set amount of money for clothing, and so forth—and do your best not to exceed that amount.

Note that savings are budgeted as a monthly expense (in section B of the above budget). If you don't budget for savings, you won't save, and saving is important for two reasons. First, savings serve as an emergency fund in case someone is laid off or becomes ill, or in case of an unexpected major expense (such as needing to replace a major home appliance or car). The unfortunate rise in layoffs that started in 2008 helps demonstrate the importance of such emergency funds. A good rule of thumb is that an emergency fund in the form of savings or other readily accessible assets should equal three to five months of your household's after-tax income. Some experts say that the emergency fund should be even greater, but at least try to save three months' worth of expenses (taking into account expenses listed in sections B, C, D, and E of the above budget). Second, once you have set up an adequate emergency fund, savings can serve as a retirement fund (in conjunction with any retirement-savings programs you enjoy through your employer), a college tuition fund, or a fund for meeting other long-term goals that your household or family may have.

In the sample budget provided above, you may have wondered why the "Committed Income" section (section E) does not list credit card payments as one of its categories. The answer is that such payments are assumed to be included as part of your expenditures for clothes, entertainment, and whatever else you pay for using credit cards. If you are living within your budget, you should be able to make credit card payments using funds from the existing categories in your budget, so they won't require a separate line item. Many people of course cannot pay their credit card balance down to zero every month. Your budget may vary depending on the level of your credit card balances. If you have a large credit card balance, you may consider making credit card payments a budget item and pay as much above the minimum required payment as you feasibly can.

After examining their budgets, many families may find that the amount of money they have available each month to pay their debts is not sufficient. In the above budget, for example, the total from section D ("Monthly income available for payments on debts that are not listed above") might be less than the total from section E ("Committed Income"). If this is the case, income must be increased or expenditures must be reduced in order to free up money for paying monthly bills. For example, some families may consider cutting back on their cable bill or dining out less or eating at less expensive restaurants. Go back and examine your two-week record of cash outflows and see exactly where you can cut spending. Eliminate the costs of, say, going bowling once a week or pursuing some other hobby. Consider writing letters or emails rather than making long-distance calls. Adopt the industry approach of zero-based budgeting: Show a real need for any expenditure above zero. In addition to cutting household cash outflows, you may be able to improve household cash inflows. For example, a spouse or teenager might take a part-time job.

If you are not able to pay your monthly bills, you may want to approach one or more of your creditors and try to reduce or defer your monthly payments without having to pay a penalty. Simply be honest: Explain your cash flow problem and ask your creditors if they can help you get back on your feet. While there is no guarantee that creditors will agree to help you, the worst thing that you can do is to try to avoid them or make promises to pay that you don't keep. If self-help efforts don't do the job, you may want to contact a consumer credit counseling service that

TALKING TO A LAWYER

Q. Is it more important to make payments on secured loans than it is to pay off credit card debt?

A. Yes. When you incur secured debt, you pledge collateral—for example, your car or your house—in exchange for a loan. If you fail to make payments on secured debts, the creditor is entitled to take and sell the collateral you pledge—often for an amount that is much less than what you owe. This means that, in addition to paying off the balance of your loan, you'll also have to replace the collateral sold by the creditor.

—Answer by Mark S. Edelman, McGlinchy
Stafford, PLLC, Cleveland, Ohio

A. To the extent you have pledged important assets as collateral for secured loans, such as a primary car or primary residence, then you may want to give these loans priority in order to preserve these assets. However, each debtor's situation is unique. You will need to set priorities based on your own particular needs and circumstances and the particular options that may be available to you—for example, borrowing temporarily from relatives; selling nonessential items or assets such as a second car (where, for example, public transportation is a viable option); moving in with family, friends, or relatives; or finding a roommate or boarder with whom to share the living expenses. (This is where seeking professional advice may be of particular assistance to you in helping you sort out your priorities and looking at all your options.)

You may also want to think twice about not making the required payments on your credit card debt. Some credit agreements governing so-called nonessential loans, like credit cards, include onerous default terms. Such terms could impose high finance charges if you are delinquent with payments; others known as "cross-default provisions" may allow satisfaction of your credit card debt with collateral that you have offered to the same creditor for an entirely different loan. Such provisions can dramatically increase your interest payments, fees, and/or payment burdens or cause you to default under the terms of a secured loan, potentially placing your secured credit—and the assets securing that credit—at risk. In addition, carrying outstanding credit card balances that are at or near the available credit limit for the credit card account will also tend to reduce your credit score, and potentially make it harder (or more expensive) for you to obtain a new refinancing loan, or a new long distance or cell phone plan, for example.

In such a case, giving low priority to a seemingly nonessential loan may dramatically change your monthly obligations or inadvertently put a secured loan or asset at risk. You need to read the terms of each credit agreement carefully in order to make the best decision for your situation. You may be better served by trying to renegotiate credit terms or by asking for payment deferral or skip-a-payment options before missing a payment.

—Answer by Michael C. Tomkies, Dreher Tomkies
Scheider, LLP, Columbus, Ohio

can help you set up a new budget. You will want to show care in selecting an appropriate credit counselor. These services are discussed in chapter 14, Credit Counselors.

One obvious advantage of a budget is that you will learn, perhaps for the first time, where your money really goes every month. It takes discipline and practice, but developing a budget is a must for many people.

HOW THIS BOOK HELPS

The first part of this book provides an overview of consumer credit, explains certain important federal laws governing consumer credit, credit cards, credit reports, credit scoring, and discusses other important terms and conditions of common credit extensions. The second part of this book discusses the different types of bankruptcy and what the process of filing for bankruptcy entails.

As you read, however, remember that bankruptcy should be a debt management choice of last resort. Many consumers can turn their financial lives around by living within a budget and incorporating lifestyle changes that allow them to live within their means.

REMEMBER THIS

- If you can only afford to make minimum payments on your credit cards, you are headed for debt problems.
- There are several other danger signs with respect to debt. They include not knowing or not wanting to know your debts, constantly making late payments, postdating your checks to cover your debts, and juggling your bills.
- If you are having debt problems, slow down the use of credit if possible. Keep careful track of your finances and try to create a budget.

CHAPTER 2

Credit: What Is It and What Does It Cost?

How the Law Protects You

You've just finished college and are about to start your first real job. You have a healthy amount of student loan debt, so you don't have much disposable income. You can barely pay your rent. But you believe that you deserve the best, so you decide to purchase a new computer, a new car, and new furniture. The problem is that you don't have the cash to buy these items. You need to get credit. You apply for several credit cards and—presto!—your problems appear to be solved. Only later do you realize that you've mired yourself even deeper in debt, as the income from your job only allows you to make minimum payments on your credit cards. Now you want to purchase a home and live the American dream. You need more credit. Welcome to what one author years ago called the "credit jungle."

In his 1971 book *The Credit Jungle*, author Al Griffin warned that "[n]ot only is credit grossly oversold to a gullible public, but debt in too many cases has become a commodity in itself." This doesn't mean that credit is a bad thing. In fact, Griffin acknowledged the importance of credit to the American economy: "[i]f for any reason consumer credit were shut off at the close of work this afternoon, by tomorrow morning this country would be in a depression that would make the Great Depression of the 1930s look like a minor recession." Sadly, Griffin's words carry added weight given the recession and credit crisis that started in 2008. Indeed, credit remains a critical part of life in the United States in the twenty-first century. Unfortunately, many people are in a credit crunch and now find it difficult to obtain any more credit. We live in an age in which many people—to borrow the title from a recent film addressing the abuses of the credit card industry—are "Maxed Out." Reports abound of credit card companies increasing rates and decreasing credit limits in this time of economic uncertainty. In December 2008, federal regulators stepped in with new rules that will limit the circumstances in which credit card interest rates may increase on both existing balances and new charges, but those new rules are not scheduled to take effect until July 2010.

Make no mistake about it—credit is vital in our economy. If you want to finance your purchase of a new home or car, you need good credit. Only a very wealthy person can afford to buy a home by paying the entire purchase price in cash; when most people purchase homes, they must depend on credit. Similarly, many people who want to attend college can't afford to pay all of their tuition in cash. Most students have to borrow money. They need good credit to do so.

Credit, a word once commonly used to mean "credibility," involves trust. It refers to your ability and willingness to make payments when they are due. "Credit" also involves acquiring money for a certain price (known as interest or finance charge). An individual uses credit to buy goods and services now and pay for them later. For example, credit lets you purchase a car or a washing machine and use it before you have fully paid for it; you pay for it while you use it. Of course, you could save money now to buy the car in the future, but you may want or need the car now—not three years from now. Similarly, you may use your credit card now to buy a pair of shoes or a dinner that you will pay for later.

However, there are costs associated with an extension of credit. People do not generally give you money or sell you products on a deferred payment basis for free. When you obtain credit, you generally owe someone else a debt. A person who extends you credit is called a **creditor**. Creditors include, for example, banks, department stores and other retail sellers, credit card issuers, and finance companies. Sometimes creditors are called **credit grantors**. Recipients of credit are called **debtors** because they owe a debt to their creditors. For example, if you apply for and receive a Visa® credit card from a bank, and then charge $500 on the card, you now owe the credit card issuer $500 plus any related finance charges. You are indebted to the credit card issuer.

Unfortunately, in what *Credit Card Nation* author Robert D. Manning calls our "culture of consumption," many consumers do not realize the dangers of overextending their credit. Consider the following data cited by the Federal Trade Commission: In 1946, outstanding consumer credit in the United States was $55 billion. In 1970, that number had risen to $556 billion. In 2007, consumer credit in the United States had risen to an estimated $2.6 trillion. As Manning writes, the "ascendance of the consumer credit society" has become "one of the most profound social and cultural revolutions of the post-World War II era."

Too many consumers live by the credo "buy now, pay later" or, even more unfortunately, "buy now and pay much later—if at all." When you obtain credit and then fail to pay your bills on time, you can easily develop a poor credit history and your debts may continue to rise. For many consumers, such a cycle can cause them to become hopelessly mired in debts. This problematic cycle has been made worse by the economic problems that came to a head in 2008, including employment layoffs, wage freezes, and a tightening of the credit markets. Some individuals stuck in this cycle may eventually have to seek relief in the form of bankruptcy.

TYPES OF CREDIT

There are three basic types of consumer credit: (1) **noninstallment credit** (sometimes called thirty-day or charge account credit); (2) **installment credit**, or closed-end credit, which is credit that is scheduled to be repaid in multiple installments over a fixed period of time; and (3) **revolving**, or open-end, credit.

With noninstallment credit, consumers must pay their balances in full within a defined period, commonly thirty days. Payment in multiple installments is not permitted; rather, payment is due in one lump sum. Travel-and-entertainment cards, such as American Express® and Diners Club International® cards, typically operate this way, as do most charge accounts with local businesses, such as service providers like doctors and plumbers. Installment credit, also known as closed-end credit, requires a consumer to repay the amount owed in multiple installments, typically (but not always) of equal amounts and over a fixed period of time. Automobile credit and personal loans are common examples of this type of credit.

Finally, revolving (or open-end) credit is an arrangement in which the consumer has the option of drawing upon a preapproved line of credit and paying off the entire balance, paying

FORMS OF CREDIT

☰ Type of Credit	Basic Operation
Charge account (30-day) credit	Balances owed on such accounts usually require payment in full within thirty days. Such arrangements are not considered installment credit, since the debt is not scheduled to be repaid in two or more installments.
Installment (closed-end) credit	A consumer agrees to repay the amount owed in two or more installments (not necessarily equal in amount) over a definite period of time.
Revolving (open-end) credit	The consumer may draw on an open-end credit line from time to time, and then pay off the entire outstanding balance, pay only a specified minimum required payment, or pay some amount in between each month. This type of credit is replenishable. The consumer may use the credit, make a payment, and then use the credit again.

the minimum required monthly payment, or paying any other amount in between each month. This arrangement is called "revolving" credit because the consumer uses the credit, makes a payment, and then uses the credit again. Most common credit cards, such as MasterCard®, Visa®, and Discover®, as well as store credit cards, are examples of revolving credit. So are equity lines secured by a second mortgage on the house.

COSTS OF CREDIT

The first thing to understand about credit is that it is far from free and often costs consumers dearly. Simple common sense tells us that a creditor will not make money if it lends a debtor $500 and then, six months later, simply asks for its $500 back. The only way a creditor can make money is if it charges the debtor a fee for extending credit. That fee is a **finance charge**, sometimes called **interest**. Interest means that you will pay back more money than you initially borrowed on credit. Finance charges can sometimes be very high, since the creditor generally has more bargaining power than the borrower. As Proverbs 22:7 reminds us: "The rich rule over the poor, and the borrower is servant to the lender." Consumers should think carefully before obtaining credit with very high finance charges. The higher the interest rate, the more money a consumer will pay in the long run. More of the consumer's payments will cover interest instead of the principal amount borrowed. It's similar to when you finance a house with a small down payment. Many consumers take out thirty-year mortgage loans because it takes that long with the interest to pay off a very large amount of borrowed principal with smaller, more affordable installment payments. For the first several years of a typical installment loan, borrowers are primarily paying interest on borrowed principal—installment payments made in the first few years of a typical installment loan do not generally reduce the unpaid principal balance significantly. The longer the principal remains outstanding (unpaid), the longer interest accrues on that unpaid principal.

Finance charges are commonly stated in **annual percentage rates** (APRs). For a given installment loan transaction, for example, the finance charge is the total dollar amount that credit will cost over the scheduled term of the loan if all required payments are made on time. For a given credit card or other revolving (open-end) credit account, the total finance charge that has accrued during a monthly billing cycle on outstanding charges is generally shown on monthly billing statements. The APR is the cost of credit (finance charge) expressed as an annual rate. The amount of the APR will directly affect the finance charge, and vice versa. Generally, the higher an APR, the higher the finance charge. Only you can decide whether it is worth the cost of the applicable finance charge to have a car or other goods and services now, rather than later.

To buy now and pay later, you generally must pay finance charges. Creditors assess finance charges because they need to make money to cover their overhead costs and stay in business. Instead of lending money to a borrower, a creditor could invest that money and earn interest on the investment; finance charges help compensate the creditor for that lost interest. Finance charges also help cover certain risks of extending credit. For example, finance charges help creditors cover losses that may occur if some borrowers do not fully repay all of the principal they owe, or if repayment occurs only after creditors have paid others (such as collection agencies or lawyers) to help collect amounts owed on debts. Debtors with good credit history are generally eligible for lower APRs than debtors with poor credit histories, because debtors with good credit history present less risk of loss (nonpayment) to creditors.

Many states regulate by law the maximum amount you may be required to pay in finance charges and provide penalties if a creditor charges more than the maximums allowed by law. However, certain types of lenders and certain types of loans (including, for example, lenders that are banks, and certain types of mortgage loans) are presently largely exempt from such regulation and may be allowed to charge high interest rates. Some states also deliberately allow relatively unregulated competition among creditors to determine how much you pay for credit. In other words, credit costs may vary significantly from state to state, from lender to lender, and depending on the type of credit. You should shop for credit as carefully as you shop for the best deal on a car or television set. The federal Truth in Lending Act and similar state laws help you to do that.

LEGAL PROTECTIONS

The federal **Truth in Lending Act (TILA)**, which is part of the **Consumer Credit Protection Act of 1968**, requires creditors to disclose to consumers the important costs and conditions of consumer credit transactions, and certain additional information, up front. In other words, creditors in consumer transactions must tell consumers the applicable APR and how much will be due in finance charges. For TILA purposes, creditors include banks, department stores, credit card issuers, finance companies, and so-called payday lenders, certain check cashers, and pawn shops. However, note that a traditional check casher that simply cashes a check payable to the consumer for a fee would not be considered a "creditor" for TILA purposes. "Deferred presentment" check cashers, on the other hand, extend credit to consumers in return for postdated checks given to them by the consumer debtors—those are credit transactions for TILA purposes. The postdated check is used as a means of obtaining repayment of the credit extension at the maturity date of the credit extension—the creditor agrees to delay or defer presenting the postdated check for payment, unlike a "traditional" check cashing transaction where the check in question is immediately presented for payment. As a general matter, TILA does not apply to extensions of credit that will be used primarily for commercial purposes. TILA also does not apply to a consumer credit transaction where the amount financed (borrowed) is greater than $25,000 unless the transaction is secured either by real property or by personal property used as the consumer's primary residence.

As TILA states, its purposes are "to assure a meaningful disclosure of credit terms so that the consumer will be able to compare more readily the various credit terms available to him and avoid the uninformed use of credit, and to protect the consumer against inaccurate and unfair credit card practices." TILA is also a **remedial statute** (a law designed to remedy a perceived problem) that courts often interpret to the benefit of consumers.

Under TILA, before you sign an installment contract, a creditor must disclose several facts to you in writing (electronic disclosure may also be permitted), including the amount being financed or borrowed, the applicable monthly payment, the number and due dates of monthly payments to be made, late payment charges, prepayment penalties, the dollar amount of the applicable finance charge, and—most importantly—the Annual Percentage Rate or APR. The APR is an annual rate that relates the total finance charge payable over the scheduled term of the installment credit contract if all required payments are made on time to (1) the amount of credit that you receive; and (2) the length of time you have to repay it. Think of the APR as a price per pound—say, 20 cents per pound for potatoes. Whether you buy five pounds of potatoes for $1 or ten pounds for $2, in either case the rate is 20 cents per pound. However, the total cost of the potatoes in dollars will depend on the amount of potatoes you buy. When you buy credit instead of potatoes, you buy a certain amount of credit for a given number of months. The total dollar amount of your finance charge will depend upon how many dollars worth of credit you obtain initially, and for how many months you use those dollars.

TILA also regulates consumer credit advertising. For example, if an automobile ad advertises a low monthly payment (giving a specific dollar figure), it must also disclose other pertinent information, such as the APR. This required disclosure under TILA is useful, since knowing the APR can also help you in shopping for credit cards and other forms of open-end credit.

In 1988, the U.S. Congress added to the Consumer Credit Protection Act of 1968 by passing the **Fair Credit and Charge Card Disclosure Act of 1988**. This law requires credit card applications and solicitations to disclose the annual percentage rates, annual fees, finance charge grace periods (if any) for purchase transactions, and how purchase balances are figured for finance charge computation purposes. This law amended the Truth in Lending Act and provides important credit card protections for consumers. Take the example of *Rossman v. Fleet Bank (R.I.) National Association* (3rd. Cir. 2002). In that case, a credit card company sent a solicitation to a prospective consumer promising "no annual fee." The consumer relied on this information to obtain the card but, less than a year later, the credit card company imposed an annual fee anyway, by sending the consumer a notice of a change to the terms of the consumer's credit card agreement. The consumer sued, alleging a violation of TILA. The credit card company defended itself, arguing that it had truthfully stated in its solicitation that there was no annual fee, but that it had reserved the right to make future changes to the agreement. The solicitation sent to the consumer also included the following statement: "We reserve the right to change the benefit features associated with your Card at any time." A federal trial court ruled in favor of the credit card company. However, a federal appeals court based in Philadelphia (the Third Circuit) reinstated the consumer's lawsuit on appeal because the solicitation may have been false and misleading. When the case was sent back to the trial court, the parties settled out of court, with the consumers getting a refund of their annual fees.

PROTECTIONS FOR CONSUMERS WHO LEASE PRODUCTS

The federal **Consumer Leasing Act**, which is part of the Consumer Credit Protection Act, applies to any lease of consumer goods lasting more than four months in which the total contractual obligation does not exceed $25,000. (It does not apply to leases of real estate, nor does it apply to consumer goods used primarily for commercial purposes, such as a car or truck leased by a business.) This law requires the **lessor**—the owner of the auto you lease, for example—to disclose certain information before you sign the lease. Among the most important required disclosures are:

• capitalized cost—that is, the cost or value of the goods being leased (the capitalized cost is negotiable, to the same extent that the price of goods would be negotiable if you were buying them instead of leasing them);

• the total amount of any initial payment you are required to make;

• the number, amounts, and due dates of monthly payments;

• the total amount for fees, such as license fees and taxes;

• any penalty for default or late payments;

• the annual mileage allowance, if applicable, and the extra charges involved if you exceed that allowance;

• whether you can end the lease early, and the method of computing the charge if you do so;

• whether you can purchase the goods at the end of the lease and for what price;

• any liability that you may have for the difference between the estimated value of the goods and their market value at the time you end the lease; and

• any extra payment that you must make at the end of the lease.

You can report apparent violations of the Consumer Leasing Act to the same agencies that enforce TILA. The Federal Trade Commission or your state or local consumer protection office may be able to help you find the proper agencies; please consult the appendix at the back of this book for the appropriate addresses and phone numbers.

CREDIT SCORING

A **credit-scoring system** attempts to determine how likely it is that a consumer will pay his or her debts. Creditors may use credit scores to determine whether you are creditworthy. Credit

DETERMINING CREDITWORTHINESS

Creditors may use any one or more of the following factors to decide whether to extend you credit. If your credit history is bad (or not good enough for the creditor—recently, creditors have become more selective in issuing credit), creditors either will not give you credit, or will charge you a higher finance charge to compensate for the added risk they assume in giving you credit.

Factor	Explanation
Ability to repay	This depends on the stability of your current job, other income sources, how much you earn, and the length of the time you have worked or will receive your current income. Creditors may also consider your basic expenses, such as payments on rent, mortgage loans or other debts, utilities, college expenses, and taxes.
Credit history	This tells creditors how much money you owe and whether you have large, unused lines of open-end credit. Additional very important considerations include whether you have consistently paid your bills on time and whether you have filed for bankruptcy within the past ten years or had judgments issued against you. Creditors also consider how much debt you currently carry on existing credit cards and whether you generally have outstanding credit card balances that are at or near the available credit limit for your credit card accounts. (If the amount you owe is at or near your credit limit, this may reduce your credit score and make it harder to obtain credit on favorable terms.)
Stability	Your stability is based on how long you have lived at your current or former address and the length of time you have been with your current or former employer. Another consideration is whether you own or rent your home.

Assets	Assets such as a car or home may be useful as collateral for an extension of credit. When used as collateral, the creditor may sell the property and use the money to pay itself if you fail to pay. Creditors may also look at what else you own that could be used for collateral, such as savings accounts or securities (stocks and bonds).

Creditors obtain information about these indicators of creditworthiness from your application and from your **credit score** (see below) or consumer credit report (credit bureau report). (For more information on credit reports, see chapter 7.)

scores range from approximately 300–400 to 800–900; a good credit score is one that is higher than 700. Your credit score may determine whether you are able to obtain a home mortgage loan, an extension of credit to buy an auto, or other credit. As mentioned in the "Determining Creditworthiness" sidebar above, a number of factors are considered when determining your credit score. These factors include: your payment history, the amount of your outstanding debt, the length of your credit history, the number of recent credit applications you have filed, and the number of credit accounts you currently have.

A California corporation known as Fair Isaac® (see www.fairisaac.com) developed credit scoring in the 1950s. Fair Isaac's version of the credit score is called the FICO® score. Fair Isaac makes FICO® credit scores available to individual consumers (see www.myfico.com) for a fee (as of January 2009, $15.95 for one credit score and one credit report from one national credit reporting agency, or $47.85 for three credit scores and three credit reports, from each of the three national credit reporting agencies). In addition, the federal Fair Credit Reporting Act requires nationwide consumer credit reporting agencies (such as Equifax, Experian, and TransUnion) to give a consumer upon request and payment of a "fair and reasonable fee," the consumer's current credit score and certain related information

FEDERAL LAWS IMPACTING CONSUMER CREDIT

There are many federal laws that provide certain protections and rights to consumers. Here is a brief description of some of the major consumer credit protection statutes:

CONSUMER CREDIT PROTECTION ACT OF 1968 (CCPA)

This law is the major federal consumer protection statute. Many well-known consumer credit laws are actually parts, or titles, of the CCPA. For instance, the Truth in Lending Act is Title I of the CCPA, while the Fair Credit Reporting Act is Title VI of the CCPA.

TRUTH IN LENDING ACT (TILA)

This is the popular name for Title I of the CCPA. TILA requires creditors to disclose important costs and conditions of credit to consumers.

FAIR CREDIT REPORTING ACT (FCRA)

This law amended the Consumer Credit Protection Act and became Title VI of the CCPA. This law regulates the furnishing and use of information in relation to credit and requires credit bureaus to maintain accurate information about consumers in so-called consumer reports (credit reports). In 1996, the law was amended to impose some requirements on businesses that furnish information to credit bureaus. The law was also amended in 2003 by the Fair and Accurate Credit Transactions Act (FACTA) (see below).

FAIR AND ACCURATE CREDIT TRANSACTIONS ACT OF 2003 (FACTA)

This law amends the Fair Credit Reporting Act to give consumers more rights, including rights to one free credit report each year, disclosure of credit scores, and the ability to dispute credit information with creditors and other businesses that furnish information about consumers to credit bureaus.

CONSUMER LEASING ACT (CLA)

This law requires disclosure of information that helps you compare the cost and other important terms of long-term (longer than four months) personal property leases (such as one- or three-year car leases). This law requires businesses that offer such personal property leases to disclose certain important facts to help you weigh the cost and terms of leasing against the cost and terms of buying on credit or with cash.

FAIR CREDIT AND CHARGE CARD DISCLOSURE ACT

This law amended the Truth in Lending Act. It requires credit card issuers to disclose certain important costs of credit in credit card applications and solicitations.

ELECTRONIC FUND TRANSFER ACT

This law amended the Consumer Credit Protection Act and became Title IX of the CCPA. This law provides protection to consumers with respect to the electronic transfer of funds to and from checking and savings accounts, including electronic direct deposit of monies to checking and savings accounts, and electronic transfers of funds from such accounts to pay creditors.

EQUAL CREDIT OPPORTUNITY ACT

This law amended the Consumer Credit Protection Act and became Title VII of the CCPA. This law prohibits creditors from discriminating against applicants for credit and borrowers on the basis of race, religion, national origin, sex, marital status, age, welfare assistance status, or the fact that an applicant or borrower has in good faith exercised any right under the Consumer Credit Protection Act.

FAIR CREDIT BILLING ACT (FCBA)

This law, passed in 1974 as an amendment to the Truth in Lending Act, describes how a credit card holder can resolve billing error disputes with credit card issuers.

FAIR DEBT COLLECTION PRACTICES ACT (FDCPA)

This law, passed in 1977 as an amendment to the Consumer Credit Protection Act, regulates the conduct of third party debt collectors (collection agencies) working on behalf of creditors during the collection of consumer debt.

HOME OWNERSHIP AND EQUITY PROTECTION ACT OF 1994 (HOEPA)

This law, which amended the Truth in Lending Act, provides certain additional protections for consumers from certain high-interest and high fee home mortgage loans.

IDENTITY THEFT AND ASSUMPTION DETERRENCE ACT OF 1998 (IDENTITY THEFT ACT)

This law criminalizes the use of another person's identity or personal identifiable information to commit fraud or theft.

REAL ESTATE SETTLEMENT PROCEDURES ACT (RESPA)

This law requires that residential mortgage borrowers receive disclosures during the residential mortgage settlement or closing process. RESPA requires mortgage brokers and/or lenders to provide borrowers applying for a mortgage loan with information on the costs of residential mortgage settlement services, a good faith estimate of settlement costs (listing the charges the borrower is likely to pay at or before closing), and a first mortgage loan servicing disclosure statement. RESPA also imposes requirements on mortgage loan property tax and insurance escrow accounts and escrow payments.

about the credit score. Consumers may also obtain at no charge, once each year, a copy of their credit report from each of the nationwide consumer credit reporting agencies. (For more information, visit www.annualcreditreport.com.) The Federal Trade Commission (FTC) has indicated that the nationwide consumer credit reporting agencies appear to be charging consumers between $4 and $8 for a current credit score (depending on the consumer's state of residence) and approximately $9 for a current credit report (if a consumer requests a copy of a credit report more than once a year from the same consumer credit reporting agency). In 2009, the FTC has set a maximum ceiling of $11 for a copy of a current credit report.

The FTC has an online publication about improving your credit report at www.ftc.gov/bcp/edu/pubs/consumer/credit/cre03 .pdf. They also have an informative article on credit scoring at www.ftc.gov/bcp/edu/pubs/articles/naps30.pdf. See chapter 7 of this book for more on credit reports.

SELECTING THE BEST WAY TO FINANCE

Let's see how you can use the information made available to you by TILA to get the best deal when financing a used car that costs $5,000 if paid for with cash. You have $1,000 in savings to make a down payment on the car, and need to borrow the remaining $4,000. Suppose that, by shopping around, you find the four possible credit arrangements shown below:

	APR	Length of Loan	Monthly Payment	Total Finance Charge
Creditor A	11%	3 years	$131	$714
Creditor B	11%	4 years	$103	$962
Creditor C	12%	4 years	$105	$1,056
Creditor D	12%	2 years	$188	$519

Let's begin with an easy decision. Notice that the four-year loan offered by Creditor B is a better deal than the four-year loan offered by Creditor C—that is, Creditor B's total finance charge is less than that of Creditor C. Creditor B's monthly payment is also less than that of Creditor C. Since the lengths of these loans are equal (four years), we know that an 11 percent loan is cheaper than a 12 percent loan for the same amount of money. Forget about Creditor C.

However, look what happens when the lengths of the loans vary. Even though Creditors A and B both charge an APR of 11 percent, Creditor B's total finance charge on the four-year loan is higher than Creditor A's total finance charge on the three-year loan. Of course, the difference makes sense, since with Creditor B you would have another year to use the creditor's money—finance charges (interest) would be owed on the unpaid principal for that extra year with Creditor B. Creditor B also has a lower monthly payment than Creditor A, because Creditor B is taking one more year in which to repay the loan. (In general, the longer the term of the loan, the smaller the monthly payment amount needed to repay the full amount borrowed with interest, since the loan would be repaid over a longer term and therefore with a larger number of monthly payments.)

In making a decision like this, you have to decide whether you would like to have the lower monthly payment that accompanies the longer loan. Note that it doesn't help to look just at the total finance charge, which is lowest on the loan from Creditor D. Creditor D charges a higher APR than both Creditor A and Creditor B—12 percent rather than 11 percent—so the only reason Creditor D's finance charge is the lowest of the four is that the length of its loan is also the shortest; you would have use of Creditor D's money for only two years. Creditor D also has the highest monthly payment amount. You might be better off with either Creditor A or B, instead of Creditor D, especially if Creditor A or B would allow you to prepay some or all of the loan ahead of schedule without penalty.

If your chief concern was the best deal in purely financial terms, without regard to length of loan, your choice would narrow to either Creditor A or Creditor B because they offer the lower APRs. Your choice would depend on how easy it would be for you to meet the applicable monthly payments. Ultimately, the biggest decision would be whether having a car today, rather than later, is worth the monthly payments at an 11 or 12 percent financing rate.

Look at More Than Just the APR

You will not be shopping wisely if you merely compare APRs. For example, in the scenario presented above, you have to decide for how long you want to owe money to a creditor. If you want to minimize that time period, Creditor D might be a good choice, although Creditor D's monthly payment amount is the highest of the four hypothetical loans shown above. If a shorter period of indebtedness is your main objective, you might consider asking Creditor A if it would make an 11 percent loan for two years instead of three. Or you might consider asking both Creditor A and Creditor B whether they would allow you to prepay some or all of the amounts due on their loans early, ahead of schedule, without penalty.

ADDITIONAL FACTORS TO CONSIDER WHEN USING INSTALLMENT CREDIT

There are several other factors to consider when using installment credit. First, consider whether the interest that you pay for the

TALKING TO A LAWYER

Q. *I understand that the Truth in Lending Act requires creditors to tell me the APR in advance, but when I applied for a mortgage, the actual APR turned out to be more than I was quoted. How does this happen? Is this permitted under the law?*

A. For certain types of mortgage loans, the Truth in Lending Act (TILA) requires lenders to give you an estimated Truth in Lending (TIL) disclosure statement within three business days of your application. This is just an estimated disclosure statement and does not necessarily reflect the actual terms of the mortgage loan you may eventually be approved for. You should generally receive a final TIL disclosure statement at or before your loan closing that more accurately reflects the actual terms of the mortgage loan you have been approved for and have agreed to accept. There are several reasons why the initial estimated TIL disclosure may have had a lower APR than your final TIL disclosure, including, for instance, the following: If you did not lock in your interest rate at the time of loan application, and the lenders' interest rate for the loan program increased after you applied but before your loan closing, the interest rate (and therefore the APR) for your loan may have increased after you applied. (For adjustable or variable rate loans, even if the initial interest rate quoted to you at or near the time of loan application is "locked" and does not increase, if the index to which future rate adjustments are tied increases before loan closing, this may also cause the disclosed APR for your loan to increase.) If you applied for a refinancing loan believing that you were applying for a loan for less than 80 percent of the appraised value of the property, but the lender received an appraisal later on indicating that the property was worth less than you had originally thought, the lender might have increased the interest rate on the loan (to reflect the fact that your loan amount was for more than 80 percent of the appraised value of the property), or the lender may have decided to charge you for private mortgage insurance (a type of finance charge that increases the APR on the loan). The initial estimated TIL disclosure also may have assumed that you would pay a certain number of "points" or loan origination fees at loan closing. If you ultimately agreed with the lender to pay a lesser number of "points" (or no "points") at closing, the lender may have increased the interest rate on the loan in exchange for receiving fewer "points" or loan origination fees at closing. Please also note that Congress has amended the TILA effective July 30, 2009, to require corrected or revised TIL disclosures to be given at least three business days before a residential mortgage loan closing in certain circumstances.

—Answer by Elizabeth C. Yen, Hudson Cook, LLP, New Haven, Connecticut

Q. *Things are tough here, and we're thinking of taking out a loan from a finance company. Are there any laws that we should know about that might protect us? What can we do to assure that we're not paying too much to get the money we need now?*

A. In many states, a law will regulate what the finance company can charge you. Federal law requires that the cost and other important terms of the loan be disclosed to you before you sign. You should read these disclosures carefully to make sure you want to go through with the loan. Before you sign, you also should check the ads for several sources of credit or ask about terms to get the best deal, just like you would shop for the best price on a car or other expensive products.

—Answer by Frederick H. Miller, Of Counsel, Phillips Murrah, P.C., Oklahoma City, Oklahoma

Q. *My son is just out of college. He asked me to co-sign a loan so he'd have money to furnish his apartment. What does co-signing mean?*

A. A co-signer on a loan is personally liable to repay the entire loan, even though the co-signer may not have directly benefited from the loan. The creditor may try to collect the full amount of the loan from the co-signer without first trying to collect from the primary borrower on the loan. The co-signer may owe late fees and collection costs on the loan if the primary borrower does not make all payments on time, as required by the terms of the loan. If the loan goes into default, the fact may become a part of the co-signer's credit record as well as the primary borrower's credit record.

—Answer by Elizabeth C. Yen, Hudson Cook, LLP, New Haven, Connecticut

credit *may* be deductible when you calculate your federal income taxes. Many homeowners may deduct for federal income tax purposes the amount of interest paid on their mortgages. Please also be aware that this area of the law concerning the deductibility of mortgage insurance premiums is complicated and could change in the near future. Also, don't assume that other debts are deductible, as many are not. For example, the interest that you pay on non-mortgage-secured credit card debt, student loans, auto loans, and other debts is no longer deductible.

If you itemize deductions in preparing your federal income taxes, you might also consider financing major credit purchases through a mortgage or home equity loan. These types of loans are discussed in chapter 11, which explains how they can have both benefits and dangers for consumers. Remember that if you use a mortgage or home equity loan, you are placing your home at risk. And if the total value of the items you are permitted to deduct for federal income tax purposes is less than the amount of your standard deduction, the interest you pay on mortgage or home equity credit will not help to reduce your federal income tax bill.

Another factor to consider is the possibility that you will pay off the loan or extension of credit early. If this is likely, you will need to figure out how your creditor calculates the rebate of any unearned finance charges and whether there is a charge (prepayment penalty) for paying early. In the case of a loan, for example, if the loan allows you to prepay amounts due, in whole or in part, without penalty, you may be able to periodically pay a larger amount than the amount due, which would result in the loan paying off ahead of schedule, and would also reduce the

CAREFULLY EVALUATE YOUR OPTIONS

The examples on these pages illustrate the importance of checking all financing options before making a decision regarding credit. Fortunately, the law allows you to obtain the information that you need to shop comparatively. You should use this information and apply it to your own situation and needs to determine which loan or credit arrangement is best for you.

total finance charges accruing on the unpaid principal balance of the loan. However, application and closing costs for installment loans, including "points" and loan origination fees paid at closing, are often not refunded or rebated if the loans are paid off early.

A final factor to consider is the penalty for failing to make a timely payment. Some creditors have established onerous penalties for consumers who make late payments. Late payments can also lead to a reduction in your credit score and your ability to obtain credit in the future.

REMEMBER THIS

• Credit is an important part of our consumer culture. Credit is obtaining money for a price. It is also defined as the ability to borrow money and defer payment of the resulting debt until later.

• Credit has its costs. A finance charge is a fee that represents the cost of consumer credit in terms of dollars. The annual percentage rate (APR) is a measure of certain credit costs over the course of a year in terms of a percentage. (Some costs of credit, such as optional credit insurance charges, and certain mortgage-related closing costs, are not required to be included in the finance charge or the APR.)

• There are three basic forms of consumer credit: (1) noninstallment credit (sometimes called thirty-day or charge account credit); (2) installment credit or closed-end credit, which is credit that is scheduled to be repaid in multiple installments over a fixed period of time; and (3) revolving, or open-end, credit.

- Creditors analyze several factors when determining whether to grant consumers credit, and often rely on credit scoring to determine whether to award a would-be consumer credit. These factors include a consumer's ability to repay the debt, credit history, stability, and debts and assets.

- Make sure to read the fine print of any credit application. Understand the penalties for late payments.

- There are many laws that impact consumer credit. Make sure to look at the Federal Trade Commission's website, which contains links to many of these laws, as well as to publications that describe them in plain English.

CHAPTER 3

Your Right to Equal Credit

Understanding How the Law Protects You

Betsy recently separated from her husband. Unfortunately, her estranged husband, Al, had been the primary breadwinner for their family. Now, Betsy seeks to establish some credit of her own. But when she attempts to apply for a loan, the loan officer asks her about her marital status, presses her for details about her future child-rearing plans, and then tells her it would be best if Al co-signed with her on the credit application.

In the scenario presented above, Betsy may have grounds for a viable federal lawsuit. Why? Because a federal law passed in 1974 known as the **Equal Credit Opportunity Act** (ECOA) prohibits discrimination against credit applicants on the basis of race, color, religion, national origin, sex, marital status, age, receipt of public assistance, or the fact that the applicant has exercised a right under the Consumer Credit Protection Act in good faith. Had Betsy felt that she was discriminated against in getting a mortgage, she might also try to seek the protections of the federal **Fair Housing Act** of 1968.

Creditors can deny you credit because you are an unacceptable credit risk. They can also deny you credit because of your poor financial history or low credit score (provided that the creditor uses a valid credit scoring system). This is common sense—why would anyone want to extend credit to someone who probably won't be able to repay it? A creditor also may deny you credit if (for example) you apply for a type of credit that is not (or is no longer) available from the creditor, or if you live outside the creditor's lending area. However, it is also common sense that people should not be denied credit for reasons that have nothing to do with their ability to repay the loan. Thus, the law provides that creditors may deny credit based on a person's creditworthiness or other legitimate business reasons, but not because of social biases.

THE EQUAL CREDIT OPPORTUNITY ACT

The Equal Credit Opportunity Act (ECOA) says that creditors may not discriminate against credit applicants "with respect to any aspect of a credit transaction." This means that it is unlawful for a creditor to discriminate against an applicant at *any* stage of the credit process—from the initial application for credit to the actual granting of credit to the refinancing or collection of debt.

The ECOA says that creditors may not discriminate against you in credit dealings based on certain factors. For example, a creditor may not use age (provided that you are old enough to enter into a legally binding contract), race, national origin, sex, marital status, religion, receipt of public aid, or the exercise of rights under the Consumer Credit Protection Act as a basis for:

- discouraging or preventing you from applying for credit;
- refusing you credit if you otherwise qualify;
- extending you credit on terms different from those granted to someone with similar credit risk factors (as determined by such factors as your ability to repay, credit history, stability, and assets); or
- giving you less credit than you asked for, if someone with similar risk factors would have received the amount you asked for or more.

The Equal Credit Opportunity Act does not, however, guarantee that you will receive credit; in order to qualify for credit, you must still meet the creditor's standards of creditworthiness and other legitimate business requirements. For example, a creditor may allocate a certain amount of funds towards a certain type of credit program (such as a student loan program or a first-time homebuyer program), and does not have to extend you credit if your request for credit would cause the creditor to go over (exceed) the creditor's funding limit for that given credit program. A creditor also does not have to extend you credit if you do not meet other legitimate requirements for a certain type of credit program (for example, a requirement that the borrower be a first-time homebuyer, or that the collateral for a loan be the borrower's primary residence).

The ECOA was passed in 1974 as an amendment to the Consumer Credit Protection Act. Initially, the ECOA only prohibited credit discrimination on the basis of sex or marital status. Many married women were unable to obtain credit unless they had the signature of their husband. Similarly, many single women were unable to obtain credit, including many women who had been recently divorced. Congress recognized this problem.

Congress expanded the scope of the ECOA by also prohibiting credit discrimination based on the other above-mentioned factors such as race, religion, national origin, receipt of public assistance benefits, and exercise of rights under the Consumer Credit Protection Act. These amendments went into effect in 1976.

Today, some state laws may be even more protective than the ECOA; for example, they may preclude discrimination on the basis of disability or sexual orientation, or on the basis that a couple has children.

GENDER DISCRIMINATION

The original impetus for the ECOA was to prohibit credit discrimination against women. Today, the law protects both men and women from discrimination that is based on gender or marital status. In general, a creditor may not deny you credit or take any adverse action, such as lowering your credit limit or raising your APR, just because of your gender or because you are married, single, widowed, divorced, or separated. More specifically, the ECOA sets forth the following prohibitions:

- A creditor may not ask your gender when you apply for credit. One exception exists if you are applying for a loan to buy

PROVING DISCRIMINATION

There are two major ways to show discrimination under federal law: disparate treatment discrimination and disparate impact discrimination.

Disparate treatment discrimination occurs when a creditor intentionally treats someone differently than otherwise similarly situated individuals who are not members of the same protected category (e.g., who are not members of the same race or sex). For example, let's say that Mr. Smith (a Caucasian) and Mr. Jones (an African-American) both apply for credit and have virtually the same income and credit history, as well as the same down payment or loan-to-value ratio. The creditor offers Mr. Smith a better finance rate than Mr. Jones and generally makes the credit application process easier for Mr. Smith than for Mr. Jones. This is disparate treatment. Mr. Jones has been treated worse (and differently) than Mr. Smith.

Disparate impact discrimination occurs when a practice that seems neutral on its face has a disproportionately negative impact on a certain protected category of people. For example, suppose a creditor refuses to grant credit to any person residing within a certain area code or ZIP code, because the creditor deems people living in that area code or ZIP code to be a high risk for default. The creditor applies this rule equally to all persons residing in the area code or ZIP code—regardless of race, gender, ethnicity, marital status, age, and so forth. However, because of housing patterns in the area, the *result* of this policy is that far more African-Americans than Caucasians are denied credit. This may constitute disparate impact discrimination. The U.S. Supreme Court recognized disparate impact discrimination as a valid form of proving discrimination in 1971 in the employment discrimination case of *Griggs v. Duke Power Co.* The Federal Reserve Board has indicated in its regulations implementing the ECOA that the disparate impact analysis used by the U.S. Supreme Court in the *Griggs v. Duke Power Co.* case should apply to a creditor's determination of creditworthiness under the ECOA, based on the legislative history of the ECOA. (See 12 C.F.R. Section 202.6(a), footnote 2.)

If a lending practice has a statistically disparate impact on one of the groups protected under the ECOA, the lender must show that the facially neutral credit practice creating the statistically disparate impact meets a legitimate business purpose that cannot be reasonably achieved as well by using different credit granting criteria that would have less of a disparate impact. (If another practice would work just as well with a lesser disparate impact, a violation may be found.) An example of a legitimate business purpose is the practice of charging a lower interest rate on mortgage loans to borrowers who make larger down payments. This might have a disparate impact on younger borrowers. However, the apparent disparate impact based on age is justified and legal because the loan-to-value ratio is a legitimate factor affecting the credit risk assumed by the creditor.

or build a home, or to repair, rehabilitate, or remodel a home, when the federal government requires creditors to ask for information about gender, race, and ethnicity in order to help the government monitor compliance with fair lending laws. However, if asked for any of this information in these circumstances, you may still refuse to answer this question. When such a credit application is taken in person (rather than online or over the phone), the government requires creditors to provide this information based on visual observation or surname.

• Normally, you do not have to use a gender title (Mr., Miss, Mrs., or Ms.) when applying for credit. Sometimes creditors may ask whether you are married, unmarried, or separated, if your marital status relates to their right to obtain repayment. For example, such a request may be made in a state with community property laws, where spouses have more rights to their partner's assets and income than in noncommunity property states. There are eight states that are considered community property states: Arizona, California, Idaho, Louisiana, Nevada, New Mexico, Texas, and Washington—and an additional two states, Wisconsin and Alaska, that have community property features in their laws.

A creditor might also inquire about a consumer's marital status if the consumer plans to pledge collateral to secure the credit. Because many state laws afford spouses certain rights in property owned by their partners, the creditor must determine whether the spouse must also agree to pledge the property to secure the loan.

• A creditor may not ask women if they use birth control or whether they plan to have children.

• You do not have to discuss child support or alimony payments that are made to you with a creditor unless you wish the creditor to consider such payments as part of your income. Note, however, that if you are required to pay alimony or child support, then the creditor will require you to disclose that information so that the creditor will know how much income you have available to repay a new debt.

The ECOA does not provide protection to those denied credit because of sexual orientation. However, some state laws do prohibit credit discrimination on the basis of sexual orientation, gender identity, disability, and other protected characteristics not included within the scope of the ECOA. In addition, courts can take a broad view of sex discrimination. Consider the federal case of *Rosa v. Park West Bank & Trust Co.*, 214 F.3d 213 (1st Cir. 2000), a case that arose in Massachusetts.

In this case, a cross-dressing bank customer alleged that the bank had refused to provide him with a loan application because he dressed in feminine clothes. He claimed that the loan officer had told him to go home and change clothes. He sued, claiming gender discrimination under the ECOA. The bank argued that it had not violated the ECOA because its employee had been legitimately unable to identify the cross-dresser, since his forms of identification showed him in traditional male attire.

A federal trial court dismissed the lawsuit, finding that the ECOA does not prohibit discrimination based on the way a person dresses. A federal appeals court, however, reinstated the lawsuit. According to the appeals court, the bank might have violated the ECOA if it treated women who dress like men differently than men who dress like women: "Whatever facts emerge, and they may turn out to have nothing to do with sex-based discrimination, we cannot say at this point that the plaintiff has no viable theory of sex discrimination consistent with the facts alleged."

How do you enforce your rights? A very good place to start is the federal, state, and local agencies that accept and investigate fair lending claims. We provide a list of such agencies in the Appendix to this book.

Another alternative is to file a lawsuit. There are some problems with this approach. Discrimination lawsuits are very difficult and costly to pursue and they are rarely successful. Talk to a lawyer if you are considering filing suit.

Marital Status and Separate Credit Accounts

Married people may open credit accounts that are not also in their spouses' names; they are not obliged to open joint accounts or take out loans with their spouses. Moreover, even if you have a joint account with your spouse, when a creditor sends information about your joint account to a credit bureau, it must report the information in each of your names, so you will not lose your separate identity for credit purposes. The credit bureau will maintain a separate file on you, so that a creditor may be able to access your personal credit history and rely on it when making a credit decision.

Specifically, a creditor may not:

• refuse to open a separate credit account just because of your gender or marital status;

• require your spouse to co-sign your account, unless you live in a community property state or unless you want your spouse to be a co-borrower with you on the account; or

• ask about your spouse or ex-spouse when you apply for credit based on your own income. However, a creditor may seek this information in a community property state, or if you are relying in part on your income from alimony, child support, or maintenance payments from your ex-spouse for the purpose of obtaining credit.

Change in Marital Status

A creditor may not require you to reapply for credit just because you marry or divorce or because your spouse has died. In addition, a creditor may not close your account or change its terms for these reasons alone. In order for a creditor to take such actions, there must be a change in your creditworthiness, such as a decrease in your income. For example, if your spouse dies or you get a divorce, and you had used your spouse's income to get a credit card or some other type of revolving (open-end) credit, a creditor may require you to reapply for credit if it appears that your income will no longer support the amount of credit currently available to you. However, the creditor must allow you to use the existing revolving credit account while considering your new application.

RACIAL DISCRIMINATION

The ECOA also prohibits discrimination based on race. Some ECOA lawsuits have alleged that persons of a particular race are treated worse than Caucasian credit applicants. For example, in the 1984 case *United States v. American Future Systems*, the U.S. Court of Appeals for the Third Circuit rejected a chinaware company's policy of extending special credit to single white females aged eighteen to twenty-one who lived in their parents' homes. Under the policy, such females would receive their merchandise immediately upon ordering it and applying for credit. The plaintiffs showed that similarly situated nonwhite women in the same age bracket were treated much differently: They had to make three payments before being deemed creditworthy and receiving their merchandise. The Third Circuit agreed that this disparate treatment violated the ECOA, determining that the company "perpetuates the past disparities between white and minority women . . . rather than helping all women it aids only white women and slams the door of equal credit opportunity in the faces of minority women."

In a recent example that, as of this writing, was still being litigated, a federal court in California refused to dismiss a claim filed by an African-American homeowner who alleged that a mortgage company discriminated against African-Americans by permitting higher discretionary loan pricing on African-Americans than Caucasians. Dana Taylor contends that she and other African-Americans had to pay higher mortgage loan rates and/or "points" than similarly-situated Caucasians, as the result of a lender policy or practice that permitted loan brokers to mark up the lender's mortgage loan interest rates and "points" using broker discretion. The brokers' discretionary markups allegedly resulted in African-Americans paying disproportionately more of a markup on their loans from the lender than otherwise similarly situated Caucasians—a disparate impact that could, if proven, violate the ECOA. In *Taylor v. Accredited Home Lenders* (2008), the federal district court reasoned that the plaintiff had adequately pled a claim under the ECOA and the Fair Housing Act that could not be dismissed at this early stage of the litigation.

In accordance with the ECOA, courts have thus expressed their unwillingness to tolerate statistically disparate race-based differences in loan pricing among applicants for credit.

There continue to be allegations that certain creditors and loan brokers discriminate against individuals based on race. Many of these claims are disparate impact claims raised in class action lawsuits, alleging that a lender engaged in policies that led to certain protected groups receiving a much higher rate on a loan than other similarly situated applicants not within the same protected group.

AGE DISCRIMINATION

A creditor may ask you your age. However, if you have reached the age of majority and you apply for credit, a creditor may not:

- refuse to give you credit or decrease the amount of credit it grants you solely because of your age;
- refuse to consider your retirement income in rating your credit application, if the creditor considers income when it evaluates creditworthiness;
- cancel your credit account or require you to reapply for credit just because you are a certain age or have retired; or
- refuse you credit or cancel your account because you cannot get credit life insurance (or a related type of credit insurance) due to your age.

However, the law does allow a creditor to consider certain age-related facts. For example, a creditor may consider how long your income will continue, or how long it will be until you reach retirement age. Consider, for example, a loan that will take a long time to pay back. If an older applicant does not provide adequate security (collateral), he or she may constitute a high credit risk. In addition, the ECOA does not prohibit creditors from inquiring about the age of an elderly person (age 62 or older) if the applicant's age is to be used in his or her favor. This provision is known as the "senior preference." For example, a creditor could give favorable consideration and more favorable loan terms to an older credit applicant than to younger applicants. The ECOA allows preference and more favorable treatment to be given to credit applicants age 62 or older.

PUBLIC ASSISTANCE

A creditor may not deny an applicant credit solely because he or she receives Social Security or public-assistance payments such as Temporary Assistance for Needy Families. However, a creditor may ask you the age of your dependents if you may lose certain public assistance benefits when they reach a certain age. A creditor may also consider whether you will continue to meet residency or other requirements for receiving benefits, and whether it can reach those benefits through legal channels if you fail to make payments on your account.

BURDEN OF PROOF IN ECOA CASES

As is the case with most other types of suits in which a plaintiff is trying to show that he or she is the victim of disparate treatment (different treatment based on an impermissible factor such as race—see page 39 for more information on disparate treatment), such as employment discrimination suits, the plaintiff in an ECOA case bears the initial burden of proof. In other words, if you want to proceed with an ECOA case, you must set forth enough facts to establish a basic or prima facie (legally sufficient) claim of discrimination. For example, in a racial discrimination claim under the ECOA, the plaintiff would have to show that: (1) he or she belonged to a specific race; (2) he or she was creditworthy; (3) he or she was denied credit; and (4) other similarly situated persons of another race were treated better.

Once a plaintiff establishes a prima facie claim, the burden shifts to the creditor-defendant to establish a legitimate, nondiscriminatory reason for the denial of credit. In other words, the creditor must show that there was a legitimate business justification for the denial of credit and that the denial was not due to the plaintiff belonging to a protected class or group or having certain protected characteristics or features. The final burden then shifts back to the plaintiff to prove that the creditor's stated justification is pretextual, or false.

DENIAL OF A CREDIT APPLICATION

Under the ECOA, a creditor must notify you whether it has approved or denied your credit application within thirty days after receiving a completed application. If the creditor denies you credit, the notice of such denial must be in writing (it can be electronic under certain circumstances), and must list the primary reasons for the denial of credit or instruct you how to request an explanation of those reasons.

Another law, the **Fair Credit Reporting Act** (FCRA), affects credit denials as well. It requires that a notice of credit denial tell you (if applicable) that the creditor relied in whole or in part upon information in a credit report (which may include a credit score) from a consumer credit reporting agency (a credit bureau) to deny you credit and (if applicable) the name and address of the credit bureau that provided the report. You are then entitled to ask the credit bureau for a free copy of your credit report within sixty days after receiving the notice of credit denial. The credit bureau will not be able to tell you why the creditor denied you credit. However, if you find inaccurate or incomplete information in your credit report, you should notify the credit bureau of the inaccurate or incomplete information and ask the credit bureau to investigate and correct the information in your credit report. These rights also apply if a creditor takes any adverse action against you after granting you credit, such as closing an existing credit account or reducing an open line of credit for reasons other than default, delinquency, or account inactivity.

Creditors that deny you credit or take other adverse credit-related action against you, due in whole or in part to information received from a credit bureau, may combine the ECOA and FCRA notices of credit denial described above in a single notice to you. If a creditor will not tell you why it has taken an adverse credit-related action against you, ask the creditor to supply a written explanation as required by the ECOA. If you think the creditor's written notice does not disclose the primary reasons it has taken an adverse credit-related action, ask for a written statement of the primary reasons credit was denied, terminated, or otherwise the subject of an adverse credit-related action. If you think the creditor has unlawfully discriminated against you, tell the creditor why you think this, and try to resolve the issue through negotiation. If the creditor continues the adverse action and has not given a satisfactory explanation, you may complain to the creditor's federal regulatory agency, the Federal Trade Commission, or the U.S. Attorney General's Office. See the Appendix of this book for contact information for all of these. In addition, the adverse action letter sent to an applicant who is denied credit should identify the creditor's primary regulator and provide the address where the regulator may be contacted with inquiries or to lodge a complaint.

DAMAGES

The ECOA provides individuals with the right to sue if they have been unlawfully discriminated against while applying for credit. Creditors who violate the ECOA can be held liable for **compensatory** or **actual damages**, which compensate people for any actual damages they sustain as a result of the violation. If the plaintiff can show the required connection between the creditor's unlawful discriminatory actions and the harm suffered by the plaintiff, then such damages could include compensation for injury to reputation, mental anguish, costs associated with finding other credit sources, and out-of-pocket expenses.

The ECOA also allows successful individuals to recover punitive damages under appropriate circumstances. **Punitive damages** are not designed to compensate the plaintiff for actual harm suffered as a result of the violation; rather, they are designed to punish the wrongdoer and deter (or discourage) such unlawful conduct in the future. Punitive damages are intended to penalize creditors for violating the law.

The amount of punitive damages awarded will depend on whether the creditor should have known it was violating the law, and on other factors such as the number of violations. In an individual case, a successful ECOA plaintiff may recover punitive damages of up to $10,000. In the case of a **class action lawsuit**— a lawsuit filed on behalf of a class of people all harmed by the same illegal conduct—the law allows punitive damages of up to $500,000, or 1 percent of the creditor's net worth, whichever is less. Many ECOA cases are brought as class action suits. In all cases, the ECOA also allows successful individuals to recover their court costs and reasonable attorney's fees expended in the litigation process.

The ECOA also allows aggrieved individuals to sue for more than just monetary damages: They can sue for injunctive and declaratory relief. **Injunctive relief** refers to an injunction, or court order, prohibiting a party from engaging in certain unlawful conduct. **Declaratory relief** refers to a court's declaration, or pronouncement, that a certain practice violates the law. In many discrimination cases, a plaintiff wishes to have the court declare, on the record, that a certain practice is unlawful, and to get an injunction (an order from the court) against the company, stopping it from ever engaging in similar conduct again.

Many courts have determined that ECOA plaintiffs are also entitled to have their cases tried before a jury.

 OTHER LAWS PROHIBITING CREDIT DISCRIMINATION

The federal Equal Credit Opportunity Act is the broadest of the existing federal credit discrimination laws, but it is not the only federal law that provides protection from credit discrimination. The **Fair Housing Act** of 1968 also prohibits discrimination, specifically in the renting, leasing, brokering, sale, appraisal, and financing of residences. In some ways, the Fair Housing Act provides greater coverage than the ECOA. For instance, the Fair Housing Act prohibits discrimination based on familial status or handicap and is not limited to transactions arising from applications for housing-related financing. Furthermore, there is no cap (limit) on punitive damages under the Fair Housing Act. A plaintiff cannot recover duplicate compensatory or actual damages (meaning the same damages twice) under both the ECOA and the Fair Housing Act if those damages occur out of the same transaction (same discriminatory conduct). However, a plaintiff can allege violations under both laws.

Victims of credit discrimination may also pursue remedies under the more general federal civil-rights statutes. For example, certain victims of intentional racial discrimination have broad remedies under a statute known as **Section 1981** (42 U.S.C. Section 1981). State laws, including state fair-housing laws and state unfair-and-deceptive-trade-practices laws, may provide additional remedies for discrimination victims.

A CASE STUDY

Credit discrimination claims are often very complicated. A case study is a good way to understand the factors at work. We are indebted to Robin K. Warren, formerly of the Bank of America of Charlotte, North Carolina, for this example.

Let's say you and your husband applied for a mortgage loan to refinance your house after a co-worker told you he'd refinanced his loan with the same creditor for a very attractive interest rate. The mortgage rate information in the newspaper the weekend before you applied for your loan showed rates for thirty-year fixed rate mortgages at about the same rate as the rate your co-worker obtained. The creditor's loan application asked you to provide information about your race, sex, and ethnicity. Then, while the loan application was being processed, you were asked to provide copies of recent income tax returns in order to prove the amount of your husband's income from the business he owns. Your application was finally approved six weeks after you submitted your application, but the approved loan amount was less than you'd asked for, and the interest rate was 0.5 percent higher than the rate your (Caucasian) co-worker got. You and your husband are African-American. You think the creditor used the information you provided about your race to discriminate against you by dragging the application process out, making the process more difficult, and by offering you a higher interest rate. What can you do about it?

It's possible that you were the victims of discrimination. It does, indeed, constitute illegal discrimination if, based on your race, the creditor discouraged you from pursuing your credit application, made the application process more difficult for you, or offered you less favorable credit terms than other credit applicants. However, it is also possible that your financial circumstances differed just enough from your co-worker's to cause the difference in your experience with your loan application and with the interest rate offered to you.

The creditor was required by federal law to ask you to pro-

TALKING TO A LAWYER

Q. I just got turned down for credit, and I think it's because of my race. They gave other reasons for turning me down, but they don't seem like the real reasons to me. What can I do?

A. First, contact the creditor to ask for a more complete explanation. Write or ask to speak to a manager or senior executive of the company who can review the actions taken by subordinates and may have greater discretion to approve your credit application. If you still are not satisfied with the creditor's actions, you can submit a complaint to the creditor's primary regulator (as noted in the appendix of this book, these are the Office of the Comptroller of the Currency, the Federal Reserve, the FDIC, the Office of Thrift Supervision, the National Credit Union Association, or the Federal Trade Commission), or to the U.S. Department of Justice, to your state's office of consumer affairs, or the state attorney general. Keep in mind that there are a number of factors a creditor will consider when evaluating a request for credit: your income; your existing obligations, including housing costs, other debt, any obligation to pay alimony or child support; your financial stability (how long you have been employed), how consistent your income level has been; how long you have lived at your current or former residences; your history of making timely payments on other debt; whether the loan will be secured by collateral (a car or a home, for example); and your equity in the collateral (in other words, the value of the collateral over and above any other loan amounts that are secured by the collateral). If your credit bureau report discloses many recent inquiries by other creditors, that might also negatively impact the creditor's evaluation of your credit.

You have the right to request a free copy of the credit bureau report upon which the creditor relied when turning you down for credit. Order a copy of the report. If you believe information on the report is incorrect, notify the credit bureau to dispute the incorrect information. If you have a good explanation for negative information that appears on the report, tell the creditor about it. The creditor is not required to accept your explanation, but it might make a difference in how the creditor views your creditworthiness.

—Answer by Robin K. Warren, formerly of the
Bank of America, Charlotte, North Carolina

vide information about your race, sex, and ethnicity. The government gathers this information pursuant to the Home Mortgage Disclosure Act so that it can monitor mortgage lending practices and detect possible violations of fair lending laws. You are not required to provide that information to the creditor, but if you fail to provide the information voluntarily, the government requires that the creditor provide that information based on visual observation and surnames.

One of the key pieces of information a creditor uses to evaluate a credit application is the borrower's income. Typically, the creditor can contact the credit applicant's employer to verify the income amount shown on the credit application. However, it is common for creditors to request copies of income tax returns to verify income when a credit applicant is self-employed or has significant non-employment income (such as investment income). Since tax returns are signed "under penalty of perjury," creditors can be reasonably confident that the information reported to the IRS is accurate.

The ECOA requires that the creditor notify you of its decision within thirty days after receipt of a completed application. An application is not considered to be "complete" until the creditor has received all the information it normally needs to render a decision, including income verifications (such as wage confirmation from your employer or a tax return for a self-employed person), property appraisals, and credit reports. For mortgage applications, the application might not be "complete" until several weeks after the initial written application form is submitted.

As for the higher interest rate you were quoted, there might be legitimate reasons for it. If you did not lock in an interest rate at the time you submitted your application, it is possible that mortgage interest rates rose during the six weeks that the creditor was reviewing (underwriting) your application. It is also possible that there were factors in your credit history (some late payments on other loans, for example) that caused the creditor to determine that you were a riskier borrower and, therefore, should pay a higher interest rate to compensate for the greater credit risk.

The reduction in the loan amount might have been due to the appraisal on your house. If it reflected a value lower than the amount you stated on your application, that could have reduced the amount of credit the creditor could offer. Creditors set maximum loan amounts based on the loan-to-value ratio on the property being mortgaged. The loan-to-value ratio is the loan amount divided by the value of the property. So, for example, if a homeowner seeks to borrow $80,000 and secure it with a mortgage on a $100,000 house, the loan-to-value ratio would be 80 percent. However, if the house was appraised at a value of only $90,000, then the loan-to-value ratio would climb to 89 percent. Many creditors will not make loans with loan-to-value ratios over 90 percent or 95 percent. If an appraisal shows that a house is worth less than the amount on the mortgage application, the creditor might offer to reduce the loan amount so that the loan can be made within the creditor's loan-to-value guidelines. Keep in mind, also, that the higher the loan-to-value ratio, the riskier the loan for the creditor and therefore the higher the interest rate you'll be charged. You have the right to request and obtain a copy of the appraisal used by the creditor.

You should ask the creditor to explain why you were offered a lower loan amount and a higher interest rate than you originally applied for. If, after considering the creditor's explanation and all the above factors, you still think you may have been a victim of discrimination, write a letter of complaint to the creditor and ask that your loan amount and interest rate be reconsidered. If you still are not satisfied, you can contact the creditor's primary regulator, the Department of Housing and Urban Development, or your state attorney general to lodge a discrimination complaint.

REMEMBER THIS

- The Equal Credit Opportunity Act (ECOA) prohibits discrimination against credit applicants on the basis of race, color, religion, national origin, sex, marital status, age, welfare assistance, or the fact that an applicant has in good faith exercised any right under the Consumer Credit Protection Act.

- The ECOA does not provide a cause of action simply because someone is denied credit. Creditors can deny credit to those that are deemed non-creditworthy based on legitimate factors. However, denying persons credit because of any of the above-mentioned criteria may well run afoul of federal, and possibly state, law.

- The ECOA is not the only law that may benefit someone victimized by credit discrimination. Other laws that may help include the Fair Housing Act, the federal civil rights statutes (42 U.S.C. Sections 1981 and 1982), and various state laws.

- A creditor must provide you with an answer to your application for credit within thirty days after receiving a completed application. If you are denied credit, it must also provide you with specific reasons for the denial.

CHAPTER 4

Applying for Credit

Information About Legal Protections in the Credit Application Process

You have just entered the job market. For years you have not had to apply for credit because you have always lived with your parents. Unfortunately, when you go to apply for credit now, you struggle to find someone willing to offer you credit, because you have never had a credit record and cannot show a history of repaying debts.

HOW TO ESTABLISH A CREDIT RECORD

First-time borrowers will quickly realize that in order to get credit, they must have a credit history. There are several ways to start building a good, solid credit history. For example, you may:

• open a checking or savings account and use it responsibly (without creating overdrafts and without writing checks against insufficient funds). When creditors see such accounts, they can judge whether you have adequate money and know how to manage it;

• apply for limited credit from a large, local department store, and use it. If you want to build a credit history, remember that some small local retailers, travel-and-entertainment cards, credit unions, and gasoline card companies may not necessarily report your credit performance to credit bureaus;

• obtain a secured credit card (a credit card secured by a bank deposit that can be applied to the debt if you do not pay) or deposit money in a bank, savings and loan, or savings bank, and then borrow against it; or

- have someone co-sign a loan with you; that person must have a favorable credit record and will be liable for the debt if you cannot or do not repay as required. Having a cosigner will make it easier for you to get a first loan, and you will also find it easier to get credit on your own after you pay back the loan. If you are asked to co-sign for another person's loan, be very careful—if that person fails to pay, the debt will be your responsibility.

The Federal Trade Commission has an online publication called "Getting Credit: What You Need to Know About Credit," that helps explain ways to establish credit, at www.ftc.gov/bcp/edu/pubs/consumer/credit/cre32.shtm.

Getting Credit In Your Own Name, Even If You Are Married

If you are married and you have your own sources of income, you should establish a credit history in your own name in case you become divorced or your spouse dies. This is also important if your spouse has a poor credit record and you do not want your credit record tarnished by his or her payment performance.

Unfortunately, many divorced or widowed persons who did not earn a separate income do not have credit histories separate from those of their former spouses. In these cases, creditors will look at the credit histories of any accounts held jointly with the former spouse. A non-earning spouse may also be able to obtain credit by showing with checks, receipts, or other records that he or she is worthy of credit. For example, the spouse can provide checks and receipts simply to show that he or she has a purchasing history and has paid off debts before. If a former spouse had a poor credit record, a non-earning spouse may show that this record does not reflect whether he or she deserves credit by producing the following: previous explanatory letters sent to creditors, copies of contracts signed only by the former spouse, receipts, or other evidence demonstrating that the bad credit was generated only by the former spouse.

CREDIT AND DIVORCE

Divorce can negatively impact people's credit for many reasons. It is important for people getting divorced to know whether their various accounts are individual or joint accounts. If an account is an individual account, then only the individual is responsible for the debts of that account except in community property states (see below). However, if the account is joint, then both persons listed on the account are responsible to repay the creditor for amounts owed on the account. This can prove costly when a spouse or ex-spouse refuses to act responsibly or does not pay his or her bills.

If you are getting separated or divorced, make sure you send a certified letter to all of your credit card companies telling them that you are leaving the relationship and directing them to take you off the joint account for any new obligations incurred after the date of the letter.

In some states known as community property states (Arizona, California, Idaho, Louisiana, Nevada, New Mexico, Texas, and Washington, though Alaska and Wisconsin also have community property features in their law), creditors may seek repayment from both spouses for debts incurred during their marriage, even in the case of individual accounts.

Just as couples getting divorced usually negotiate settlements in which they agree to divide their property, couples dividing responsibility for debts usually negotiate as well. If a couple can't agree on a settlement, a court will divide the couple's assets and debts. However, this will not prohibit creditors from going against either party to collect joint debts.

CREDIT INSURANCE

Credit insurance is insurance that some consumers buy to repay their loan if they are or become disabled or involuntarily unemployed. There are many different types of credit insurance. **Credit life insurance** will pay off the balance owed on covered debt in the event of your death. **Credit accident and health in-**

surance will make minimum monthly payments on the covered debt for the period of time that you cannot work as a result of accident or illness. However, such coverage may not become available until after you have been disabled for a specified number of days. Occasionally, you may be offered **unemployment insurance**, which would provide for payments on covered debt during a period in which you were involuntarily unemployed. Again, such coverage may require a waiting period.

There are certain basic rules that creditors must observe in offering you any of these forms of credit insurance:

• Whether or not you accept credit insurance available through the creditor should not be a factor in the creditor's decision to approve your application for credit, and that fact should be disclosed to you in writing, although electronic disclosure is permitted under some circumstances.

• The cost of any credit insurance offered must be disclosed to you in writing (in some circumstances, electronic disclosure is allowed). If a creditor requires credit insurance, the cost must be disclosed and included as part of the finance charge. However, if the creditor does not require credit insurance, a creditor does

---

 TALKING TO A LAWYER

Q. I'm just out of a bad marriage, and my ex screwed up the finances beyond belief. How do I get credit in my own name with this history? What can I do to show that I am responsible?

A. You can open a checking or savings account and establish a responsible record. You can also open a limited credit account from a department store, or apply for a secured credit card and use it responsibly. If you can find a person to co-sign with you for your credit and establish a successful payment history, this can help rebuild or establish a good credit history.

—Answer by Frederick H. Miller, Of Counsel, Phillips Murrah, P.C., Oklahoma City, Oklahoma not have to disclose the cost of the insurance as part of the finance charge if certain other conditions and disclosures are met. The bottom line is that generally the creditor must reveal the cost of any credit insurance available through the creditor.

• You must provide an affirmative, written indication of your desire to purchase such insurance. Usually this means that you must check the "yes" box on the credit agreement and sign or initial a form or a section of a form indicating that you want the insurance.

Do You Have to Get Credit Insurance? Should You?

Consumers generally do not have to purchase credit insurance. However, if you do not have other insurance that will cover your death, disability, or involuntary job loss, buying credit insurance could be a wise choice. If nothing else, it might provide peace of mind.

Whether or not you should buy credit insurance is a personal decision. Surveys of consumers who have purchased such insurance indicate that they have done so because they did not have much other life insurance and did not wish to leave their families with the obligation of paying off their debts. Generally, the cost per $100 of credit insurance will be higher than the cost per $100 of, say, a decreasing term life insurance policy.

However, credit insurance may generally be used to cover much smaller amounts than a life insurance policy—a fact that may be useful if you wish to obtain coverage for a $5,000 auto loan. (The minimum amount of life insurance you can purchase is usually $50,000 or $100,000, depending on the insurer.) Thus, although you should expect to pay more per $100 of coverage for credit insurance than for life insurance, part of that added cost can be chalked up to convenience—just as you would expect to pay more per ounce for a glass of milk in a restaurant than for a gallon of milk at the supermarket.

Credit insurance may also be appropriate for consumers who would have difficulty obtaining disability or life insurance on their own—for example, because of poor health, a serious medical condition, or other circumstances that would make it difficult (or very costly) for certain individuals to obtain similar insurance on their own. However, some consumer advocates argue that credit insurance is not a good deal for consumers. If possible, you should decide ahead of time whether or not you want to buy credit insurance; otherwise, once you are at the point of sale, you may feel pressured to accept it, just as you may feel pressured in a sales situation to buy a more expensive TV set or more options on a car. Be sure that your decision is respected when it comes to credit insurance. Tell the salesperson whether or not you want the insurance. If you are told to "sign here, here, and here," be sure to study the credit agreement to ensure that your wishes regarding credit insurance have been observed. When you are at the final closing, check again. If you have made arrangements over the phone for a loan, and have specified that you do not wish to purchase credit insurance, check the loan document when you go to the lender's office to collect the loan. If you have stated that you do not want to purchase credit insurance, but find that such insurance is provided by the loan agreement, don't sign the agreement—even if the lender says that the form will have to be completely redone and that the loan closing will be delayed as a result.

As for credit insurance for credit cards, remember that credit insurance makes only the minimum payment each month, even though you may have been paying a larger amount toward your credit card bills before the disability or unemployment that triggered the benefit.

If you think credit insurance might make sense for you, you should also investigate purchasing decreasing term life insurance. Though you may have to purchase a high minimum amount, and pay more upfront, such insurance may protect your family better since it will last for as long as you continue to pay the premiums (and will not automatically terminate once the loan has been repaid), and since its benefits will not be tied to the amount you owe on a particular loan.

The Federal Trade Commission has a publication on credit insurance that is accessible online in English or Spanish at www .ftc.gov/bcp/edu/pubs/consumer/alerts/alt118.shtm.

REMEMBER THIS

- In order to obtain credit, you need a credit record. Opening both a checking and a savings account with a local bank is a way to establish a credit record.
- Credit insurance is insurance consumers may buy to help them pay a creditor for a loan if they die or become disabled or involuntarily unemployed. There are many different types of credit insurance.
- You do not have to purchase credit insurance from or through a creditor in order to obtain a loan from that creditor. Think carefully before purchasing credit insurance—many consumer advocates believe it is not a good deal, and insurance policies with better coverages could be available at comparable or lower cost from other insurance sources.

CHAPTER 5

Applying for a Credit Card (and Choosing the Right Card)

Credit Cards, Their Cost, and Their Potential Effect on Your Credit Rating

A credit card company sends you an attractive mailing. It says you are a select customer, preapproved for a gold or platinum card. It offers enticing cash advances, balance transfers with little or no transaction fees, and no annual fee. It also offers you the chance to redeem points for gifts and products. What could be wrong with this picture?

It sounds nice and easy, but there may be more to such a mailing than meets the eye. With credit card offers, you must look beyond the cover letters and examine all of the relevant information; remember to keep reading after the asterisks at the bottom of the first page. What happens with the balance transfers and cash advances when the introductory period runs out? How are the payments applied? What is the interest rate?

Many cards have high APRs (annual percentage rates), charge high penalties if you miss any payments, and charge even higher rates for cash advances. Even sending in a payment a day late could trigger a higher APR. In addition, card companies offering initial low rates may increase those rates if you miss a payment.

Many Americans rely—or over-rely—on credit cards. A 2007 Cardtrak.com survey found that the median average of credit card debt carried by Americans was more than $6,000. Among those who carried credit card debt, more than one in ten carried more than $25,000 in debt.

REVOLVING CREDIT

Revolving (open-end) credit is popular in this country, as more people have credit cards than ever before. Discover®, Master-Card®, Optima®, and Visa® are just a few of the many credit cards issued by banks, savings banks, and credit unions. When shopping for a credit card, you need to recognize that cards with the Visa® and MasterCard® logos are issued by thousands of different institutions; hence, if you do not like the terms on one Visa® card, you can always check with other issuers to see if their terms are preferable. Major retailers issue their own credit cards (or make special arrangements with banks or other third parties to have their store credit cards issued by third parties), and oil companies also have their own cards, although many oil companies do not offer revolving credit—only thirty-day credit (except on purchases of tires, batteries, and accessories).

BASICS OF CONTRACT LAW

It is important to understand that the agreement you sign when you apply for a credit card is a legally enforceable contract. A valid contract requires the parties to mutually agree to the basic contract terms. A mutual agreement consists of a valid offer and acceptance. When a credit card company sends you a preapproved credit card solicitation, the company has made an offer (subject to the conditions disclosed in the offer). When you accept the card and later sign your name or use the card, you have accepted the offer. Many believe that if you don't sign a credit card agreement, you have not signed a contract. This is false, as there are several ways to accept a credit card solicitation, including keeping and using the card.

A valid contract also requires that the agreement be supported by consideration, which consists of a type of bargained-for exchange in which each side to the contract receives possible benefits and/or detriments. The credit card company extends you

HISTORY OF THE CREDIT CARD

In the 1920s, several businesses began issuing credit cards to their customers for use only at their respective businesses. In 1946, John C. Biggins offered the first third-party credit card, called Charg-It, which was available for use in a two-block neighborhood in New York City. In 1949, the Diners Club® offered a credit card called the "Diner's Card" for entertainment expenses. American Express® issued a card in 1958 that is still known for its famous slogan, "Don't leave home without it."® In 1959, Bank of America in San Francisco issued its first BankAmericard®, which became available in other states in 1966. The original BankAmericard became known by its present name, Visa®, in 1976. Competing banks began offering the card known as MasterCard® in 1969.

---

credit but you must pay back the credit extended, together with certain fees, interest, and if you miss a required payment or pay late, there is a possibility for greater fees. Remember that a credit card solicitation—if accepted—can form a binding contract.

CHOOSING A CREDIT CARD

Selecting a credit card is like selecting a suit or dress: you want a good "fit." Because there are many card issuers, you have a wide variety of cards from which to choose. In this section, we will examine terms that banks and other issuers of credit cards typically offer consumers. Excerpts from example solicitations will help you to understand whether a card offered to you is a good fit for your own credit needs.

First, be aware that it is illegal for a card issuer to send you a credit card unless you have asked for it, or unless it replaces a card for which you previously asked. However, this doesn't mean you can't receive credit card solicitations and invitations to apply for credit cards. Second, under the federal Truth in Lending Act (TILA), every solicitation and application for a credit card must contain a brief disclosure statement (in the form of a table or chart), summarizing some (but not all) of the important fees, annual percentage rates (APRs), and other terms that apply to the credit card account. More extensive disclosures should be provided (often as part of the credit card customer agreement) before you use a credit card you have requested, and specific disclosures about finance and other charges and transaction fees are also required to be included as part of your periodic billing statements, which are usually sent monthly.

Annual Percentage Rate

The law requires a creditor to quote the APR of a credit card and to tell you the balance calculation method it uses to figure the finance charge you owe on credit card purchases. Since different creditors may use different methods to compute the balances to which APRs are applied, creditors who quote identical APRs may end up charging you different dollar finance charges each month. Each finance charge will depend on how you use the applicable account and on how the creditor calculates the unpaid balance for purposes of assessing its finance charge.

 ## ONLINE HELP IN CHOOSING CARDS

There are several places online where you can get information that could help you choose your credit cards. These include:

Federal Reserve on Choosing a Credit Card: www.federalreserve.gov/pubs/SHOP/

Federal Trade Commission on Choosing a Credit Card: www.ftc.gov/bcp/edu/pubs/consumer/credit/cre05.shtm

CardWeb.com: www.cardweb.com

Card Offers.com: www.cardoffers.com

Bankrate.com: www.bankrate.com

CreditCardSearchEngine.com: www.creditcardsearchengine.com

Computing the Balance

When figuring the finance charge you must pay for each billing period, credit card issuers may compute your account balance in a number of different ways. In the most common method, card issuers determine your **average daily balance** owed for the monthly billing period, and then apply the monthly periodic rate (corresponding to the APR divided by twelve) to that average figure to determine the amount of interest you owe for the monthly billing period. Credit card offers typically use the following language to indicate that this method will be used:

> *Method of Computing the Balance for Purchases*: Average Daily Balance (including new purchases)

Beginning in mid-2010, credit card offers may use the following language:

> *How We Will Calculate Your Balance:* We use a method called "average daily balance (including new purchases)."

A variation on the average daily balance method is the **daily balance method**. Instead of calculating the average daily balance owed for a monthly billing period and then applying a monthly periodic rate to this average daily balance to determine the finance charge owed for a monthly billing period, the daily balance method takes each daily balance owed during the billing period and applies a daily periodic rate (corresponding to the APR divided by 365) to the daily balance, to come up with the finance charge owed for each day in the billing period. Then, all of these daily finance charges are totaled to come up with the finance charge owed for the billing period.

Finance charges owed under the average daily balance and daily balance methods for a billing period will generally be very similar if the APRs and daily account balances are the same—minor differences between these two methods are largely due to the fact that the daily balance method figures finance charges owed for each day in a billing period, and some monthly billing periods are a few days shorter or longer than other monthly billing periods, while the average daily balance method generally applies a monthly periodic rate (corresponding to the APR divided by twelve) to monthly billing periods and disregards the fact that some monthly billing periods are slightly longer or shorter than other monthly billing periods. In addition, minor differences between the average daily balance and daily balance methods may occur due to rounding (since finance charges must be imposed and paid in whole cents, and card issuers may not all round fractions of pennies in exactly the same manner), even if APRs and daily account balances are the same.

Occasionally, retailers will use the **adjusted-balance method**, in which they compute your balance for finance charge calculation purposes by subtracting payments made or credits given during the billing period from the total amount you owed as of the start of the billing period. Other creditors may use the **previous-balance method**, in which any payments you make during the billing period are not subtracted from the total amount that you owed at the start of the billing period for finance charge calculation purposes. The previous-balance method can cost you more than the other three methods discussed above, depending on how you use your account. (See the chart below for examples that further explain the differences between these balance calculation methods.)

Credit card issuers may use other methods to compute your balance and finance charge, but these methods are the most common. There are also variations within these methods; for instance, some card issuers charge interest on unpaid interest, and essentially treat unpaid interest or finance charge as the equivalent of a transaction charged to the account until the interest or finance charge is paid.

Let's look at an example that demonstrates the major differences between these methods. For each method, assume that your credit card has a billing period of one month and an APR of 18 percent, you have a previous balance of $500, you make a payment of $400 on the sixteenth day of your billing period, and no other fees or charges are posted to the account during the billing period:

	Average Daily Balance Method	**Daily Balance Method**
APR	18% (corresponding monthly periodic rate of 1.5%)	18% (corresponding daily periodic rate of 0.0493%)
Previous balance	$500	$500
Payment on 16th day (of a 30-day billing period)	$400	$400
Calculation of finance charge	$300 x 1.5% equals $4.50. (During the billing period, the daily account balance was $500 for 15 days and $100 for 15 days, assuming no new purchase or other transactions during the billing period,* for an average daily balance of $300, multiplied by the monthly periodic rate of 1.5%.)	$500 times the daily periodic rate of 0.0493% equals $0.2465 daily finance charge for each of the first 15 days of the billing period (for a subtotal of $3.6975 in finance charges for the first 15 days). $100 times the daily periodic rate of 0.0493% equals $0.0493 daily finance charge for each of the last 15 days of the billing period (for a subtotal of $0.7395 in finance charges for the last 15 days). The total finance charge for the 30-day billing period is $4.437 (rounded to $4.44).**

*The average daily balance may be substantially higher than $300 in this example, if there were new purchases or other transactions charged to the account during the billing period, in which case the finance charge for the billing period would also be higher.

If the billing period in this example had an extra day in it (i.e., a 31-day billing period), with a daily balance of $100 on that extra day, there would have been an extra $0.0493 daily finance charge for that extra day, increasing the total finance charge for the billing period to $4.4863 (from $4.437) under the daily balance method, for a total finance charge of **$4.49 after rounding. (Under the average daily balance method, the average daily balance would have been $293.55 in this particular 31-day billing period example, for a total finance charge of $4.40.) In contrast, if the daily

Adjusted-Balance Method	**Previous-Balance Method**
18% (corresponding monthly periodic rate of 1.5%)	18% (corresponding monthly periodic rate of 1.5%)
$500	$500
$400	$400
$100 x 1.5% equals $1.50. (The amount owed as of the start of the billing period, minus payments made during the billing period multiplied by the monthly periodic rate of 1.5%.)	$500 x 1.5% equals $7.50. (The amount owed as of the start of the billing period, multiplied by the monthly periodic rate of 1.5%.)

balance had been $500 for that extra day, the total finance charge for the billing period would have increased by $0.2465 under the daily balance method, bringing the total finance charge for the billing period to $4.6835 (**$4.68** after rounding). Under the average daily balance method, the average daily balance would have been $306.45 in this particular 31-day billing period example, for a total finance charge of $4.60.

As you can see from these examples, finance charges may vary greatly depending on how the creditor calculates the balance that is subject to its finance charge.

PROTECT YOUR CREDIT CARDS AND KNOW YOUR RIGHTS

1. Sign new credit cards as soon as they arrive. Cut up and throw away expired credit cards. Destroy all unused preapproved credit card solicitations and applications.

2. Keep a list of your credit card numbers, expiration dates, and the toll-free telephone number of each card issuer in a safe place, so that you can report missing or stolen credit cards and possible billing errors (see chapter 9 for information about identity theft).

3. Don't lay your credit card down on a counter or table. Hand it directly to the clerk or waiter. Keep an eye on your card after you give it to a clerk. Make sure that he or she imprints only one charge slip and, if he or she makes an error and has to imprint a second charge slip, make sure he or she tears up the first one. Take your card back promptly after the clerk is finished with it, and make sure that it is yours. If the vendor is still using the old machines that produce carbon copies, tear up any carbons when you take your credit card receipt.

4. Never leave your credit card in the glove compartment of a car. Never leave your credit card in an unlocked desk drawer, grocery cart, or hotel room.

5. Never sign a blank credit card receipt. Draw a line through any blank spaces above the total when you sign receipts.

6. Open credit card bills promptly, and compare them with your receipts to check for unauthorized charges and billing errors. If your monthly statement doesn't arrive on time, call the issuer immediately.

7. Write or telephone the card issuer promptly to report any questionable charge. As a practical matter, most consumers would prefer to call the card issuer's toll-free 800 number for billing questions, and most disputes can be settled in this way. (You can find the correct 800 number on your billing statement.) However, written inquiries will leave a paper trail that might be helpful in certain situations. Written inquiries will better preserve your legal rights because the Fair Credit Billing Act only protects written—not telephone—inquiries.

Billing error inquiries should not be included with your payment. Instead, check the billing statement for the correct address for billing questions. Either a written or telephone inquiry must be made within sixty days of the statement date to protect your rights under the federal Fair Credit Billing Act, which is part of the Consumer Credit Protection Act.

8. Never give your credit card or checking account number over the telephone unless you have placed the call yourself. Never put your credit card number on a postcard or on the outside of an envelope.

9. Do not write your credit card number on a check (except for the checks paying your credit card bill), and do not allow any merchant who takes your check to do so either.

10. If any of your credit cards is missing or stolen, report the loss as soon as possible to the card issuer. Follow up your telephone calls with a letter to each card issuer. Send each letter by certified mail and keep a copy. Each letter should contain your credit card number, the date the card went missing, and the date you called to report the loss.

11. If you report the loss of a credit card before it is used by another party, under federal law the issuer cannot hold you responsible for any subsequent unauthorized charges. If a thief uses your card before you report it missing, the most that you will owe for unauthorized charges on each credit card is $50, though if you lose a number of cards you could be out hundreds of dollars. However, this limitation of liability does not apply to debit cards (cards that access funds in your checking or savings account and where greater delay may subject you to greater loss). Some banks may give you a limited guarantee against fraud connected with the use of your debit card, but such guarantees may allow them to investigate for a couple of weeks before refunding your money, and such guarantees also may include exceptions and exclusions for gross negligence or fraud and delay in reporting unauthorized use.

12. This may seem obvious, but it happens—don't lend your credit card to a family member or friend. You're liable for the charges, which may be way more than you expected.

Finance Charges

Many credit cards offer a finance charge grace period for purchases (but typically not for cash advances or balance transfers), which is the time between the end of the billing period and the date by which you must pay the entire account balance shown on the bill in full to avoid paying a finance charge on new purchases charged to the account during the billing period. This finance charge grace period for purchases is usually between twenty and twenty-five days. The finance charge grace period for purchases may be disclosed on a credit card solicitation or application in the following manner:

> *Grace period for repayment of the balance for purchases*: 25 days on average.

Beginning in mid-2010, credit card offers may use the following language:

> *How to Avoid Paying Interest on Purchases*: Your due date is at least 25 days after the close of each billing cycle. We will not charge you interest on purchases if you pay your entire balance by the due date each month.

In this example, note that the grace period starts on the billing date (the first day of the billing period). Thus, by the time you receive the bill, you may have only two weeks left to make your payment before the finance charge grace period ends. You must be careful to ensure that your payment is received (not just postmarked) before the end of the finance charge grace period. Also, be aware that the full account balance must be paid each month to avoid finance charges on purchases and that the grace period typically applies only to purchases. Thus, if you obtain, say, a cash advance with your credit card, you will almost always have to pay finance charges on the advance from the date you obtain it until the advance is repaid in full, and probably a cash advance transaction fee as well.

Some creditors may adjust the grace period using a method called the retroactive or two-cycle average daily balance method. Under this method, if you paid the last month's balance in full by the payment due date (so that no finance charges are imposed on new purchases that appeared on last month's billing statement—called the "Month A" billing statement), and then you make new purchases but do not pay your entire bill in full the following month (called the "Month B" billing statement), your next monthly statement (called the "Month C" billing statement) could include a finance charge not just for the new purchases that appeared on the "Month B" billing statement (because you did not pay the entire account balance in full during the finance grace period after receiving the "Month B" billing statement), but also could retroactively include finance charge for the new purchases on the "Month A" billing statement from the dates that they were posted to your account to the dates on which they were repaid. The two-cycle average daily balance method is prohibited for most credit card issuers as of July 1, 2010.

Here is how the Federal Reserve Board recently described the two-cycle average daily balance method of figuring finance charge:

> This method generally does not result in additional finance charges for a consumer who consistently carries a balance from month to month (and therefore does not receive a grace period) because interest is always accruing on the balance. Nor does the two-cycle method affect consumers who pay their balance in full within the grace period every month because interest is not imposed on their balances. The two-cycle method does, however, result in greater interest charges for consumers who pay their balance in full one month but not the next month (and therefore lose the grace period).
>
> The following example illustrates how the two-cycle method results in higher costs for these consumers than other balance computation methods: Assume that the billing cycle on a consumer credit card account starts on the first day of the month and ends on the last day of the month. The payment due date for the account is the twenty-fifth day of the month. Under the terms of the account, the consumer will not be charged interest on purchases if the balance at the end of a billing cycle is paid in full by the following payment due date (in other words, if the consumer receives a grace period). The

consumer uses the credit card to make a $500 purchase on March 15. The consumer pays the balance for the February billing cycle in full on March 25. At the end of the March billing cycle (March 31), the consumer's balance consists only of the $500 purchase and the consumer will not be charged interest on that balance if it is paid in full by the following due date (April 25). The consumer pays $400 on April 25, leaving a $100 balance. Because the consumer did not pay the balance for the March billing cycle in full on April 25, the consumer would lose the grace period and most institutions would charge interest on the $500 purchase from the start of the April billing cycle (April 1) through April 24 and interest on the remaining $100 from April 25 through the end of the April billing cycle (April 30). Institutions using the two-cycle method, however, would also charge interest on the $500 purchase from the date of purchase (March 15) to the end of the March billing cycle (March 31). (See 74 Federal Register 5489-5584, 5535 [January 29, 2009].)

As noted earlier, as of July 1, 2010, most credit card issuers will be prohibited from using the two-cycle average daily balance method.

By paying credit card balances in full every month within the finance charge grace period, you may be able to avoid pay-

HOW MANY CARDS SHOULD YOU HAVE?

Consumers are often deluged with credit card solicitations in the mail and over email. It is easy and often tempting to apply for more credit cards, but you should think carefully before taking on more than one. Having too many credit cards could lower your credit score because you could be deemed to be at risk of having too many credit repayment obligations and being overburdened with respect to your disposable income. Remember that a key aspect of your credit score is the relative ratio of your debts to your assets. It is a mistake to open new credit accounts to increase your available credit.

ing finance charges on purchases (although not on cash advances or most balance transfers). If you are able to pay your credit card balances in full every month, the annual percentage rates charged by your credit card issuer on purchases may be less important to you. Instead, the finance charge grace period for purchases, the APRs for cash advances and balance transfers, and the dollar amount of any annual fee, overlimit fee, late and returned payment fees, and other fees (including cash advance and balance transfer fees) may be more important.

Variable APRs

Often a credit card will have a **variable-rate provision** in which the credit card issuer sets an APR that varies based on some interest rate index, such as the market rate on three-year U.S. Treasury bills (T-bills) or the prime rate charged by banks on short-term business loans. Where such a provision applies, the issuer must disclose in its solicitation to you that the rate may vary and how the rate is determined. This may be done by describing the applicable index and the spread (sometimes also called the margin) that is the number of percentage points added to the index rate to determine the rate you will pay. A current typical disclosure for a variable-rate credit card solicitation or application might look something like this:

Variable Rate Information: Your Annual Percentage Rate may vary. The rate will be determined monthly by adding 9% to the Prime Rate as published in The Wall Street Journal. The rate will not go below 15.0% or exceed 19.9%.

However, important changes to variable rate information are scheduled to take place on July 1, 2010. As of that date, the Federal Reserve Board limits the variable rate information that may be included as part of credit card solicitation and application disclosures, in an attempt to streamline such disclosures, reduce the risk of "information overload" in such disclosures, and focus consumer attention on other important information contained in such disclosures.

Beginning on July 1, 2010, credit card solicitations and applications may describe the variable rate feature along the following lines (sample language for a variable rate APR applicable to credit card purchase transactions appears below for illustration purposes only):

Annual Percentage Rate (APR) *for Purchases:* **8.99%**, **10.99%**, *or* **12.99%** *introductory* APR *for one year, based on your creditworthiness.*

After that, your APR *will be* **14.99%**. *This* APR *will vary with the market based on the Prime Rate.*

The Federal Reserve Board has determined through focus group testing that consumers do not generally use the detailed variable rate information historically included with credit card application and solicitation disclosures when shopping for credit cards. The Federal Reserve Board has revised the credit card application and solicitation disclosure requirements to prohibit including detailed information about the index and margin as part of these application and solicitation disclosures.

Detailed information about the index and margin may (but is not required to) appear outside of these application and solicitation disclosures as additional optional supplemental information. Detailed information about the index and margin will continue to be included as part of the actual credit card agreement. The above sample disclosure is based on a model disclosure form prepared by the Federal Reserve Board as guidance to creditors concerning the disclosure rules that will take effect in 2010. It is important to note the requirement that the APRs for purchases appear in at least 16-point type when appearing as part of required credit card application or solicitation disclosures.

While the above example speaks of annual percentage rates of 8.99, 10.99, and 14.99, some credit card companies charge annual percentage rates of nearly 30 percent to certain consumers. If you make late payments to credit card companies, your rates can rise. Fortunately, federal regulations that go into effect in July 2010 will offer some protection and should curb the most abusive practices of credit card issuers.

It is important to note that issuers of fixed-rate cards can also

IF YOU'VE GOT BAD CREDIT

You'd like to have a credit card, but you've got bad credit. Be careful—you might not like the deal you're offered. Consumers with bad credit may get credit card solicitations promising a card if they pay an up-front fee. These fees can be very high, and the interest rates on the cards can be very high too.

Maybe a better approach is to get your spending under control, improve your credit rating, and then apply for a card—maybe a secured card. Also, if you cannot pay off the entire balance on your credit card, you should pay as much of that balance as you can afford. If you pay only the minimum amount due each month, it may take you more than ten years to pay off your credit card debt, even if you never use your card again.

change their rates from time to time, in accordance with the applicable cardholder agreements and with state and federal law, often simply by sending the cardholder fifteen days' advance written notice of a rate increase. Again, changes are afoot: after July 1, 2010, credit card issuers must give cardholders at least forty-five days' advance written notice of most rate increases.

Annual Fees

A credit card solicitation or application must disclose any annual or other periodic fee that applies to your account, as well as certain other fees such as transaction, cash advance, and late fees, if they are imposed.

Few, if any, credit cards issued by or through retailers have annual fees. However, such fees are common in the case of credit cards issued by financial institutions. Annual fees usually range from $15 to $25, and perhaps from $35 to $60 or more for "premium cards" that provide higher lines of credit. Charge cards, such as American Express® or Diners Club®, are different from credit cards in the sense that full payment is due when you are billed. They have annual fees that often exceed annual fees charged for credit cards. If you pay your credit card account balance in full each month and thus do not generally expect to pay finance charges on purchases, you should shop for a credit card with either no annual fee or an annual fee that is low. If you often don't pay your balance in full, a low APR may be more important to you than a low annual fee. Some credit cards have a minimum finance charge even if you pay in full each month.

Other Fees

Assuming that transaction, cash advance, over-the-limit, and late fees are a part of your credit card plan, the credit card solicitation or application disclosures may include a statement that looks something like this:

> *Transaction fee for cash advances, and fees for paying late or exceeding the credit limit*: **Transaction fee for Cash Advances:** 2% of the amount of the advance ($1.00 minimum; $10.00 maximum). **Late payment fee:** $15.00, if the amount due is $2 or more. **Over-the-limit fee:** $15.00.

Beginning in mid-2010 credit card offers may use the following language (sample language appears below for illustration purposes only):

> *Transaction fees:*
> **Balance Transfer:** Either **$5** or **3%** of the amount of each transfer, whichever is greater (maximum fee: $100).
> **Cash Advance:** Either **$5** or **3%** of the amount of each cash advance, whichever is greater.
> **Foreign Transaction:** 2% of each transaction in U.S. dollars.

> *Penalty fees:*
> **Late Payment: $29** if balance is less than or equal to $1,000; **$35** if balance is more than $1,000.
> **Over-the-Credit limit: $29**
> **Returned Payment: $35**

Unless you expect to be late with your payments, your choice of a card should not be heavily influenced by the size of its late

CHOOSING THE *RIGHT* CREDIT CARD

A credit card must fit your financial habits. If you often do not pay your account in full each month, you should pay more attention to the annual percentage rate (APR) than someone who pays in full every month and never owes a finance charge. That person will be more concerned with an annual fee that might be levied.

Just knowing the APR is not enough, since there are different ways of calculating the balance against which the APR is applied. If you don't think your income will rise if interest rates go up, you might prefer a credit card with a fixed APR rather than one with a variable rate. However, it is important to remember that the APR on a fixed rate credit card may still go up after the card issuer gives you advance written notice of the rate increase.

If you expect to use your credit card to obtain cash advances, the card's cash advance fee and cash advance APR should be important considerations. Moreover, if you have a hard time keeping track of charges on your credit cards, cards with high over-the-limit fees may be worth avoiding. Finally, if late fees promise to be a major problem for you, perhaps it is in your best interest to refrain from taking on a credit card account.

fees. Note that your credit card plan may provide for other fees as well, such as replacement card fees, copy fees, wire transfer fees, and telephone payment fees, that are not required to be disclosed as part of a credit card solicitation or application.

Most credit card issuers set a limit on the amount of credit they are willing to provide you at any one time. To encourage you not to exceed this limit, some card issuers may charge over-the-limit fees. Unless you keep careful track of your charge slips, it may be difficult for you to know how much you owe in relation to your credit limit. Thus, if you believe that you might be close to your credit limit from time to time, you might want to shop for a credit card that does not have over-the-limit fees, or that has a very low over-the-limit fee.

ARBITRATION AWARENESS

Consumers should be aware that many credit card companies require consumers to submit claims to arbitration. Many consumers unknowingly enter into contracts requiring them to resolve their disputes through mandatory arbitration. The consumer watchdog group Public Citizen refers to this as the "Arbitration Trap." They write in their 2007 report that "binding mandatory arbitration is a rigged game in which justice is dealt from a deck stacked against consumers." See Public Citizen's 2007 publication at www.citizen.org/documents/ArbitrationTrap.pdf. On the other hand, some credit professionals argue that consumers do derive benefits from using arbitration instead of litigation. Like most things, it is difficult to draw absolute conclusions about arbitration.

The Federal Arbitration Act generally permits mandatory arbitration provisions to be included as part of consumer contracts. Many federal court cases have held that such provisions are permitted under the Federal Arbitration Act. (See, for example, the U.S. Supreme Court decisions in *Green Tree Financial Corp. v. Randolph*, 531 U.S. 79 [2000] and *Buckeye Check Cashing, Inc. v. Cardegna*, 546 U.S. 440 [2006].) Some courts have, however, refused to enforce certain specific aspects of mandatory arbitration clauses (such as provisions limiting a consumer's ability to recover punitive damages).

IN CASE OF REJECTION

What if the credit card company turns you down? You may want to consider applying for a **secured credit card**. This is a credit card issued by a bank or other financial institution that is secured by a savings account that you have deposited with that particular institution. You need to shop carefully for the best terms. Try to avoid having to pay an application fee for a secured credit card. Your line of credit will typically be limited to between 90 and 100 percent of the balance in the savings account that is securing the credit card. As you shop around for a secured card, compare the rates paid on savings accounts, the APR charged on the credit card account, and the fees that may be charged on both the savings account and the credit card account. Especially important are the amounts of late fees and any over-the-limit fees, which can sometimes be quite high with secured credit cards.

Secured cards are something like training wheels on a bicycle: Once you have shown that you can use them, you should be allowed to move on to the "real thing." Once you have shown that you can handle a secured credit account, you should ask the institution that issued you the secured credit card to offer you the opportunity to switch to an unsecured card with more favorable terms. If your request is declined, even after you have established a good credit record, you should take your business elsewhere and apply for a regular credit card from another financial institution.

 ## THE CYCLE OF DEBT STARTS EARLY

Credit card companies have learned that the key to growth in their industry often lies with young people. According to recent statistics cited by Congress, 75 percent of college students have a credit card. As of 2002, nearly 50 percent of college students have significant credit card debt, with an average debt of more than $3,000 per student. As of 2007, 56 percent of college students had four or more credit cards with an average balance of nearly $3,000. The number of bankruptcies filed by people between the ages of 18 and 24 has escalated dramatically.

Many consumer groups have been formed to teach young people about finances and credit, including Jump$tart Coalition for Personal Financial Literacy, which offers a number of resources online at www.jumpstart.org.

It is important to learn about credit early in life, particularly in an era where credit card marketers target young people as customers.

PROTECTIONS FOR THE CONSUMER

Truth in Lending Act

As explained in chapter two, the federal Truth in Lending Act (TILA) helps you to choose credit wisely by requiring creditors to give you plenty of information before you make a choice. However, the law alone cannot protect you fully; you have to do your part by being an informed consumer.

TILA does not set finance charges, nor does it tell if rates are fair or unfair. In some states, laws exist to prevent you from paying finance charges that are thought by legislators to be too high, but often these laws are not applicable to every bank in the state. In any event, in most cases it is simply marketplace competition that serves to keep credit card rates in line. But for competition to continue as an effective mechanism for controlling rates, consumers must reward with their business only those credit card companies that offer the most favorable terms. Thus, you the consumer must use the information provided by creditors to select the credit card that best fits your needs.

Violations of TILA

A creditor violates TILA if it fails to disclose required information in a timely manner, or if it provides you with required disclosures that are inaccurate. In the event of such a violation, you should inform the proper federal enforcement agency. The consumer protection office of your state or local government should be able to help you find the appropriate agency; you can also use the appendix of this book to find the appropriate agencies to contact. To enforce your rights under TILA, you have the right to bring a lawsuit for actual damages (any money loss you have suffered as a result of the violation). Under TILA, you may also sue for an amount equal to twice your finance charge or $100, whichever is greater. Even if your finance charge is high, however, the most you can recover under TILA is $1,000 for an account that is neither secured by real estate nor by any type of residential property (such as a manufactured home), unless you are able to prove actual damages arising from the inaccurate or delayed disclosures. Should you win your lawsuit, TILA also entitles you to recover your court costs and reasonable lawyers' fees.

Regulation Z is the rule, issued by the Federal Reserve Board, which implements the federal Truth in Lending Act. In the American system of law, Congress—as the legislative branch of our federal government—passes laws that generally affect a set of actions or a particular aspect of society. However, these laws often grant the power to implement and expound them through additional rules or regulations to different administrative agencies of the executive branch of our federal government. Regulation Z is one such regulation. Regulation Z governs how creditors must disclose terms of credit, compute credit costs, and resolve certain credit card and revolving credit account disputes. Its stated purpose is "to promote the informed use of consumer credit by requiring disclosures about its terms and cost." For example, TILA and Regulation Z generally prohibit creditors from issuing credit cards unless consumers request the cards. Regulation Z also provides that creditors must disclose finance charges and other important terms. It also provides remedies for certain credit card and revolving credit account billing errors and limits liability for unauthorized charges, as described in the next chapter.

Under some state laws, a violation of TILA may be considered an unfair or deceptive act or practice or a violation of other state law, in which case other state law remedies may be available. For instance, some state laws may impose greater penalties, such as treble (triple) damages, upon violators in certain instances. You should contact your state's Office of Consumer Protection (or a similar office), or your state attorney general's office for more information on relevant state laws, since deciding whether to proceed under federal or state remedies is often a complex issue that requires learned guidance.

Limiting Finance Charges

Shopping carefully for credit plays a key role in minimizing the finance charges that you will eventually have to pay, regardless of whether you are looking for closed-end credit (installment credit) or open-end credit (revolving credit). And even though many states impose rate ceilings on various creditors or types of credit—for example, state law usually limits the rates that finance companies may charge—careful shopping can still save you money.

When shopping for the best terms for you, check the *Wall Street Journal* and other newspapers that frequently publish shopping guides to credit cards from financial institutions. Such guides typically cover all of the relevant terms discussed in this chapter. In addition, you can easily shop for credit cards and compare terms by logging on to www.cardweb.com and other sites that provide information on credit cards. The Federal Reserve Board also gathers credit card rates for publication.

 TALKING TO A LAWYER

Q. My card issuer just raised my rate—which I thought was locked in—with no explanation. When I called them they said it was because I had become a worse credit risk (even though I'm paying off my balance with them regularly). How did this happen, and how can I prevent it from happening again on another account?

A. Your credit card agreement may have included a provision allowing the card issuer to increase your annual percentage rate (APR) if you have become past due on other accounts you have, either with the card issuer or with another creditor, or allowing the card issuer to increase your APR if the card issuer has good reason to believe that you now pose a higher risk of nonpayment than before (for instance, because your credit report might show a larger number of accounts past due now than before, or because your credit report might show a larger dollar amount of total debt outstanding now than before). In addition, your credit card agreement may allow the card issuer to increase your APR by giving you fifteen days' advance written notice of the increase. You should review your credit card agreements carefully to determine the circumstances in which your card issuers may have reserved the right to increase your APR. You may also wish to consider transferring the balance you presently own on a higher APR credit card account over to a lower APR credit card account, and discontinue using the higher APR account. Please also note that new rules scheduled to take effect on July 1, 2010, limit the circumstances in which an APR increase may apply to pre-existing outstanding account balances, and require forty-five (instead of fifteen) days' advance written notice of most APR increases.

—Answer by Elizabeth C. Yen, Hudson Cook, LLP, New Haven, Connecticut

Q. *Credit card applications are full of small print and stuff I don't understand. What should I look for? What can I do if I find something I don't agree with?*

A. Look for universal default clauses, arbitration clauses, grace periods, how payments are applied, the method of computing the finance charge, and the manner in which the terms of the agreement can be changed. If you find terms you do not like, don't accept the card and let the card company know why.

—Answer by Marc S. Stern, Law Offices of Marc S. Stern, Seattle, Washington

Q. *Is it worthwhile to sue under TILA? It doesn't seem like you can recover much money.*

A. As a general rule, suing is never a good idea unless you feel strongly that you have been harmed. As for TILA, it depends upon the circumstances. If it involves a $50 credit card charge, maybe not. If it is your house involved, probably yes.

—Answer by Marc S. Stern, Law Offices of Marc S. Stern, Seattle, Washington

High Credit Card Rates

Many states impose rate ceilings on store credit cards. A rate ceiling is the uppermost rate that an institution extending credit can charge. However, these limits do not always apply across the board. For example, under federal law, national banks may export their finance charge rates and related fees on credit cards from their home state to residents of other states. This means that if a national bank is located in Delaware and the consumer is located in Arkansas, the national bank can charge the higher interest rate allowed in Delaware even if that rate exceeds Arkansas law. State-chartered, federally insured banks generally have the same rate and fee exportation rights as national banks. Thus, a national bank or a state-chartered FDIC-insured bank may issue credit cards from headquarters located in (for example) South Dakota, enabling it to charge its cardholders in Iowa any rate the credit card agreement specifies, since South Dakota does not have a rate ceiling on bank-issued credit cards. While most retailers selling to Iowa consumers may not charge rates on their store credit cards higher than Iowa law permits, some major retailers have made arrangements with banks headquartered in South Dakota (or other states with no rate ceiling on bank-issued credit cards) to have those banks issue credit cards for use only at the retailers' store locations. In such instances, the bank-issued store credit cards are generally subject to the laws of the state where the bank is headquartered. Of course, competition forces banks and retailers to keep their rates in line with those charged by other financial institutions and retailers. In this particular South Dakota example the pressures of the marketplace—the choices made by informed consumers—set the rates. The law does not set them.

Nonetheless, if you believe that you are being charged a rate that violates state law, you should report your case to your state's Office of Consumer Protection (or a similar office), your state's attorney general, or the federal authorities for national banks or federal credit unions (depending on whether the credit card is issued by a national bank, a federal credit union, or some other type of financial institution). Consult the appendix of this book

TALKING TO A LAWYER

Q. When I checked in at a hotel I gave them one card, but when I paid I gave them another—and now I'm having a problem with the first card company. They've earmarked an amount to pay the bill, so I'm blocked from using that money till they're satisfied that the bill has been paid. What can I do?

A. Hotels and car rental companies often estimate the amount they will eventually be charging to your credit card, and ask the credit card company to place a "hold" on your account for that estimated amount. This is done to ensure that you will have enough available credit on your account to cover the total amount owed to the hotel or car rental company when you check out or when you return the rental car. If you make your payment with a different credit card from the card you used when you first checked in, the first card company (the company that issued the card you used when you checked in) may still be waiting for the hotel or car rental company to post the final charge to your account, and may not agree to release the "hold" on your account until the hotel or car rental company authorizes them to release the "hold" (by telling them that you have paid your bill with a different credit card). Ask the hotel or car rental company to contact your credit card company about releasing the "hold" on your account, or give your credit card company a copy of your final hotel or car rental bill and a copy of your credit card charge receipt showing that you used a different credit card to pay that bill.

—Answer by Elizabeth C. Yen, Hudson Cook, LLP,
New Haven, Connecticut

for information about where to go in the event of such problems. As explained above, competition and enforcement activities usually prevent such violations on the part of credit card issuers, but if there is a violation, you may be able to recover some or all of your finance charges plus a penalty, depending upon the applicable state's law.

In December 2008, the Federal Reserve adopted new rules that limit some of the more egregious practices of credit card companies, including the raising of interest rates retroactively on old purchases and raising interest rates in the first year of issuance. The new rules will not go into effect until July 1, 2010. For more information on these new rules, see the Federal Reserve's news release at www.federalreserve.gov/newsevents/press/bcreg/20081218a.htm.

REMEMBER THIS

- All credit cards are different. Selecting one is a decision that should be made carefully. You want and need a good fit.
- Remember that federal law requires credit card companies to disclose the costs of credit to you, the consumer. They must tell you the APR, finance charges, how finance charges are computed, and a host of other financial information.
- Bear in mind that the Truth in Lending Act (TILA) is primarily a disclosure statute. It does not set limits on the interest rates that credit card companies may charge, although it does impose certain requirements and restrictions on such things as how a card issuer may change certain terms applicable to a credit card account after the account is opened. For example, effective July 1, 2010, the Federal Reserve Board's regulations implementing TILA increase (from fifteen days to forty-five days) the period of advance written notice cardholders generally must receive in connection with certain changes to their credit card account terms. The circumstances under which rates may be increased on pre-existing account balances are also restricted effective July 1, 2010.
- Some cards do not offer fixed APRs. Many cards have variable rates, usually tied to an interest rate index. Sometimes these rates can soar to as high as 30 percent if you do not make timely payments every month. It's important to note that as of July 1, 2010, higher penalty or default APRs may apply to pre-existing outstanding credit card balances if a payment becomes or remains more than 30 days past due after advance written notice

of intent to impose the higher penalty or default APR is given. If you plan to use your card for cash advances, carefully consider the cash advance fee. Credit card companies use different methods to calculate the balance upon which you pay finance charges. Pay attention to this methodology when you receive a credit card advertisement.

• The APR, fees, finance charge grace periods, and other terms and conditions of a credit card may change after the account is opened. Many of these changes can happen after the credit card company gives you fifteen days' advance written notice of the change. As of July 1, 2010, this fifteen-day advance notice requirement is being increased to a forty-five-day advance notice requirement.

• Identity thieves would love to get their hands on your credit cards. Guard your cards and know where they are at all times.

• If you have too many credit cards, you could increase the chance that your total credit repayment obligations might exceed your disposable income, and you could lower your credit score and overall credit rating.

CHAPTER 6

How to Correct Billing Mistakes

Your Rights Under the Fair Credit Billing Act and Other Consumer Protection Laws

You receive your credit card bill and are surprised to find it contains a charge for an item you bought and returned the next day. There was plenty of time for the store to reverse the charge before the credit card bill was sent, but it didn't happen. What can you do? Does the law offer any help?

After you have established credit, the best way to remain in good standing is to repay your debts on time. If you fail to pay a bill, the relevant creditor can hurt your credit record by reporting your delinquent account to credit bureaus.

However, what happens if the creditor makes an error on your bill? What if you are billed for an item that you did not buy or for a product that you returned as defective? This chapter discusses what you can do to correct creditors' mistakes on your credit card or other revolving (open-end) account billing statement.

BILLING ERRORS

Fair Credit Billing Act

Your credit rating will not suffer if there is an error on your account and you promptly bring the error to the attention of the creditor. However, if you don't pay, and you don't swiftly bring the error to the attention of the creditor, your rating could suffer.

The Fair Credit Billing Act, passed in 1974, requires revolving (open-end) account creditors, such as credit card issuers, to correct billing errors promptly. It defines a billing error as a charge on your credit card or other revolving account:

• for something that you didn't buy, or for a purchase made by someone not authorized to use your account;

• that is not properly identified on your monthly account statement, or that is for an amount different from the actual purchase price; or

• for something that you refused to accept on delivery because it was unsatisfactory, or that the supplier did not deliver according to your agreement.

Billing errors may also include:

• errors in arithmetic;

• failure to reflect a payment that you made or other credit to your revolving account; or

• failure to mail an account billing statement to your current address (if the creditor received notice of that address at least twenty days before the end of the billing period).

For a summary of the Fair Credit Billing Act, a sample dispute letter and common billing errors, see the Federal Trade Commission's short publication, "Fair Credit Billing," available online at www.ftc.gov/bcp/edu/pubs/consumer/credit/cre16.shtm.

In Case of Billing Errors

If you think your revolving (open-end) bill is incorrect, or if you simply want more details about it, you should take the following steps:

1. In order to preserve your legal rights, notify your creditor in writing of the potential billing error. Many creditors readily handle billing complaints over the phone, and calling is a lot faster and easier than writing a letter—be prepared to provide your name, address, account number, and a description of the error. However, it is safer to send a letter as well, because sending a letter will trigger the protections of the Fair Credit Billing Act.

2. If you aren't satisfied with the results of your phone call, note the name of the person you talked to and send a letter to the address your creditor has supplied for billing error purposes

on your bill, so that the creditor receives the letter within sixty days after the bill was mailed. The sixty-day period is very important. Use the address for billing error inquiries on your account statement—do not send your letter to the address for account payments. If you don't do this, you may lose your rights under the Fair Credit Billing Act. The letter should contain your name, address, and account number. State that you believe your bill contains an error, describe the error and explain why you believe your bill is wrong, and include the date and the suspected amount of the error.

For an example of what may happen if a consumer does not provide sufficient written notice of a billing error to a credit card issuer, see *Conn-Burnstein v. Saks Fifth Avenue & Company*, 85 Fed. Appx. 430, 2003 U.S. App. LEXIS 26600 (6th Cir. 2003), affirming 208 F.Supp.2d 765 (E.D. Mich. 2002). In that case, the federal appeals court upheld a lower court ruling in favor of a store credit card issuer, where the jury had found that a customer's letter did not provide the credit card issuer with enough information to enable the card issuer to identify and investigate the customer's alleged billing error. The court noted that, al-

 KEEP SALES RECEIPTS

One reason to keep sales receipts is so that you may return an item in the event that it is defective, damaged, or the wrong size or color. Another reason to keep sales slips is to protect against billing errors. Most credit and charge card companies do not provide sales slips with your monthly statement; rather, your statement usually gives only the date and amount of purchases and the store where you bought each item. Therefore, you need to keep all sales slips, at least until you have checked them against your monthly credit and charge card billing statements. Keeping your receipts will also enable you to determine whether some unauthorized person is charging purchases to your account.

though the consumer claimed her account had been double-billed for certain purchases, her "letter failed to identify any specific instances of double-billing and failed to specify the amount of any alleged billing error." The court's opinion explained that a consumer's written correspondence to a creditor must do three things in order to trigger a creditor's responsibilities under the Fair Credit Billing Act. The letter must:

(1) set forth or otherwise enable the creditor to identify the name and account number (if any) of the obligor,

(2) indicate the consumer's belief that the account statement contains a billing error and the amount of such billing error, and

(3) set forth the reasons for the consumer's belief (to the extent applicable) that the account statement contains a billing error.

In the case of *Langenfeld v. Chase Bank USA, N.A.*, 537 F.Supp.2d 1181 (N.D. Okla. 2008), the federal district court held that a letter that did not dispute any specific extension of credit or the dollar amount of any specific extension of credit, and that did not request supporting documentation for any specific extension of credit, but that only generally disputed the credit card issuer's legal right to impose any finance charges at all on the credit card account from the date the account was first opened, did not raise a billing error dispute under the Fair Credit Billing Act. (The letter was also sent years after the account had been opened, and therefore was not received by the credit card issuer within sixty days after the first monthly account statement showing disputed finance charges had been mailed.)

Duties of the Creditor After Notice

The law requires a revolving (open-end) account creditor to acknowledge your billing error letter within thirty days. (This does not apply if the creditor fixes the billing error within thirty days.) The creditor must investigate and correct your revolving (open-end) account within two billing periods. Fixing the error should never take more than ninety days from the time the creditor receives written notice of your billing dispute. If the creditor does not correct the error, it must tell you in writing why it believes the bill is not wrong.

If the creditor reviews your bill and does not find an error, it must promptly send you a statement explaining why the creditor believes the original bill was correct, and explaining what you still owe and when payment is due on the amount you had questioned. On this statement, the creditor may include any finance charges that accumulated and any minimum payments you missed while you were disputing the bill.

In some cases, consumers may not have to pay finance charges on the contested amounts owed on their revolving accounts under the Fair Credit Billing Act, provided they have sent a timely written billing error notice. There are two possible outcomes. If the bill is not correct, you do not have to pay the finance charges on the amount that was improperly billed to your account. If you have already paid these amounts, the creditor should refund them. If the bill is correct, you must pay the amounts owed, including related finance charges.

Effect on Credit Rating

A creditor may not threaten your credit rating because you didn't pay a disputed amount, a related finance charge, or other dispute-related charges owed on a revolving account while you're trying to resolve a billing dispute. Once you have taken the required steps described above by writing down your question and sending it to the creditor, the law prohibits the creditor from reporting the account as delinquent because you have not paid the disputed amount or related charges. Until the creditor answers your written billing error notice, the law forbids it from taking any action to collect the amount in dispute. You must, however, continue to pay any undisputed amounts.

However, if the creditor finds that the disputed bill is correct, then you must pay the bill. If you fail to pay, then the creditor may take action to collect the amount and may report you to credit bureaus as overdue for the amount in question.

If the creditor finds that the disputed bill is correct, but you still disagree with this finding, notify the creditor of your views in writing within ten days of receiving the creditor's written explanation to you of why the creditor believes your bill is correct. Then, if the creditor reports your account as past due because of the billing dispute, it must also report that you have challenged the bill and must give you written notice of the name and address of each person who has been told by the creditor that your account is past due because of the billing error dispute. When you settle the dispute with the creditor, that outcome must be reported by the creditor to each person who was previously told by the creditor that your account was past due because of the billing error dispute. If you are unable to settle the dispute to your satisfaction, you may want to consult a lawyer.

If the creditor does not follow each of these rules within the time limits required by the Fair Credit Billing Act, then the creditor cannot collect the first $50 of the disputed amount, even if the disputed bill turns out to be correct and the amount is thus money you truly owed. In addition, the creditor is subject to any applicable remedies available for violations of the Truth in Lending Act (as discussed in chapter 2).

DEFECTIVE GOODS OR SERVICES

The Fair Credit Billing Act (FCBA) also provides some assistance to certain consumers who purchase certain defective goods or services with a credit card. If you use a credit card to purchase shoddy or damaged goods or poor-quality services, the FCBA might help. If you have not already paid off your credit card balance relating to the defective or damaged or otherwise disputed goods or services, the FCBA allows you to withhold payment that is still due to the credit card issuer for the disputed goods or services, provided that you first notify the card issuer or retailer of your claim or defense and have made a real attempt to solve the problem with the retailer. You can demonstrate such an

TALKING TO A LAWYER

Q. This chapter has a lot of information on legal protections regarding credit cards, but in practical terms, how can someone best protect himself in disputes with a credit card issuer?

A. Write a letter, send it certified mail, and keep a copy.

—Answer by Marc S. Stern, Law Offices of Marc S. Stern, Seattle, Washington

attempt by providing the card issuer with, for example, a copy of a letter you have sent to the retailer's complaint department, or with notes you took at the time you made a phone call to the complaint department, including the name of the person with whom you spoke.

You have the right to withhold payment relating to defective, damaged, or otherwise disputed goods or services if you bought the goods or services with a bank card such as Visa® or Master-Card®, or with a travel or entertainment card, or a store credit card. For example, if you purchase a tour or air travel ticket using your credit card, and the tour or airline goes bankrupt before your trip, you may be able to withhold payment on that charge. However, when you use your credit card, the law generally limits your right to withhold payment in connection with defective, damaged, or otherwise disputed goods or services to credit card charges greater than $50, which took place either in your home state or within 100 miles of your home address. (The $50 limit and the home state/100-mile rule do not apply to a purchase charged to a credit card that was issued by the retailer or by a company related to the retailer and also do not apply to goods or services charged to a credit card as the result of a direct mail solicitation made or participated in by the credit card issuer.)

If you refuse to pay for a charge on your credit card statement because goods or services are defective, the credit card issuer might sue you for payment. If a court finds the goods or services to be truly defective, you probably won't have to pay for the credit card charge, provided that you tried in good faith to resolve your dispute about the defective goods or services directly with the retailer. Moreover, during the dispute period, the card issuer cannot report the disputed amount to a credit bureau as delinquent.

LOST OR STOLEN CREDIT CARDS

The Truth in Lending Act limits your liability in the event that your credit cards are lost or stolen. It is very important that you notify the credit card company as soon as you notice the loss or theft of one or more of your cards, since you are not responsible for any unauthorized charges made after such notification. Moreover, under TILA, the most you will have to pay for any unauthorized charges made before you notify the credit card company is $50 on each card. However, this TILA limitation of liability does not apply to debit cards (cards that access funds on deposit in checking or savings accounts) or prepaid (stored value) cards such as prepaid gift cards—different rules apply to lost or stolen debit cards and prepaid (stored value) cards. For a summary of the different federal law limitations on your liability for unauthorized charges made with credit and debit cards, please see the Federal Trade Commission's short publication, "Credit, ATM and Debit Cards: What to do if They're Lost or Stolen," available online at www.ftc.gov/bcp/edu/pubs/consumer/credit/cre04.shtm.

Being Prepared for Lost or Stolen Credit Cards

As noted in chapter 5, it is a good idea to keep a list of all your credit cards, their account numbers, and the information needed to notify the credit card issuers of theft or loss. Since you may lose credit cards when traveling, always take a copy of this list with you and keep it separate from your credit cards. And be sure to keep the list itself in a safe place, since someone with your account numbers may be able to make purchases on your account, even if he or she does not have the actual cards. Also, you should keep your Social Security number separate from your credit cards, since some issuers of credit cards use Social Security numbers to check the identities of card users.

REMEMBER THIS

• The Fair Credit Billing Act is the federal law that governs billing errors and the rights of consumers when disputing errors on credit card or other revolving (open-end) accounts. The law establishes time limits for consumers and creditors that are designed to establish a framework for resolving such disputes.

• Make sure that you give written notice of a billing error to the creditor within sixty days after you receive an erroneous bill. This is an important time limitation for consumers. Generally, creditors have thirty days to acknowledge a consumer's written dispute of a credit card charge.

• The Fair Credit Billing Act also provides a degree of protection to consumers who purchase defective goods or services with a credit card.

• The Fair Credit Billing Act also requires the prompt crediting of payments and provides rights with respect to credit (positive) balances on your account (if you pay more than your outstanding account balance).

• The Truth in Lending Act limits your liability for lost or stolen credit cards.

CHAPTER 7

Credit Records

Your Rights Under the Fair Credit Reporting Act

You receive an invitation in the mail for a credit card with an excellent APR, no annual fee, and other favorable terms. You believe this is a good deal and apply for the card. Unfortunately, a short while later you receive a letter from the credit card company denying you credit. You are shocked, because you know that you have excellent credit, have always paid your bills on time, and do not carry large balances. You are mystified as to this development and recognize that your credit report must be flawed. You are not alone. Many people have mistakes on their credit reports.

In 1990, former Illinois Congressman Frank Annunzio said in the House of Representatives, "a poor credit history is the 'Scarlet Letter' of twentieth-century America." The same is true in the twenty-first century. Bad credit can harm many aspects of your life. More recently, Julie Sturgeon in an article for Bankrate.com wrote that bad credit can harm a consumer's chances for car insurance, a car loan, a job, housing, utilities, cell phones, elective medical procedures, school loans, and even marriage.

Imagine that you are denied credit based on a bad credit history. In denying you credit, the creditor relies on a negative consumer report from a major credit bureau or credit-reporting agency. You request a copy of the credit report from the credit bureau and, much to your dismay, find that the report contains items relating to another individual with the same name, information more than ten years old, and other inaccuracies. What can you do to correct these mistakes on your credit report?

Fortunately, a federal law known as the **Fair Credit Reporting Act (FCRA)** is designed to protect consumers from inaccurate information in consumer reports, as well as to protect the

PRIVACY PROTECTION UNDER THE FCRA

The FCRA regulates consumer-reporting agencies to protect the accuracy and privacy of credit information. Chapters 5 and 6 have discussed the accuracy requirements at length. But privacy of credit information is also a very important topic, particularly in this age of identity theft (discussed in chapter 8). In 1996, Congress added a series of amendments to the FCRA that provided additional privacy protection for consumers. As a result, the FCRA now protects consumers' privacy in a number of ways. For example, it prohibits any person from obtaining a credit report without a permissible purpose. The law also limits the release of credit reports to those with a "legitimate business need" for such reports. A "legitimate business need" might arise, for example, if you applied for life insurance, a job, or an apartment, in which case a person might legitimately need to examine your credit report.

The FCRA also generally prohibits so-called target marketing, which occurs when credit issuers make unsolicited contacts with consumers. In a long-running battle between the Federal Trade Commission and TransUnion (one of the three main credit-reporting bureaus), a federal appeals court has ruled that the FTC can prohibit credit bureaus from selling target-marketing lists, which target potential consumers for certain goods and services. The court determined that the ban on target-marketing lists serves the substantial state interest of protecting privacy.

Even though the FCRA prohibits target marketing, it does allow pre-screening—the process of selecting individuals for firm (that is, guaranteed) offers of credit or insurance.

The FCRA does, however, recognize the need for consumer privacy with respect to prescreening. To this end, the law provides that any prescreening must allow consumers a way to opt out of future prescreening. This means that if you receive a prescreened offer, the credit solicitation must include some information in the offer telling you how to avoid receiving such offers in the future.

privacy of that information. The law, passed in 1970, provides that "whenever a consumer reporting agency prepares a consumer report it shall follow reasonable procedures to assure maximum possible accuracy of the information concerning the individual about whom the report relates." The FCRA regulates the behavior not only of credit-reporting agencies, but also of "users" of credit reports prepared by such agencies, such as a car dealer using a credit report to decide whether to finance a retail installment on the family car.

CREDIT BUREAUS

Credit bureaus (sometimes called **credit-reporting agencies** or **consumer-reporting agencies**) maintain records of your financial-payment histories, public-record data, and personal-identifying data. (They do not maintain information about your medical history.) There are three major competing credit-reporting agencies: Experian, Equifax, and TransUnion Credit Information Company. You can find the bureaus serving your area simply by looking online or by looking for "credit-reporting companies" in the yellow pages of your phone book. The Fair Credit Reporting Act governs activities of credit bureaus, and several states have enacted similar laws.

Credit bureaus do not make credit decisions. Instead, they provide data to creditors for use in making such decisions. How does this work? Creditors provide information on their customers' debts and payment habits to credit bureaus, usually on a monthly basis. Credit bureaus then make this data available, sometimes online, to other creditors to whom you apply for credit. For this reason, a good credit record is very important to your ability to obtain credit for purchasing goods and services, renting an apartment, or buying a home. Credit reports may also be used when you apply for insurance or for employment.

The availability of credit history information is a key driver in making credit widely available to the American consumer. The information credit bureaus provide to creditors enables the creditors to make credit available to all kinds of consumers quickly, conveniently, and relatively easily. Without credit reports, creditors would be hard pressed to approve credit requests made by telephone or online, where there is no face-to-face opportunity to verify the credit applicant's identity and creditworthiness. We all appreciate the convenient access to credit. However, as with most good things, there are some downsides to this system. Negative information in a credit report (whether accurate or inaccurate) can adversely affect a consumer's ability to obtain credit, or it can cause the consumer to pay a higher price for credit. Also, unscrupulous identity thieves can hijack a consumer's credit record, leaving the consumer with a poor credit history that may take many months to correct.

Because credit reports contain highly confidential information, the law permits credit bureaus to disclose credit reports only under very specific circumstances when the requester (such as a creditor) has a legitimate purpose for obtaining the information in connection with a transaction with a consumer. Among the authorized purposes for which credit reports may be furnished are when:

• a consumer applies for credit or insurance,

• maintenance or collection of a credit account takes place, and

• certain credit offers known as prescreened solicitations (like those preapproved credit card offers that sometimes arrive in the mail) occur.

The law punishes unauthorized persons who lie to obtain credit reports, or credit bureau employees who supply credit reports to unauthorized persons. Such persons may receive fines or prison terms, or both, if they are found guilty. In addition, they may also face civil liability, in the form of money damages imposed on them by a court. The law has also been amended to provide protection in relation to identity theft.

Since your credit record is critical to obtaining credit, it is very important that you check to make sure that each item in your credit record accurately reflects your own credit history,

FURNISHERS OF INFORMATION

The FCRA regulates more than the behavior of credit-reporting agencies or credit bureaus; it also regulates the behavior of those companies that furnish information to credit bureaus. It imposes a duty on furnishers of information to provide accurate information. The law provides that "[a] person shall not furnish any information relating to a consumer to any consumer reporting agency if the person knows or consciously avoids knowing that the information is inaccurate." If a consumer disputes a debt, then the furnisher of information must provide notice of the disputed debt to the credit bureau. Furnishers of information have a further duty to correct and update information.

The **Fair and Accurate Credit Transactions Act of 2003**, better known by the acronym **FACTA**, amended the FCRA. A key change made by the new law is that now consumers may dispute inaccurate information directly with the furnishers of information, as well as with the consumer-reporting agency, as was previously required. Under FACTA, consumers can dispute directly with furnishers, who must investigate all disputes and cannot report negative information while an investigation is pending. To preserve your rights, however, you must dispute the information with the consumer reporting agency, too.

---

and not that of another person. Whenever you apply for credit, you should use the same name. Thus, if you are James R. Jones, Jr., always append the "Jr.," and do not use "J. Randall Jones" sometimes and "J. R. Jones" other times. If you use the same name with every credit application, then your complete credit record will be under one name. You will typically be asked for your Social Security number on a credit application. If you are asked, you should provide it. The request is not made to invade your privacy, but to assure that your credit records do not get mixed in with those of some other person named James Jones. (But remember that you should only give out your Social Security number and other confidential information if you have initiated the communication and you are sure about whom you are talking to. Never give out your Social Security number or other confidential information to anyone who calls you or sends you an email.)

YOUR CREDIT REPORT

Understanding Your Credit Report

Contrary to popular belief, a credit bureau neither tracks all aspects of your personal life nor explicitly evaluates credit applications. Credit bureaus are simply organizations that collect and transmit four principal types of information: identification and employment data, payment histories, credit-related inquiries, and public-record information.

Though credit bureaus don't evaluate your credit per se, the fact that creditors can request a **risk score summary** from credit bureaus does suggest that such bureaus have a significant effect on your ability to acquire credit.

As required by the Fair and Accurate Credit Transactions Act of 2003, creditors must disclose credit scores to mortgage loan applicants. Later in this chapter, we discuss how to improve a credit score with which you are dissatisfied.

A good credit report is vital to ensuring your access to credit. Therefore, it is important for you to understand and find out what your credit report contains, how to improve your credit report, and how to deal with credit problems.

Checking Your Credit Report

You have the right to know the content of credit files that contain information about you, and many consumer credit experts suggest that you examine these credit files about once a year. A periodic checkup will enable you to find out what information credit bureaus will provide to credit issuers about your credit. Whenever you ask to learn the contents of your file, you will need to provide adequate identification to the credit bureau to ensure that you receive your own report, and not the report of someone with a similar name. These identification procedures also help ensure that others with similar names will not see your credit report inadvertently.

The FCRA allows you to review your file at any time, and it is particularly important for you to do so if you plan to apply for an apartment, a job, a home mortgage loan, or some other major loan or credit purchase. Historically, under the FCRA, a credit bureau was permitted to charge you a reasonable fee for providing this service. However, the Fair and Accurate Credit Transactions Act (FACTA), which was signed into law in December 2003, amended the FCRA in several respects. One of these amendments provides that consumer-reporting agencies must provide consumers with one free credit report per year. Consumers can obtain their free credit report from the nationwide agencies simply by making a phone call. The FCRA and FACTA allow credit bureaus to charge a "reasonable fee" for providing additional credit reports. As of 2009, the FTC set the maximum fee for a credit report at $11.

Also as required by FACTA, the Federal Trade Commission issued a rule that requires the nationwide consumer-reporting agencies—Equifax, Experian, and TransUnion—to create a "centralized source" for accepting consumer requests for credit reports. This source includes a website, a toll-free telephone number, and a mailing address. The FTC's website has helpful information pertaining to this. Visit the FTC website at www.ftc.gov; you'll find the credit information by clicking on "For Consumers," then on "Credit." Free credit reports can be obtained at the credit bureaus' centralized site, which is now up and running: Access www.annualcreditreport.com or call 877-322-8228.

The FTC cautions that this is the "only authorized source for you to get a free credit report under federal law." See www.ftc.gov/freereports. To obtain the free credit report, do not contact any of the three agencies directly. Instead, contact the centralized site at www.annualcreditreport.com or complete the

Annual Credit Report Form and mail it to: Annual Credit Report Request Service, P.O. Box 105281, Atlanta, GA 30348-5281. Some experts contend that the best method to receive your report is to call.

As noted above, a creditor may turn down your application for credit or take other adverse credit action because of a report from a credit bureau. If you are denied credit or if you are offered less favorable credit terms on the basis of information contained in your credit report, the law requires that the creditor give you the name and address of the bureau from which it obtained your report. You are allowed to request information from the credit bureau by phone, by mail, or in person. If a creditor has denied you credit within the past sixty days because of information sup-

 TALKING TO A LAWYER

Q. It's maddening to find the same mistakes over and over again in a credit report. How can you get rid of information that's just plain wrong?

A. If you have notified the credit bureau and the creditor that the information is being reported incorrectly and the mistake has not been corrected, you can file a complaint with the Federal Trade Commission (which regulates the credit bureaus) and with the creditor's regulator. If you still are unable to get this problem resolved and if the erroneous information has caused you harm or could cause harm in the future, you might consider suing the credit bureau and/or the creditor for failing to fulfill their responsibilities under the Fair Credit Reporting Act to investigate disputed information and make appropriate corrections. FCRA authorizes recovery of your actual damages, plus your attorney's fees and other costs to bring the action and, if the noncompliance with the FCRA is determined to have been willful, punitive damages.

—Answer by Robin K. Warren, formerly of Bank of America, Charlotte, North Carolina

plied by a credit bureau, the bureau must provide your credit report information free of charge (even if you have previously received your one free annual credit report).

Finally, still another provision of FACTA requires that a financial institution that extends you credit must send you a notice before or no later than thirty days after it furnishes negative information about you to a credit bureau. Such negative information includes information about late payments, missed payments, partial payments, or any other form of default. Most creditors provide this notice at the time credit is extended or soon thereafter, informing customers of their practice and what they report to the credit bureaus.

Format of a Credit Report

Credit reports will vary slightly, depending on which of the three national credit-reporting bureaus compiles them. Generally, however, the same types of information will be on every credit report, including:

• Identification and employment data: Your name, birth date, Social Security number, addresses (present and former), and employment history.

• Your residential information, including how long you have resided at your current location.

• Public-record information: Events relating to your creditworthiness that are a matter of public information, such as bankruptcies, foreclosures, tax liens, or court cases, such as a record of a dispute between a consumer and an appliance dealer that was settled in small-claims court.

• Payment history: Your account record with different creditors, showing how much credit has been extended and how you have repaid it.

• Inquiries: Credit bureaus maintain a record of all creditors who have checked your credit record within the past six months, including for prescreening purposes. Prescreening occurs when, for example, credit bureaus enable issuers of credit cards to develop mailing lists to which they can distribute preapproved offers for their cards. Credit bureaus typically do not include credit-prescreening inquiries in credit reports for credit issuers, though they will provide records of prescreening inquiries to consumers as part of their disclosure duties under the law.

• Credit score: Your credit score and a list of the factors that most affected that score. Such factors could include the number of delinquencies with which you are credited, the average balance on your revolving accounts, and the collection amounts you owe.

Correcting Your Credit Record

If you find that information in your credit report is inaccurate, incomplete, or outdated, you may challenge its accuracy or completeness by notifying the credit bureau. You can contact the agencies by phone or online, as follows:

Equifax: 1-800-685-1111, or www.equifax.com
Experian: 1-888-397-3742, or www.experian.com
TransUnion: 1-800-916-8800, or www.transunion.com

These companies also have information on their websites explaining how to correct a mistake on your report. For example, Equifax has a section on its site called "How to correct errors in your credit file." Visit www.equifax.com and type "correct credit report errors" into the search field.

Unless it believes that your request is "frivolous or irrelevant," the credit bureau must reinvestigate and either verify the disputed information within thirty days or delete the information from its files. (The "frivolous-or-irrelevant" provision is there in part to deal with certain credit repair clinics, discussed in chapter 14, that challenge all negative information in a person's credit report, whether there is a basis for such a challenge or not.) If your complaint is justified, the credit bureau will automatically notify the other bureaus of the change and, if you request it, notify you of any creditor that has checked your file in the past six months. The bureau will also notify you of anyone who has made an employment-related check of your credit within the last two years.

STATING A CLAIM UNDER THE FCRA

The vast majority of courts have determined that the FCRA provides a private right of action for individual consumers. A "private right of action" means the ability of an individual to bring a lawsuit against a person or company or the government. In order to make a claim under the FCRA, a consumer must establish that: (1) inaccurate information was included in his or her credit report; (2) the inaccuracy was caused by the consumer-reporting agency's failure to follow reasonable procedures to assure maximum possible accuracy; (3) he or she suffered an injury; and (4) the injury was caused by the inaccuracy in his or her credit report.

Credit-reporting agencies are not strictly liable for posting inaccurate information. In other words, the mere fact that there is inaccurate information on a person's credit report does not automatically mean that a credit-reporting agency must pay that person monetary damages. If a credit-reporting agency shows that it followed reasonable procedures under the circumstances, it will not be liable. (Note: There is a two-year statute of limitations for bringing claims for inaccurate information under the FCRA [meaning after two years from the posting of the inaccurate information, you cannot file a suit]. There is a concept in law called the discovery rule that sometimes will extend the tolling, or running, of a statute of limitations to when a consumer reasonably discovered the information. It is important to stay on top of information in your credit report because the discovery rule may not be applied by a reviewing court.)

Your Right to Sue

Under the Fair Credit Reporting Act, you have the right to bring a lawsuit against any credit bureau or creditor that violates any provisions of the Act. This includes any credit-reporting agency that fails to observe the restrictions about who may access your credit file, and any credit bureau that does not properly

TALKING TO A LAWYER

Q. The law says you can put up your version of a dispute on a credit report, but does anyone pay attention to that? What can I do to avoid having a dispute hurt my credit rating—besides paying the disputed amount, of course?

A. If you dispute an item on your credit report, it is always a good idea to make sure that the report gives your side of the story. Creditors will look at that information and will consider it, but if you are turned down for credit, you should contact the creditor to call attention to the dispute and make sure that your side of the story was considered. Keep in mind that a single isolated adverse item on a credit report ordinarily can be overcome if all the other reported credit accounts show that you have a history of making timely payments.

—Answer by Robin K. Warren, formerly of Bank of
America, Charlotte, North Carolina

Q. I was laid off from my job last year and had trouble keeping up with payments on my loans and credit cards until I was able to land a new job. I'm thinking about buying a home, but I know that my credit history will hurt me. I've gotten solicitations from a company that says it can repair my credit history. Can they really help me clean up my credit record?

A. There is little that a credit repair clinic can do to alter the payment history reflected on your credit report. Beware of firms that claim that, for a fee, they can clean up your credit record. These firms will sometimes try to get you to "game" the system by repeatedly disputing legitimate information on your credit report so that reporting on the negative items is suspended while your "disputes" are being investigated. If you apply for credit while the negative information is suspended, they contend that what your prospective creditors can't see won't hurt you. Some credit repair companies will charge sizable fees up front and then either will not do anything you can't already do yourself (like disputing erroneous information on your credit report) or will engage in conduct of questionable legality.

Assuming that the information being reported about your payment history is accurate, the best thing you can do to clean up your record is to continue building a current record of paying your bills on time. Pay down or pay off any credit card debt as soon as you are able. The best cure is time (usually a minimum of twelve months) and a current record of prompt payments and paying off credit card debt. Before you make an offer on a house you want to buy, go talk to a mortgage lender to explain your situation and find out what the lender will want you to show in order to overcome the negative credit history while you were unemployed.

—Answer by Robin K. Warren, formerly of Bank of America, Charlotte, North Carolina

Q. I am recently divorced. When I went to apply for a car loan recently, I discovered that my credit report shows a delinquent payment history on my mortgage loan. The mortgage loan was a joint account in my name and my ex-spouse's name. Under our divorce agreement, my ex-spouse was responsible for making the mortgage payments. What can I do to delete this negative information from my credit report?

A. Even though you and your ex-spouse agreed that he or she would be responsible for making payments on the mortgage, the mortgage lender did not agree to release you from responsibility for the loan. Although you might not be able to get the negative history removed from your credit report, there are some things you can do. First, the Federal Reserve's regulations that implement the Equal Credit Opportunity Act require the creditors to consider, at your request, information that indicates that the credit history on the credit report does not accurately reflect your creditworthiness. You should explain your situation to the auto lender. Be prepared to provide a copy of the legal agreement or court order that makes your ex-spouse responsible for paying on the account. The auto lender must take this information into consideration, but that doesn't necessarily mean that the lender must or will disregard the negative information.

—Answer by Robin K. Warren, formerly of Bank of America, Charlotte, North Carolina

investigate and correct inaccurate data in your file that you have disputed. However, if an agency has followed reasonable procedures, it has obeyed the law.

If you win a lawsuit brought under the FCRA, you are entitled to receive actual damages (which might include lost wages for a job you did not get or the amount of additional interest you paid because you could not obtain a loan on the best credit terms). These are subject in some cases to a minimum but also to a maximum amount. You may be entitled to punitive damages if you prove the violation was intentional. If you are successful, you will also receive court costs and a reasonable amount for lawyers' fees.

Effect of Time on Credit Reports

Under the FCRA, most negative information (such as late payments, accounts charged off, and so forth) may only be main-

 TALKING TO A LAWYER

Q. Is it worthwhile to sue a credit-reporting agency if its incompetence hurts you?

A. Suing is rarely worthwhile, but sometimes it's something that you need to do. You need to decide how much damage the reporting agency's incompetence costs you and, more importantly, what this continued incompetence will cost you in the future. You must then weigh this against the cost of a lawsuit, which will consist of the attorney's fees and costs. They also include the amount of time you will have to spend dealing with the issue, the stress it will cause in your life, and emotional distress that being involved with the lawsuit will bring.

Is it worthwhile, then? This is a subjective decision that incorporates all of the above.

—Answer by Marc S. Stern, Law Offices of
Marc S. Stern, Seattle, Washington

Q. I recently applied for a credit card and was shocked when I was turned down because of loans that were "charged off" or in "collections." I have always paid my accounts on time and I'm not aware of any that were in collection status. What can I do about this?

A. If you were turned down for credit because of information in a credit report, you have the right to request that the credit bureau send you a free copy of the report. The creditor should have sent you an adverse action letter that shows the name and address of the credit bureau from which the creditor purchased a credit report on you. When you get your report, check to see if all of your accounts accurately report your payment history. If any account histories are incorrect, contact the creditors on those accounts immediately to dispute the information and request that the creditor investigate and correct the information reported. You may initiate this request by phone, but be sure to follow up in writing because the law imposes obligations on the creditors and credit bureaus only when they receive written requests.

When you get your credit report, you may discover that it lists accounts with which you are unfamiliar. Could these be accounts that you co-signed or guaranteed for someone else (for example, a relative or a close friend)? If so, then the creditor has correctly included those accounts in your credit history. If the person for whom you co-signed did not pay on time or failed to pay at all on an account, you are legally responsible. Contact the creditor to find out the current status of the account. The creditor might agree to remove the account from your credit history or remove the negative information about the account if you agree to bring the account current or pay it off.

If there are unfamiliar accounts that you know you neither opened nor co-signed or guaranteed, it is possible that you have been the victim of identity theft. Someone may have used your good name and credit history to get credit and then leave you holding the bag. If that's the case, you should notify the credit bureau and the creditor immediately that the account is not yours. For more information on what to do if you are a victim of identity theft, see chapter 9.

—Answer by Robin K. Warren, formerly of Bank of
America, Charlotte, North Carolina

tained on your credit record for seven years. There are a few exceptions, which include: criminal convictions (no time limit); bankruptcy information (generally ten years); information provided in response to an application for a salaried job of more than $75,000 per year (no time limit); information provided in response to an application for more than $150,000 worth of credit or life insurance (no time limit); and information about a lawsuit or unpaid judgment (seven years or the length of the applicable statute of limitations—whichever is longer).

REMEMBER THIS

• The Fair Credit Reporting Act (FCRA) gives consumers the right to sue to ensure that their credit reports contain accurate information.

• Most would-be creditors obtain information about consumers from major credit bureaus or credit-reporting agencies when making credit decisions, as well as in connection with the maintenance and collection of credit accounts. These credit bureaus possess files detailing your financial-payment history, data from public records, and personal-identification data. Your credit history should not contain any medical information.

• Since the passage of the Fair and Accurate Credit Transactions Act of 2003, consumers are entitled to one free annual credit report per year. It is important to review your credit report annually in order to confirm that the information being reported about you is accurate and to make sure that you have not been a victim of identity theft.

• The FCRA imposes duties upon creditors and credit bureaus to submit and maintain accurate information on consumers. If you dispute items in your credit report, the applicable credit bureau must either verify the disputed information within a reasonable period of time or remove the information from its files.

• Negative information does not stay on your credit report for life. Most information must be removed after seven years. However, records of bankruptcies can be reported for ten years.

CHAPTER 8

Electronic Payments and Credit

Your Rights in an Electronic World

Every month, you balance your checkbook using your bank statements. Much to your chagrin, one month you notice that your bank statement includes two identical withdrawals from an ATM on the same date, but you know that you only made one withdrawal on that day. Obviously, an error was made. You go to the bank to speak to a representative, who assures you that you are in error. What recourse do you have? How can you contest what you believe to be double-dipping from your bank account? Fortunately, a law passed in 1978 known as the Electronic Fund Transfer Act provides some relief to consumers in such situations.

The Electronic Fund Transfer Act focuses on deposit accounts, including checking and savings accounts, and other types of consumer "asset" accounts (not consumer "credit" accounts such as loan accounts) involved with electronic fund transfers. The world of electronic withdrawals and electronic fund transfers is fluid and ever-changing, and we take the opportunity in this chapter to discuss a wide range of transactions under new technology.

In the past, commerce primarily consisted of transactions using cash, checks, and credit cards at merchants' physical places of business. Today, commerce has changed dramatically, and many consumers now shop for their goods over the Internet, using credit cards to make online purchases. Other consumers use debit cards for their online transactions, simply entering their debit card numbers and having the money for their purchases immediately debited from their checking accounts.

According to the Federal Reserve Board, use of electronic payment methods (including credit and debit cards) surpassed the use of checks in 2003. Electronic commerce or "e-commerce" creates greater ease and convenience for us as consumers.

But problems can arise in the world of e-commerce, just as in the world of physical commerce. Ultimately, even a marketplace that relies heavily on computers is not immune to human error.

ELECTRONIC FUND TRANSFER ACT

In 1978, Congress amended the Consumer Credit Protection Act through passage of the Electronic Fund Transfer Act (EFTA). The stated purpose of the EFTA was "to provide a basic framework establishing the rights, liabilities, and responsibilities of participants in electronic fund transfer systems." Its primary objective, as the law itself states, is "the provision of individual consumer rights."

Recent amendments to the EFTA require automated teller machines (ATMs) to disclose to you any fees that you must pay the ATM owner or operator to withdraw money from the ATM or to obtain account balance information. Usually, a consumer who does not have an account with a particular bank must pay an extra $1.50 or $2 to withdraw money from one of that bank's ATMs or to obtain account balance information from that bank's ATM. (However, account balance information is not always available from ATMs owned or operated by companies with which you do not have the account in question.)

In addition, the EFTA applies to several kinds of electronic fund transfers (EFTs) to and from consumers' checking and savings accounts, including ATM transactions, point-of-sale purchases, certain pay-by-phone transactions, and automated clearinghouse transactions. The Federal Reserve Board recently extended coverage of the EFTA to certain "payroll card accounts" to which employers directly deposit wages on a regularly recurring basis and from which employees may withdraw or transfer (pay out) their wages using their payroll cards, and to electronic check conversion services where information from your paper check is used to initiate an electronic fund transfer, rather than submitting your paper check for processing and payment (and instead of processing your payment with a debit card). The EFTA also applies to direct deposits—transactions in which an employer, insurance company, or pension plan sends monthly paychecks or monthly or quarterly disability or retirement payments directly to your checking or savings account.

The EFTA is an important law, particularly given recent exponential growth in the number of electronic fund transfers. The Electronic Payment Association reports that the use of debit cards has been growing at about a 25 percent rate per year in the past several years; the association reports that electronic payments are rising at about a 13 percent rate per year. According to TowerGroup, the use of debit cards grew three times faster than the use of credit cards in the years 2005–2007.

Another provision of the EFTA provides that neither creditors nor employers (nor anyone else) may require you to repay loans "by means of preauthorized electronic fund transfers" from a consumer-purpose checking or savings account, nor can they require consumers to set up an account for receipt of electronic fund transfers with a particular financial institution as a condition of employment. Lenders may, however, offer cost-related incentives (such as interest rate or closing cost reductions) under the EFTA to encourage borrowers to agree to repay their loans automatically each month by electronic debiting of their checking or savings account. Employers may require employees to have their wages electronically deposited to checking accounts under the EFTA, if their employees can choose the financial institutions where they will maintain checking accounts for this purpose. (State labor and employment laws may further regulate the extent to which employers may electronically pay wages.)

Paying Bills Online

Almost all banks now offer a service enabling consumers to pay certain of their bills online. Consumers can usually arrange payments of regular bills—including car loan payments, mortgage payments, and insurance payments—and bills that change every month, like utilities. Many banks offer incentives to consumers who make the change from writing checks to paying bills online. According to banks, online customers tend to be better customers, in that they save administrative costs by receiving online statements instead of paper, and make fewer calls to call centers.

If you pay your bills online, you will not always receive a separate receipt for each electronic payment you've pre-authorized. This may mean that you'll need to pay extra careful attention to your bank statement to ensure that the right amount has been paid. You can stop a scheduled regular EFT payment by giving oral or written notice to your bank three business days or more before the next scheduled transfer. If you give oral notice, your bank may require written confirmation of your oral notice within fourteen days. If you want to permanently stop all future scheduled EFT payments to a particular company, you should notify that company in writing and make other payment arrangements with that company.

Consumer Liability

If there is an unauthorized electronic fund transfer from your checking or savings account, you can generally limit the amount of your loss to $50 if you notify the bank of the unauthorized EFT within two business days after you discover the loss or theft of your ATM or debit card or your personal identification number (PIN). However, if you fail to provide such notification, you could be liable for up to $500 in unauthorized EFTs. If you do not provide notification to the bank of an unauthorized EFT within sixty days after the bank sent you the account statement showing that unauthorized EFT, you could lose an even greater amount of money. For this reason, you must take great pains to make sure that you retain control over your debit and ATM cards and PINs at all times, and you must carefully review your checking and savings account statements for possible unauthorized EFTs immediately after you receive those statements.

The law provides guidelines for identifying and correcting EFT errors. You have sixty days from the time a periodic account statement is sent to dispute an EFT shown on that statement. The bank then generally has ten business days to conduct an investigation, though it can take up to forty-five days (or up to ninety days in certain cases, including cases involving point-of-sale transfers, EFTs that were initiated outside the United States, and EFTs to or from new accounts) if it provisionally recredits the money to you in the meantime. (If you dispute an EFT orally, the bank may require you to send your dispute to the bank in writing within ten business days and, if the bank does not receive your written dispute within ten business days, the bank does not need to provisionally recredit the money to you while it investigates your dispute. For new accounts, the bank may investigate for up to twenty business days before provisionally recrediting the account with the amount in dispute.)

If the bank determines there was an error, it must correct the error within one business day, and notify you within three business days, after it determines that an error occurred. If the bank determines that there was not an error, it must notify you in writing within three business days of making that determination. (See the side bar below, "The Law in Action," for details about what can happen if a bank fails to provide the required notice.) The bank must also supply an explanation and notify you of your right to receive a copy of the documents that the bank used to make its findings.

Under the EFTA, consumers must first consent to automatic deductions from their account and can order banks to stop making such deductions. If a consumer requests a stop payment of a particular regularly scheduled automatic payment three business days or more before the scheduled date of the automatic deduction, the bank must comply with the request. (To permanently stop future automatic payments to a particular business from your checking or savings account, you should notify the business and make alternative payment arrangements with the business.)

If you notice a discrepancy or error with respect to an automatic payment deduction, contact your financial institution im-

mediately. Document your discussion; it is usually prudent to follow up telephone requests with written documentation. Specifically, the Federal Trade Commission recommends that you notify
the financial institution by certified letter, return receipt requested, so you can prove that the institution received your letter,
and that you keep a copy of the letter for your records.

The Federal Trade Commission offers several tips for consumers who make electronic fund transfers with debit or ATM
cards. One FTC publication suggests that you should keep your
EFT receipts and compare them to your periodic bank statements,
just as you compare your credit card receipts with your monthly
credit card statements. For more information about what to do if
your ATM or debit card or PIN is lost or stolen, you may wish to
look at the following FTC consumer brochures: "Credit, ATM and
Debit Cards: What to do if They're Lost or Stolen," copy available
at www.ftc.gov/bcp/edu/pubs/consumer/credit/cre04.shtm, and "A
Consumer's Guide to E-Payments," copy available at www.ftc.gov/
bcp/edu/pubs/consumer/tech/tec01.shtm.

THE LAW IN ACTION

FACTS

The 1986 case *Bisbey v. D.C. National Bank* involved a bank customer who
set up monthly debits from her account to pay for life insurance premiums.
For two consecutive months, her account had insufficient funds to make
the required payments, and no transfers were made to cover her insurance
premiums. In each case, her bank made the required payment and sent
the customer an overdraft notice. The customer, however, having forgotten her nonpayment in the first month, believed that the bank had erro-
neously made two payments from her account in the second month.

The customer informed a bank employee of what she thought was a
double-withdrawal error and confirmed her complaint in writing. Ten days
later, an official of the bank telephoned the customer and explained to her

that there had been no improper duplication of her premium payments. The customer remained unsatisfied, and eventually filed suit under the EFTA. The bank argued that it had not violated the EFTA, in part because the consumer had not been harmed. In fact, the bank argued, the consumer had benefited because the bank had paid her insurance premiums, which otherwise would have remained unpaid.

DECISION

In finding for the customer, Bisbey, the court focused on the plain language of the EFTA, which provided in pertinent part:

> If [a] financial institution determines after its investigation . . . that an error did not occur, it shall deliver or mail to the consumer an explanation of its findings within three business days after the conclusion of its investigation, and upon request of the consumer, promptly deliver or mail to the consumer reproductions of all documents which the financial institution relied on to conclude that such error did not occur. The financial institution shall include notice of the right to request reproductions with the explanation of its findings (793 F.2d 315 (D.C. Cir. 1986).

Though admitting it seemed "odd" for the consumer to win her case when the bank's disputed transactions had actually benefited her, the appeals court nonetheless sided with the consumer based on the statute's plain language. Specifically, the appeals court noted that the bank had not complied with the provision of the EFTA quoted above, because it had provided the customer only with oral, and not written, notice. (Today, under certain conditions, the notice may be electronic, but that does not include oral notice.) Furthermore, the bank had failed to give the consumer notice of her right to request reproductions of the documents on which it had relied to reach its conclusions. The appeals court remanded the case to a lower court, ordering the bank to pay attorney's fees and what would likely be only a nominal damage award to the plaintiff.

The lesson of the Bisbey case is that banks and other financial institutions must comply with the statutory language of the EFTA or face civil liability for attorney's fees.

Electronic Checks

More and more businesses are converting the paper checks you write into electronic payments from your checking account. Under this process, a store clerk processes your paper check through an electronic system that records your checking account information and the number and amount of the paper check. The store processes the paper check and then gives you a receipt for your records. (Sometimes the paper check is returned to you—you should *not* reuse this paper check.) The store presents the information it obtained and processed from your paper check to your bank electronically, and the bank transfers the funds electronically to the store's account. The paper check used as the basis for the electronic payment is *not* itself presented to any bank for payment. The store must tell you if they are processing your paper checks electronically and, in many instances, you may be able to pay for your purchase with a credit card or a debit card, if you do not want to have your paper check converted to an electronic payment.

Consumers should realize that there is no "float" period for electronic payments. Payments processed electronically are processed immediately. This means that you don't have an extra day or two to deposit funds into your account to cover the amount of an electronic check. If a paper check you write is converted to an electronic payment, and the electronic payment bounces, both your bank and the store may charge you fees. And, of course, bounced checks (including bounced electronic payments) can hurt your credit record and lower your credit score.

Much of this "float" discussion applies equally to "substitute checks" created as a result of federal Check 21 legislation. Check 21 is a federal law that is designed to enable banks to handle more paper checks (and to handle paper checks more efficiently) by transferring digital images of paper checks electronically instead of by paper. Because of this law, paper checks may be processed faster by banks, meaning less of a "float" period, even if paper checks are not converted to electronic payments or EFTs.

For more information about electronic payments and electronic checks, you may wish to look at the following FTC consumer brochures: "Electronic Check Conversion," copy available at www.ftc.gov/bcp/edu/pubs/consumer/credit/cre31.shtm, and "Check 21: Substitute Checks, Electronic Processing, and What It Means to You," copy available at www.ftc.gov/bcp/edu/pubs/consumer/credit/cre37.shtm.

INTERNET LOANS

Obtaining a loan used to require a trip to the bank or other lending office to speak with a bank manager or loan officer. In the past, this process often required several trips. Now, in the twenty-first century, the process is much easier. People can obtain certain types of loans right over the Internet from consumer direct-lender

---

 ## AUTOMATIC-DEBIT SCAMS

The Federal Trade Commission has warned consumers about an automatic-debit scam perpetrated by some telemarketers. The scenario works like this: A telemarketer calls to say that you have won a free prize or have qualified for a major credit card. At some point during the call, the telemarketer asks for your checking account number, which he or she explains the offer or prize requires. Then he or she puts that number on a computer-printed paper "demand draft." This is processed like a paper check but, unlike a check, does not require a signature. The telemarketer is then able to withdraw funds from your account.

As a precaution, the FTC warns that you should never give out your checking account number over the phone unless you know the company requesting it and the reason they have requested the number. Also be wary of e-mail spam messages that appear to be from banks and credit card companies requesting your personal information. These could well be scams from would-be identity thieves. (See also chapter 9.)

companies and/or companies such as E-Loan, Inc.®, which has a website at www.eloan.com. On various websites, consumers can apply for a whole range of loans: mortgage loans, home equity loans, personal loans, and much more, including extensions of credit to buy a car. If you type "online loans" into your favorite web search engine, you will find a plethora of companies that offer loan applications. Many people use these online loans as payday advances to simply serve as a bridge between paydays.

Internet loans are a part of the growing field of e-commerce, which accounts for billions of dollars in consumer spending each year. Just as the credit card industry revolutionized the way consumers spend money, Internet loan sites have made it that much easier for consumers to acquire more credit. A potential pitfall of this convenience is that consumers now have a heightened ability to overextend themselves financially. (This problem may be minimized at least slightly in the current economic slowdown when many lenders are more reluctant to offer credit.) Another potential pitfall of e-loans is the problem of identity theft, to be discussed in chapter 9.

REMEMBER THIS

• The Electronic Fund Transfer Act is a consumer protection statute designed to provide a remedy for consumers when monies are wrongfully taken from their checking or savings account through some type of electronic-payment transaction.

• If you report an electronic payment loss within two business days after you discover the loss or theft of your ATM or debit card or your personal identification number (PIN), you generally will not be responsible for more than $50 of any unauthorized use of your card or PIN (e.g., someone steals your ATM card and withdraws a large amount of money). If you report the loss within sixty days after your bank sent you the account statement showing the unauthorized transfer, your maximum exposure is generally $500 for unauthorized use of your card or PIN. If you miss the sixty-day deadline, you could lose all the money in your account.

- If you notice a discrepancy or error with respect to an automatic-payment deduction, contact your financial institution immediately. Document your discussion; it is usually prudent to follow up telephone requests with written documentation.

- Be careful with easily accessible Internet loans. These can leave you open to over-extending yourself financially and to possible identity theft.

CHAPTER 9

Identity Theft

What It Is and How to Protect Yourself

You open your mail and suffer a horrible shock. You have re-ceived a credit card statement for a card you never asked for and, worse yet, the statement includes a bill for thousands of dollars worth of merchandise that you never purchased. Wel-come to the not-so-wonderful world of identity theft.

You should be aware of the ever increasing problem (some have called it an epidemic) of **identity theft**, or **ID theft**. The Identity Theft Resource Center (www.idtheftcenter.org) and others have referred to ID theft as the "nation's fastest growing crime" and "the crime of the new millennium." ID theft reached such proportions that in May 2006, President George W. Bush issued an executive order creating a President's Task Force on Identity Theft to examine the problem and ways to combat it. The task force released a seventy-page report in April 2007 that identified thirty-one recommendations in four key areas: (1) data protection, (2) avoiding data misuse, (3) victim assistance, and (4) deterrence. Clearly, the federal government would not have marshaled so many resources and agencies together if identity theft was not a major problem in our society.

There are different types of identity theft, a term that is used to cover a variety of fraudulent activities. The FTC and others label lots of different kinds of fraud "identity theft." The problem is that using this one label for everything blurs important distinc-tions that have ramifications for consumers. Consumers' rights and liabilities can vary depending upon which of three types of fraud they've been the victims of. Here are three major types of "identity theft" and their legal ramifications:

1. **Basic Fraud:** Someone uses your credit card or debit card number to make purchases you haven't authorized. This can hap-pen either through loss/theft of the card or by someone using

your card number to make telephone or online purchases (or to produce a phony credit card). This can happen fairly easily. If your credit card is ever in the hands of another person—for example, a waiter at a restaurant—that person could easily run it through a small device designed to read and store the magnetic strips on the backs of credit cards. Such devices, called "skimmers," are readily available, and sell for around $100. The thief could then load the data from your credit card onto another credit card and use it at his or her will. Though there may be some fraudulent transactions on your account, your identity hasn't been compromised. Your credit report, for example, will not show any accounts that aren't truly your accounts.

If fraudulent (or other unauthorized) credit card or debit card transactions appear on your account, you should notify the card issuer immediately. For unauthorized credit card transactions, the Truth in Lending Act limits your liability to no more than $50 for unauthorized transactions. Many credit card issuers will waive the $50 liability and not hold the consumer liable for any of the unauthorized transactions. (See chapter 6 for additional information on your rights under the Truth in Lending Act.)

Unauthorized debit card transactions are covered by the Electronic Fund Transfer Act (EFTA). Under EFTA, you can have unlimited liability for unauthorized transactions if you do not notify the debit card issuer within sixty days after an unauthorized transaction first appeared on an account statement. Liability for debit card transactions that occur prior to that sixty-day window is generally limited to $50, but can be as much as $500 if you were aware that your debit card was lost or stolen and failed to report it within two business days to the debit card issuer. (See chapter 8 for additional information.) As with TILA liabilities, many debit card issuers voluntarily waive their rights and do not hold consumers liable for any unauthorized debit card transactions if the consumer provides prompt notice and did not negligently facilitate the unauthorized transactions.

It is important, therefore, to be on the lookout for your monthly account statements and notify the card issuer if a statement fails to arrive when expected or reflects erroneous or unauthorized transactions. Review your account agreements or contact your card issuers to learn whether they offer greater protections than those afforded by TILA or EFTA.

2. **Account Takeover**: Someone, posing as you, contacts your card issuer, bank or other financial services company (including insurance companies) to notify it of a change of address. The financial services company begins mailing your account statements or bills to a new address. Some time after changing the address on your account, the fraudster, again posing as you, requests a new credit or debit (or insurance) card to be mailed to him or her at "your" new address. The fraudster is betting that it may be several months before you notice that you haven't received a bill or account statement. Meanwhile, the fraudster is racking up hundreds or thousands of dollars worth of purchases and they're being billed to your account.

As with basic fraudulent transactions, your liability for these transactions is generally limited by TILA or the EFTA or other applicable federal or state laws. If you want to avoid potentially unlimited liability for debit card transactions, be sure that you maintain an awareness of when your checking account statement should arrive each month and notify your bank if the statement doesn't arrive when you expect it.

There's another risk with account takeover, though. Because you aren't receiving your account statement each month, you might not be aware that you are incurring other charges, like late payment fees or overlimit fees on your credit card or overdraft charges on your checking account. Your card issuer should reverse those fees after you notify it that you've been the victim of an account takeover. Be sure to insist that the card issuer also update any credit reports it furnished to the credit bureaus to delete any slow payment or overdraft history previously reported as a result of the fraudulent activity.

To help detect fraudulent (unauthorized) change of address requests, many financial institutions mail a change of address notification or confirmation to the original (old) address after they receive a change of address request. You should read all notifications sent to you by your financial institutions carefully, and contact your financial institutions immediately if you believe any unauthorized or fraudulent activity may have occurred or been attempted regarding one of your accounts.

3. **True Identity Theft**: Someone, posing as you, opens one or more accounts in your name. They use your personally identifiable information, such as your Social Security number and other confidential information, to open up new accounts in your name. These accounts can include credit card accounts, automobile purchases they've financed in your name, cell phone accounts, or checking accounts in your name but using someone else's mailing address and other contact information. The bottom line is that someone is using your good name to get access to money, goods, or services.

Identity thieves will sometimes keep these accounts current and in good standing for months at a time, usually by fraudulently obtaining new credit to pay the old credit. Often, it can be months before the victim discovers that these accounts have been fraudulently opened in the victim's name. Maybe you learn about it when you start getting calls and letters from collectors about accounts you know nothing about. Maybe you learn about it when you apply for credit and get turned down because of negative information on your credit report. Maybe you learn about it when you order your free credit report. In at least one truly awful instance, a grandmother discovered she was the victim of identity theft only after she was arrested. A warrant for her arrest had been sworn out by a merchant after the ID thief had written a bad check on an account opened in the victim's name.

Because accounts established as the result of true identity theft are not yours and were never yours, you have no liability for any of them—not the first $50, not the first $500, not the first penny. And the creditors who established the accounts (who, like you, have been victimized by the ID thief) should update their records so that these accounts are not reported to the credit bureaus in your name.

The rest of this chapter focuses on the laws dealing with true identity theft and what you can do to protect yourself from it.

THE WAYS AND MEANS OF IDENTITY THIEVES

Consumers need to realize that their personal information is a valuable commodity. Many identity thieves are resourceful and will employ a variety of means to obtain information to wreak havoc on the unsuspecting, trusting, and unaware. If Social Security numbers, bank account numbers, or credit or debit card numbers fall into the wrong hands, they can easily be used by imposters to rack up fraudulent charges in unheard-of amounts.

Identity thieves use a variety of methods to obtain information. Some will steal a person's mail to obtain his or her important information. Others will complete change-of-address forms to send an unsuspecting person's mail to a location that the thieves can access. Sometimes thieves will steal records from victims' employers, hack into an organization's computers, or pose as employers themselves. Some identity thieves will even rummage through trash cans or Dumpsters to locate account numbers and other personal financial information in a practice called **Dumpster diving**.

When they obtain this information, identity thieves may go on spending sprees, buying up lots of merchandise before finding new victims. Some identity thieves will open up new accounts, thus leaving their theft victims with damaged credit reports—through no fault of the victims. Thieves may even take out loans in a victim's name, or open up a bank account in a victim's name and use it to write bad checks.

PREVENTING IDENTITY THEFT

There are several steps you can take to minimize your exposure to identity thieves:

• Be careful to whom you reveal personally identifiable information such as your Social Security number. Do not give out this kind of information over the phone or online, unless you know the person or institution with whom you are dealing.

• Be guarded about releasing your Social Security number and other confidential personal information. When asked to provide your Social Security number and other confidential information, ask why the person, business, or employer needs it, how it will be used, how the person or business will protect it, and what will happen if you refuse to provide it.

• Make a mental note of the dates each month you receive your regular bills and account statements. If you do not receive a bill from a regular creditor around the date you expect it, contact your creditor to make sure that it still has your current address. An identity thief may have changed your billing address so that he or she could use your account to run up charges without you noticing.

• Use passwords for your bank and credit card accounts. Do not use easily obtainable passwords such as your mother's maiden name or the name of your spouse. If you write your password down, keep it in a safe place, separate from your actual cards.

• Guard your mail, and even your trash, from theft. When you throw away credit card and loan application offers, make sure that you thoroughly tear up all of the relevant paperwork. Don't make it easy for identity thieves. Inexpensive home paper shredders are readily available and are a good investment. Shred paper account statements, checks, or other confidential information before disposing of them.

• Make sure that your computer is updated with the latest antivirus protection. Some viruses may cause your computer to release or send out your personal information or files. Use a firewall on your computer if you have access to the Internet. A firewall will make it much harder for a hacker to invade your computer and files.

• Avoid using automatic log-ins on Internet sites that contain your personal information, such as Internet banking or shopping sites. While it might be easier to log in using automatic features, such features could also make it easier for unauthorized users to access your accounts. Make sure to log off every time you are done with an Internet site.

• Pay attention to the privacy policies of various websites. Learn what personal information these sites acquire from you, and how that information is used.

• As soon as you become aware that one of your credit or debit cards (or card or account numbers) has been stolen, immediately notify the card issuer or other financial services company. Also consider taking advantage of state security freeze laws, which enable consumers to ask credit reporting agencies

 CREDIT ALERTS

In 2003, Congress amended the Fair Credit Reporting Act to enable consumers to add a **fraud alert** to any personal credit files maintained by a nationwide consumer reporting agency. These alerts include an **initial alert** and an **extended alert**. The initial alert lasts ninety days and the extended alert lasts seven years. Consumers may have to provide evidence that they have been a victim of identity theft. A third type of fraud alert is available to active duty military personnel. Fraud alerts are designed to help protect consumers who fear that they have been or are about to become victims of identity theft (for example, when a consumer's wallet is stolen). When consumers place fraud alerts in their consumer report files with a nationwide consumer reporting agency, anyone who requests information from that file, including a credit score, also receives a notification about the alert. Creditors who receive this notification must take reasonable steps to verify the identity of the credit applicant before proceeding with the credit request. In other words, the fraud alert directs users of consumer report information to proceed with caution and to ensure that they are dealing with the right consumer, rather than with an identity thief.

PHISHING

Consumers should be aware of a type of identity theft called **phishing**. Phishing (pronounced "fishing") involves the fraudulent acquisition of someone's personally identifiable information from the Internet. A typical example involves an Internet user receiving an e-mail telling him or her to update his or her bank or credit card account information. Such e-mails typically contain an Internet link. If the user clicks on this link, he or she will be directed to a copycat website (i.e., a website that looks like but is not the bank or credit card issuer's website) that asks for personal account information, user ID, password, and similar confidential information. A user who provides his or her information as requested by the copycat website unwittingly provides an identity thief with tools to commit his or her crime. For more information on this phenomenon, see the FTC's website at www.onguardonline.gov/topics/phishing.aspx.

(credit bureaus) to freeze or lock access to their credit files (generally for a fee). This makes it harder for others who might try to open up new accounts and get more credit in your name. However, you should be aware that a security freeze may cause you disadvantages. If there is a security freeze on your credit file, it may make it difficult or near impossible for you to receive cell-phone service, long distance telephone service, and other needed services. Because of this, some states have laws that allow for the temporary unfreezing of credit files for specific transactions. The bottom line is, think carefully before using the "security freeze" option. The Connecticut State Attorney General's Office has a helpful publication on credit freezes that can be viewed by visiting www.ct.gov/ag and search "identity theft alerts."

• Check your credit report at least annually to verify that no one has established unauthorized accounts in your name. (See www.annualcreditreport.com.) It's not unusual for an account opened by an identity thief to be active for several months before the unsuspecting victim discovers what has happened.

WHAT TO DO IF YOU ARE AN
IDENTITY THEFT VICTIM

If you are the victim of identity theft, take the following steps as fast as you can:

- Place a fraud alert on your credit reports and accounts.
- Notify all creditors, banks, and other businesses where fraudulent accounts were opened in your name. Many of them will ask you to complete an affidavit swearing that the accounts are not yours, providing any information you might have about when or how the accounts were established or who the identity thief might be, and agreeing to cooperate with prosecution of the thief when and if he or she is found and brought to justice. (You'd be surprised how often the thief turns out to be a family member or close friend.)
- Close any and all accounts that have been compromised by an identity thief. Ask for copies of the applications or other records related to the fraudulent accounts. The Fair and Accurate Credit Transactions Act (FACTA) requires creditors to furnish this information to you.
- Notify the police and file a police report (if the local police are unsure how to categorize the nature of your report, ask them to classify your report as a "Miscellaneous Incidents" report). Keep copies of the police report so that you can send copies to your creditors, banks, nationwide consumer reporting agencies, and others who may ask to see your police report.
- Get a copy of your credit report so that you can determine how many other fraudulent accounts there might be.
- Notify the Federal Trade Commission's toll-free ID Theft hotline at: 1-877-IDTHEFT or online at www.ftc.gov/bcp (click on "File a Complaint").

For more information about how to protect yourself against

identity theft, also read a brochure prepared in 2008 by the federal bank, credit union, and thrift (savings association) regulatory agencies, called "You Have the Power to Stop Identity Theft," available at www.ncua.gov/Publications (scroll down to "You Can Fight Identity Theft").

 TALKING TO A LAWYER

Q. How can I prove that I'm not a deadbeat but the victim of identity theft?

A. There are several things you can do. Request a copy of the account records, including the documents used to establish the account. The Fair and Accurate Credit Transactions Act entitles you to get these records from the company that opened the account. By reviewing those records, you'll probably find a number of ways to show the account is fraudulent: for example, the signature on the account agreement is not yours. File a police report and send a copy of the report to the company that opened the account. Contact the credit bureaus and make sure they put a fraud alert on your credit report. Creditors will usually request that victims of identity theft or other kinds of fraud complete a form affidavit. The affidavit asks you to swear that the account is not yours and was not established on your behalf and that you did not benefit from the account. The affidavit may also ask you to provide any information you might have about how the identity theft occurred (for example, your credit card was taken when your wallet was stolen) or about who the thief is (for example, a former roommate who took some of your personal property and had access to your personal information). Finally, the creditor will ask you to verify that you will cooperate with authorities in prosecuting the ID thief if he or she is apprehended. The affidavit, because it is a sworn statement, is an additional indicator of your honesty and good faith in asserting that you have been a victim of identity theft.

—Answer by Robin K. Warren, formerly of Bank of America, Charlotte, North Carolina

LEGISLATION COMBATING
IDENTITY THEFT

There are numerous federal and state laws dealing with identity theft. Depending on the type of identity theft involved, consumers can have different remedies. The law on identity theft continues to evolve, as more federal and state laws are passed to address the different forms of identity theft. Those who commit identity theft often will also be in violation of other federal or state laws, such as laws preventing identification fraud, credit card fraud, computer fraud, mail fraud, wire fraud, and mail theft.

You can contact a local consumer protection agency or attorney general's office to learn more about applicable laws in your jurisdiction. See the appendix of this book for a listing of state consumer protection agencies and the credit reporting bureaus.

There are several federal laws that deal with the problem of identity theft. For example, the **Identity Theft and Assumption Deterrence Act of 1998** provides that someone commits a crime when he or she "knowingly transfers or uses, without lawful authority, a means of identification of another person with the intent to commit, or to aid or abet, any unlawful activity that constitutes a violation of federal law, or that constitutes a felony under any applicable state or local law."

In December 2003, President George Bush signed into law the **Fair and Accurate Credit Transactions Act (FACTA)**. We have discussed other provisions of that law in earlier chapters. Part of that law also addresses the problems created by identity theft. FACTA provides that consumers can issue a "one-call" fraud alert to one of the three nationwide consumer reporting agencies. If one of the three nationwide consumer reporting agencies receives a fraud alert from a consumer, it must refer that fraud alert information to the other two nationwide consumer reporting agencies. A military consumer going on active duty can similarly issue an active duty alert to one of the nationwide consumer reporting agencies. That agency must then notify the other nationwide agencies about the active duty alert. Another provision of the law requires financial institutions and creditors to institute "reasonable policies and procedures" for "red-flag" guidelines regarding identity theft. This is to help detect and prevent possible identity theft by monitoring certain "red flag" indications of potential identity theft. FACTA also requires consumer reporting agencies (credit bureaus) to block the reporting of information in their consumer report files identified as resulting from identity theft and allows consumers free copies of their consumer reports maintained by a nationwide consumer reporting agency after a fraud alert has been placed on their consumer reports.

In 2004, President Bush signed into law the **Identity Theft Penalty Enhancement Act**, which provides greater penalties for identity thieves. It creates the crime of "aggravated identity theft," punishable by up to two years in prison when committed in connection with other felonies, and imposes a special five-year prison term for committing identity theft in connection with terrorism.

Many states have passed ID theft laws. Arizona passed the first such law in 1996. This law prohibits persons from "knowingly tak[ing] or us[ing] any personal identifying information of another person, without the consent of that other person." State laws may give you greater protection than the federal laws; contact your consumer protection agency or state attorney general to find out what protections exist in your state.

The U.S. Congress continues to debate other measures designed to combat identity theft. In the 111th Congress, both Houses of Congress are considering identity theft legislation, including (for example) possible increased penalties for misuse of Social Security numbers.

REMEMBER THIS

• Identity theft is a growing problem. Guard your personally identifiable information, such as your Social Security number, and release it only when necessary.

• Make yourself aware of your state laws on identity theft. Many states allow you to "freeze" or "lock" your credit report through laws sometimes referred to as security freeze laws.

• You can take many steps to reduce the threat of identity theft. These steps include installing a firewall on your computer system, not giving out your passwords to anyone, guarding your mail and trash from theft, and contacting creditors if you don't receive a bill or account statement on time.

• If you have been the victim of identity theft, take the following steps: (1) place a fraud alert on your credit reports and accounts; (2) close all accounts that have been compromised; (3) contact the police and report the problem; and (4) file a complaint with the Federal Trade Commission.

CHAPTER 10

Unfair Lending

How to Protect Yourself from Loans You Can't Afford

Bill Jones has faced some unexpected expenses this month. He has no way of getting money until his next payday, which is not for another two weeks. He has no family or friends who can lend him money. He walks into a "cash advance" establishment and writes a check for $380 that he postdates by two weeks to his next payday. The check casher gives Mr. Jones $300, and tells him that the establishment will hold his check for two weeks until payday. On payday, however, Mr. Jones cannot afford to pay the entire $380 that he owes the check casher, so he has to pay an additional $20 "rollover" fee to continue the loan for another two weeks. It may be six months before he is able to repay his total debt. He needed money badly, but now he has a loan he can't pay back and the loan balance is increasing.

There are many opportunities for consumers to obtain cash advances that appear to be cheap and easy, but instead turn out to be expensive short-term loans. State and federal laws require comprehensive disclosures of costs and terms of loans, but these disclosures are highly technical and often are not available to the consumer until he or she has already decided to enter into the transaction.

Loan terms that a consumer has agreed to sometimes may seem unfair or inappropriate in hindsight. In the worst cases, a consumer may have been subjected to unfair treatment, such as "bait and switch," heavy sales pressure, or even misrepresentation by the lender or a loan broker. These worst cases may include instances of unfair lending, as a byproduct of the wide availability of high-priced credit arrangements aimed at unaware lower-income consumers. A 2006 report by the Center for Responsible Lending states that predatory short-term payday lending may have cost Americans $4.2 billion a year in excessive fees. (See "Financial Quicksand," by Uriah King, Leslie Parrish and Ozlem Tanik, Center for Responsible Lending (November 30, 2006). A copy is available at www.responsiblelending.org and by searchong for "Financial Quicksand."

Much of the charges of predatory lending stem from the mortgage industry. As the Department of Housing and Urban

 BROKERS AND MORTGAGE BROKERS

A **broker** is a party who serves as a bridge or intermediary of sorts between a buyer and a seller. Brokers usually receive a commission for their efforts in facilitating the exchange of property or commodities. There are many different types of brokers, including investment brokers, insurance brokers, and mortgage brokers. We emphasize mortgage brokers because the real estate market is one that has been subject to most of the charges of predatory lending. This is not to suggest that all mortgage brokers are unethical or engage in predatory lending. On the contrary, most probably do their jobs efficiently and fairly. However, there is no denying that charges of predatory lending have arisen vigorously out of the real estate market.

A mortgage broker is someone who helps a borrower find an appropriate mortgage loan. A mortgage broker does not make the loan or extend credit; he or she simply helps the borrower obtain a mortgage loan by matching the borrower with a loan mortgage lender. A potential problem for borrowers is that mortgage brokers may collect fees from lenders as well as borrowers. It may not be clear to the borrower whether the broker is working for the lender or the borrower. In some cases the fees paid by lenders to brokers may be higher if the interest rates on the mortgage loans referred by the brokers are higher than prevailing market rates or higher than the interest rates at which lenders would be willing to close loans to borrowers with the assistance of brokers. Also, many mortgage brokers only refer to a limited number of mortgage lenders. It is possible for an unscrupulous broker to work against the best interests of borrowers.

Development (HUD) explains on its website (www.hud.gov/offices/hsg/sfh/pred/predlend.cfm): "too many families are suffering today because of a growing incidence of abusive practices in a segment of the mortgage lending market." Predatory mortgage lending practices strip borrowers of home equity and threaten families with foreclosure, destabilizing the very communities that are beginning to enjoy the fruits of our nation's economic success." For that reason, we discuss predatory lending in general in chapter 10 (though there will be some discussion of predatory lending in the mortgage area) and then a more focused discussion of predatory lending in the mortgage area in chapter 11.

Consumers should be especially aware of the unfair lending practices often collectively referred to as "predatory lending." The problem of predatory lending has escalated within the past fifteen years. As Margot Saunders and Alys Cohen wrote in a 2004 piece published by the Joint Center for Housing Studies at Harvard University, "[w]hile abusive and fraudulent credit scams have always been a problem in a commercially oriented culture, the problems in the past fifteen years caused by the explosion of predatory lending are new in the history of personal credit." (See Saunders and Cohen, "Federal Regulation of Consumer Credit: The Cause or the Cure for Predatory Lending?" March 2004, copy available at www.jchs.harvard.edu/publications/finance/babc/babc_04-21.pdf.) Groups such as the National Association of Consumer Advocates (www.naca.net) and the National Consumer Law Center (www.nclc.org) exist in order to protect consumers from unfair and deceptive practices. They attempt to provide financial and consumer credit advice, budget planning, debt counseling, and debt consolidation strategies.

There is no universally accepted definition of "predatory lending"! Nonetheless, there are many accounts of predatory lending practices. As Tania Davenport writes in the 2003 article "An American Nightmare: Predatory Lending in the Subprime Home Mortgage Industry," 36 Suffolk University Law Review 531, 545 (2003), unfair lending may involve "targeting, threatening, deceiving, manipulating, and defrauding the most vulnerable borrowers." A key element of the unfair lending process involves targeting people most in need of money—people who often do not qualify for prime borrowing rates and terms. Unfortunately, some of the worst abuses have occurred in home mortgage lending. Any consumer must be absolutely certain he or she can afford to repay any loan on his or her home, because, as we saw during 2007 and 2008, the consequences of nonpayment may be loss of the consumer's most important asset.

Many states and even cities have passed laws that limit certain loan practices and terms. These outlawed practices include fraud and misrepresentation in soliciting or marketing loans, charging very high interest rates, imposing excessive prepayment penalties, and steering consumers into multiple refinances.

THE "SUBPRIME" MARKET

Consumers who cannot qualify for a conventional loan may find credit available on "subprime" terms. **Subprime lending** is defined as the provision of credit to borrowers with past or recent credit problems. Subprime loans are often made at a higher cost or on other less favorable terms than "prime" loans available to borrowers in the "conventional" credit market. In other words, a borrower who is deemed a higher credit risk is often charged a higher, "subprime" rate than those with better credit. It is important to note that subprime loans are rarely labeled as subprime loans when the consumer is applying. It must also be recognized that not all subprime lending should be considered predatory per se.

Theoretically, subprime lending helps people with credit problems to obtain homes and increases their access to credit. In fact, in a 2000 study titled "Curbing Predatory Home Mortgage Lending" (which can be found at www.huduser .org/publications/hsgfin/curbing.html and www.huduser.org/ Publications/pdf/treasrpt.pdf), the Department of Housing and Urban Development (HUD) and the Department of Treasury (Treasury) noted the widespread growth of subprime lending and remarked that subprime lending "serves an important role, by providing loans to borrowers who do not meet the credit standards for the prime mortgage market." The study further noted that "By providing loans to borrowers who do not meet the credit standards for borrowers in the prime market, subprime lending provides an important service, enabling such borrowers to buy new homes, improve their homes, or access the equity in their homes for other purposes. A majority of mortgages in the subprime market are used for consumer debt rather than housing purposes." However, in some cases, subprime loans appear to have been made to borrowers without sufficient attention to whether the loans are in the borrowers' interests and without sufficient attention to whether the borrowers could reasonably be expected to repay.

Subprime lending makes loans available to borrowers who have blemished credit. Some experts have said that subprime lending contributed to the 2008 economic downturn. Whatever its overall impact, there is no doubt that predatory lending has had a negative impact on many individual borrowers. Some borrowers do not fully understand the terms of higher-cost loans and the risks these loans can pose to them and their families. For example, another HUD study points out a downside to the widespread availability of credit to borrowers of all types of credit standing. That is, there may be unscrupulous lenders drawn into a business once dominated by community banks and savings associations:

> Since subprime lending often operates outside of the federal regulatory structure, it is a fertile ground for predatory lending activities, such as excessive fees, the imposition of single premium credit life insurance and prepayment penalties . . . And predatory lending can have disastrous consequences for the unknowing borrower. At the very least, equity is stripped from the home. In more egregious cases, homeowners may lose their home altogether.

See "*Unequal Burden: Income and Racial Disparities in Subprime Lending in America,*" April 2000, www.huduser.org/publications/fairhsg/unequal.html.

Disturbingly, predatory home mortgage lending practices may target low-income persons and the elderly. Congress has considered legislation to provide protections to consumers victimized by such practices (see sidebar), and the Federal Reserve Board has enacted some anti-predatory home mortgage lending regulations, generally effective October 1, 2009. State legislatures are also active in regulating high cost loans, and some of them have recently enacted additional consumer protection laws supplementing federal law.

 CONGRESS ON THE SUBPRIME MARKET

Congress is continuing to consider bills to strengthen federal laws that fight predatory or unfair lending practices within the mortgage industry. For example, Congress passed the Mortgage Forgiveness Debt Relief Act of 2007 (H.R. 3648) and President George W. Bush signed the legislation in December 2007 (Public Law 110-142). This act amends certain provisions of the Internal Revenue Code concerning the federal income tax treatment of residential mortgage indebtedness that is discharged (forgiven) by mortgage lenders. "The Mortgage Forgiveness Debt Relief Act of 2007 will protect families from higher taxes when they refinance their homes," President Bush noted upon signing the legislation. Congress also passed the Mortgage Disclosure Improvement Act (part of Public Law 110-289) in 2008, and President Bush signed the legislation in July 2008. This act amends certain provisions of the Truth in Lending Act (TILA) to (among other things) require certain residential mortgage loan TILA disclosures to be provided earlier to consumers, more in advance of closing. These TILA amendments are scheduled to take effect on July 30, 2009. Additional provisions of the Mortgage Disclosure Improvement Act (expanding upon certain existing variable rate TILA disclosure requirements) are scheduled to take effect on January 30, 2011 (or on any earlier compliance date that may be established by the Federal Reserve Board). You can monitor the progress of congressional bills through the regular congressional site—www.gpoaccess.gov/hob/index.html.

PREDATORY LENDING PRACTICES

There are many types of predatory lending practices, including flipping, packing, and stripping. We discuss these more fully in chapter 11, but briefly, loan **flipping** is a process in which a creditor encourages a consumer to refinance a loan several times in a relatively short period of time, each time adding more points and fees to the outstanding unpaid principal. **Packing** involves adding fees to a new loan for optional loan-related services or products such as credit insurance (see chapter 4), or adding the borrower's old debt into the new loan. This tactic gets its name from the fact that lenders "pack" old debt or new fees into new loans, which can make it more difficult for borrowers to repay. **Stripping** refers to the practice of basing the terms of a loan on a borrower's equity in his or her home, rather than on the borrower's ability to repay the debt. If the mortgage loan amount and the required periodic loan payments are too high for the borrower, eventually, foreclosure and sale of the property will occur, and money received from the foreclosure sale is rarely enough to cover the debt secured by the owner's property. Any equity the owner had in the mortgaged property is "stripped" through foreclosure and given to the lender for repayment.

Another example of predatory lending occurs when home improvement contractors go door-to-door, seeking to induce people to take out mortgages to pay for home improvements (sometimes including improvements that the homeowner may not even need).

In many cases, consumers may not be aware that they are the victims of predatory lending practices. The Center for Responsible Lending (www.responsiblelending.org) has identified several possible initiatives to combat predatory lending, including:

• Prohibiting creditors from financing credit insurance as an up-front payment.

• Limiting direct and indirect fees charged to borrowers to 3 percent of the loan amount. The more fees imposed on a consumer to obtain a loan, the more likely the consumer's payments will be more than he or she can pay.

• Addressing the issue of "steering" by making sure that borrowers receive the lowest-cost loans for which they qualify. Borrowers must be aware that loan brokers can steer customers to particular finance companies with which they have a profitable arrangement. Borrowers should find out whether the loan broker is working for them or the finance company. Borrowers should only be guided toward the lowest-cost loans for which they qualify or to the most appropriate loan for their own financial circumstances.

• Avoiding mandatory arbitration clauses in home loan agree-

 TALKING TO A LAWYER

Q. Are advances on tax refunds actually expensive loans? I'd always like the money earlier, but not if the cost is too much.

A. Rates charged in connection with "refund anticipation loans" or "refund anticipation checks" may be higher than for other loans, such as unsecured loans from finance companies. Be sure you review all of the documents and disclosures provided by your tax preparer that related to the loan transactions.

—Answer by Donald C. Lampe, Womble Carlyle Sandridge
and Rice, PLLC, Charlotte, North Carolina

Q. My bank offers bounce protection. What is that? Is it different from overdraft protection—and is it worth getting?

A. Overdraft protection or "bounce protection" is a feature that your bank may offer you to protect against overdraft fees and the consequences of bounced checks. These plans function like short-term loans, so be sure you understand the costs and charges, especially compared with the time that you have the use of the additional funds to cover overdrawn checks.

—Answer by Donald C. Lampe, Womble Carlyle Sandridge
and Rice, PLLC, Charlotte, North Carolina

ments. Arbitration can be a costly process, and many arbitration clauses have cost-splitting provisions, which require the parties to share the costs of arbitration. Companies can afford these fees, but many borrowers and individuals cannot.

• Prohibiting "flipping" of borrowers through repeated fee-loaded refinancings.

The Special Problem of "Payday Loans"

So-called "payday loans," sometimes known as deferred-presentment check cashing, may result in a borrower paying more for credit than is appropriate under the borrower's circumstances. In a common example of this practice, as detailed in the hypothetical at the beginning of this chapter, you have no money until your next payday, and you go to a check-cashing establishment and write a postdated check for, say, $380 in order to obtain $300 cash. You must then pay back the $380 on payday, or be charged further fees. Check-cashing businesses may charge extremely high annualized interest rates. Many commentators believe that payday lenders target low-income persons.

Nearly twenty states have laws that establish small-loan interest caps on payday loans. The Center for Responsible Lending has encouraged states to enact small-loan interest caps "at or around 36 percent." (See, for example, "Springing the Debt Trap," Uriah King and Leslie Parrish, Center for Responsible Lending [December 13, 2007]; a copy of this executive summary is available at www.responsiblelending.org/pdfs/springing-the -debt-trap-exec-summary.pdf.) In states that have no usury limits, the annual percentage rate (APR) for such payday loans can be higher than 300 percent. For example, the Arkansas Supreme Court recently ruled in *McGhee v. Arkansas State Board of Collection* (2008) that the Arkansas Check-Cashers Act, which allows payday loans, violates the Arkansas state constitution, which sets a 17 percent maximum interest rate for all loans and credit sales. However, out-of-state (non-Arkansas) lenders may make loans to Arkansas residents and charge interest rates higher than

17 percent per year pursuant to the laws of the lenders' home states. (See, for example, *Evans v. Harry Robinson Pontiac-Buick*, 336 Ark. 155, 983 S.W.2d 946 [Arkansas Supreme Court 1999].)

In some cases, courts have ruled that check-cashing businesses have violated the federal Truth in Lending Act by misrepresenting the interest charges imposed upon consumers. For example, in *Turner v. E-Z Check Cashing of Cookeville, TN, Inc.*, 35 F.Supp.2d 1042, a 1999 federal district court case that arose in Tennessee, a court ruled that a check-cashing service violated the Truth in Lending Act by misstating its finance charges and APR. In that case, the check-cashing service stated the APR was 24 percent when it was actually 400.2 percent.

Professor Creola Johnson writes in the 2002 Minnesota Law Review article "Payday Loans: Shrewd Business or Predatory Lending?" that Congress should enact legislation that accomplishes the following:

> (1) places a ceiling on the maximum interest rates and fees that payday lenders can charge; (2) prohibits banks from partnering with nonbank payday lenders; (3) forbids the collection of treble damages from defaulting customers; (4) bans the criminal prosecution of defaulting customers; and (5) prohibits loan rollovers using the same or multiple lenders.

The past several Congresses have considered (but not passed) such bills as the Payday Borrower Protection Act, which would limit annual interest rates to 36 percent and would prohibit the refinancing or "rolling over" of any payday loans. As Congressman Bobby Rush noted in introducing the legislation, "[m]ost loans made are small, usually no more than $100 to $500, but the interest rates can soar from 390 percent to 913 percent. Only loan sharks lend money with such high interest rates and loan sharking is illegal." Of course, loans of small amounts for short periods must carry a rate of interest high enough to earn enough dollars to cover the lender's costs and some profit. Long-term large real estate loans can earn enough dollars at low rates to be profitable. Payday loan fees might be better compared to credit card cash advance fees, which may be

3 percent of the cash advance (with both the cash advance and the cash advance fee accruing interest, typically at an APR higher than the APR that applies to credit card purchases, until the cash advance and cash advance fee are repaid in full). A 3 percent cash advance fee on a small credit card cash advance that is repaid within a month could cause the effective annual percentage rate charged on the cash advance to exceed 50 percent or 80 percent, depending on the exact facts. See, for example, "TILA 'Finance' and "Other' Charges In Open-End Credit: The Cost-of-Credit Principle Applied To Charges For Optional Products Or Services," Ralph J. Rohner and Thomas A. Durkin, 17 Loyola Consumer Law Review 137 (2005). Congress passed legislation in 2007 that limited the rates and fees that may be imposed in connection with certain payday loans made to members of the military on active duty. The measure, part of the National Defense Authorization Act, includes an effective annual interest rate cap of 36 percent for payday loans made to members of the military on active duty. Congress is still considering various measures regulating payday loans for members of the general public.

Consumers should avoid cash advances from check-cashing services and use them only as a last resort. The quick fix of a cash

"SUBPRIME" CREDIT CARDS

As many as 40 million Americans have a hard time getting credit because of past bankruptcies, loan defaults, or low income. Some credit card issuers will give these high-risk borrowers credit cards, but at a price: high rates of interest and big up-front fees. And delinquency rates are high—as many as 20 percent of these cardholders ultimately can't pay their credit card bills, compared with 2 to 5 percent of lower-risk cardholders. Moreover, the card companies often go after delinquent accounts with very aggressive collection practices. For some consumers, easy credit may turn out to be quite expensive and potentially very troublesome.

advance easily may result in costly credit on terms that may create further hardship for the consumer.

Other Types of Loans That Can Be Predatory

The term "predatory lending" refers to a series of lending practices; it does not refer only to one type of lending. Other types of loans susceptible to abuse include home improvement loans (discussed in chapter 11), rent-to-own purchases, auto title loans, and income tax refund anticipation loans.

Rent-to-own purchases are short-term, renewable rentals of consumer appliances or similar items on a weekly, bi-weekly, or monthly basis. Consumers with limited resources often rent television sets, washers and dryers, or furniture because they don't have the money to pay for such items in full. If you renew your rental of a rent-to-own product enough times, you can actually purchase it; however, you will have paid far more than the purchase price by making multiple rental payments, which include the equivalent of finance charges. Legislation in many states regulates these transactions, and a number of court cases have treated these types of transactions as extensions of secured credit, even though they are ostensibly in the form of a short-term (often four months or less) automatically renewable lease with an option to purchase after a certain number of lease payments have been made. Often, the ultimate cost of one of these rent-to-own contracts is not clear to the consumer.

Auto title loans are another type of short-term loan ripe for abuse by unfair lenders. Auto title loan establishments are often located next to pawnshops and often operate in ways that disadvantage the poor. These short-term transactions are structured as pawn transactions and often carry a high rate of interest. A person needing money can visit one of these establishments and turn over the title to his or her vehicle as collateral for a loan. When the loan is repaid in full, the lender returns the vehicle's title to the consumer. The term of an auto title loan is typically six months or less. The problem with these transactions is that the interest rates for auto title loans are high, compared with other types of credit. In many states, auto title loan establishments face little state and local regulation. In Tennessee, for instance, it has been reported that some auto title loans have interest rates as high as 264 percent.

Your best defense against falling prey to such loans is being aware of the risks and, if you are forced to seriously consider one, examining its terms fully to understand what you will ultimately pay. When you see what an auto title loan really costs, you'll have extra incentive to find the money somewhere else or find a way to get by without borrowing money.

Income tax refund anticipation loans (RALs) are short-term loans intended to be repaid by the proceeds of a pending income tax refund. RALs are often offered through income tax preparation services. The amount owed in connection with a RAL is typically scheduled to be repaid at the time an income tax refund is scheduled to be deposited into the borrower's bank account. It is important to note the following concerning RALs: In many cases, if the borrower's income tax return is filed electronically and the borrower asks for the income tax refund to be deposited electronically to the borrower's bank account, the borrower may receive the tax refund within a few weeks after the tax return is filed. (For example, the Internal Revenue Service [IRS] Web site indicates that an income tax refund would generally be issued approximately three weeks after the IRS receives an electronically filed income tax return. However, longer income tax refund processing time periods apply to certain types of federal income tax returns, including income tax returns with errors or missing information, amended or corrected tax returns, and returns filed with the IRS by mail.) RAL-related interest and fees are generally paid for a loan that will be due and payable when you receive your income tax refund, in some cases a month or less after you receive the RAL loan proceeds. (As an example of the possible cost of a RAL, Connecticut limits the interest rate on RALs to 60 percent per year for the first twenty-one days of a RAL, and 20 percent per year for the remaining term of a RAL until the RAL is paid. However, RAL-related fees may cause the annual percentage rate of a RAL to be higher than the interest rate on the RAL.) It is also important to note that a RAL borrower is responsible for repaying a RAL (including all principal, interest, and any other RAL-related fees) even if the pending income tax refund is not received, or is less than what the borrower anticipated, or is frozen, attached or garnished by other creditors or governmental authorities (for example, to pay for past due taxes, past due child support, or to repay certain governmental benefits).

REMEMBER THIS

- Consumers should be especially careful of the unfair lending practices often collectively referred to as "predatory lending."
- Predatory lending takes many forms, including "flipping," "packing," "stripping," charging excessive interest rates and fees, and misrepresenting the need for credit insurance.
- Avoid payday loans and cash advance loans if at all possible. Such loans often charge high interest rates and fees for very short periods of time. Also watch out for provisions calling for mandatory arbitration in cases of disputes.

CHAPTER 11
Mortgage and Home Equity Loans

An Area Ripe for Abuse by Predatory Lenders and Brokers

Two door-to-door salesmen knock on the door of the home of a 75-year-old woman living on a small fixed income. The salesmen convince the woman that she needs to make significant repairs to the siding and roofing of her house. The repairs will cost more than $10,000.

The salesmen, who work in conjunction with a mortgage broker, tell the woman that all is not lost if she does not have the funds immediately available to pay for the home improvements. They convince her to obtain a loan using the equity in her home as collateral. What they don't tell her is that the monthly payments under the loan may be higher than her disposable monthly income and that there is a large final payment, called a "balloon" payment, required at the end of the loan. She may well wind up losing her home.

The largest financial decision many people make in their lives is the decision to purchase a home. Unless you are wealthy, you'll probably have to finance the purchase—that is, take out a large loan, or mortgage, in order to own a home. This is a huge financial commitment for most of us, but the good news is that there are legal protections for consumers during the mortgage loan/home-buying process.

MORTGAGE LOANS

A mortgage deed is a document that gives a creditor rights in your real property (including land and the buildings and other improvements on the land) as security for the repayment of a

RISING FORECLOSURE RATES

Foreclosures continue to soar in this country. There were about 250,000 households that were foreclosed in 2006. That number jumped to more than 400,000 in 2007, and the final number will be even higher for 2008—more than a million. The U.S. foreclosure problem reached such epic proportions that it became a major issue in the presidential campaign of 2008. With these increases, and recent changes to federal and state laws, it is even more important today that you understand your rights and responsibilities when you enter into a mortgage or home equity loan.

debt. (In some states, a "deed of trust" may be used for this purpose instead of a mortgage deed.) That means that if you don't make the required loan payments, the creditor has the right to take the property, sell it, and use the money in repayment. This is called **foreclosure**.

Not only is a mortgage home loan probably the single biggest extension of credit most people will ever take out in their lifetime, it can result in loss of the mortgaged home under a worst-case scenario. Obviously it makes good sense to be very careful in making this commitment.

The Federal Trade Commission writes: "A mortgage—whether it's a home purchase, a refinancing, or a home equity loan—is a product, just like a car, so the price and terms may be negotiable." This means that consumers should pay close attention and read the fine print to make sure they are receiving a good deal. Consumer self-education is the best policy.

Consumers have rights during the mortgage/home-buying process. For example, the **Real Estate Settlement Procedures Act (RESPA)** requires that mortgage borrowers receive disclosures during the real estate settlement or closing process. RESPA requires mortgage brokers and/or lenders to provide borrowers applying for a mortgage loan with information on the cost of real estate settlement services, including a good faith estimate of settlement costs (listing the estimated charges the mortgage borrower is likely to pay at or before the closing of the mortgage loan), a final settlement statement (listing the actual charges the borrower is paying at or before the closing of the mortgage loan), a mortgage servicing disclosure statement (for certain first mortgage loans), and (if applicable) certain property tax and property insurance escrow account information (if the mortgage lender is requiring such an escrow account in connection with the mortgage loan).

Under RESPA, a mortgage lender/broker generally must deliver a good faith estimate (GFE) of the approximate costs of the mortgage loan to be paid by the borrower at or before the time of closing, within three business days after the borrower submits an application for a mortgage loan. A final settlement statement (sometimes called a "HUD-1" or "HUD-1A") showing the actual charges the borrower is paying at or before the closing of the mortgage loan should generally be provided to the borrower at the mortgage loan closing, before the actual mortgage loan contract documents (including the mortgage deed and promissory note or other consumer credit contract) are signed. The GFE and the final settlement statement are not, however, required to be provided in connection with home equity lines of credit (sometimes called HELOCs), as long as the home equity line of credit borrower receives certain required Truth in Lending HELOC disclosures within three business days of application and at closing. Beginning in January 2010, revised RESPA regulations issued by the Department of Housing and Urban Development (HUD) will limit the extent to which certain (not all) of the estimated fees shown on a GFE may differ from the actual fees shown on the final HUD-1 or HUD-1A settlement statement—that is, the extent to which actual fees shown on the final settlement statement may be significantly higher than the originally estimated fees on a GFE will be limited as of January 1, 2010. Before January 1, 2010, RESPA regulations require a GFE to reflect the mortgage lender/broker's good faith estimate of the borrower's likely mortgage loan-related application and closing costs, but do not require the fees on the borrower's final settlement statement to fall within a certain range of the originally estimated fees on a borrower's GFE.

RESPA also prohibits brokers and lenders from giving or accepting a fee or kickback in exchange for referrals of business involving home mortgage closing-related services or home mortgage loans. Another section of RESPA prohibits sellers of property that will be purchased with mortgage loan proceeds from forcing home buyers to use a particular title insurance company. (Many state laws also prohibit mortgage lenders from requiring borrowers to use a particular title insurance company.) Title insurance offers protection against losses that might arise with problems connected to the title of your property. Title insurance is a requirement if you have a mortgage.

Individuals can bring lawsuits under RESPA for certain (but not all) violations of the law. For some violations, case law has established that individuals cannot file lawsuits—in legal terms called a private right of action. However, government officials can file claims for violations. The Department of Housing and Urban Development, state attorneys general, or state insurance officials may also bring actions to stop certain violations of RESPA. Those who believe they have a complaint under RESPA should send a complaint to:

Director, Office of RESPA and Interstate Land Sales
U.S. Department of Housing and Urban Development
Room 9154
451 7th Street, SW
Washington D.C. 20410

Consumers have rights in addition to those under RESPA. The federal Truth in Lending Act (TILA) contains a provision that generally gives consumers three business days after loan closing in which to cancel most home equity (non-purchase money) mortgage loans that are secured by mortgages on primary residences (excluding mortgage loans used to purchase or build a primary residence). Separate federal and state laws give consumers three business days in which to cancel many transactions that are closed in your own home or somewhere other than the place of business of the company you're dealing with. This means that if something is bothering you about a non-purchase money mortgage loan secured by your primary residence, or the mortgage lender has engaged in questionable behavior, you may be able to release yourself from your mortgage loan obligations within the first three business days after the mortgage loan clos-

 ## POINTS

Points are fees paid to the lender and/or broker for the loan at or before loan closing and are usually a percentage of the principal amount of the loan. For example, one "point" is 1 percent of the principal amount of the loan. Points are prepaid finance charges and can greatly increase the total cost of credit. The total number of points you pay at or before loan closing is often linked to the interest rate of the loan. Normally, the more points you pay the lender, the lower your interest rate will be. Many lenders quote loan interest rates that assume a certain number of points will also be paid. For instance, a lender might quote loan interest rates on the assumption that the borrower will also pay 1-½ points (1.5 percent of the principal amount of the loan). If the borrower is willing to pay more points (sometimes referred to as "discount points"), the lender might quote a lower interest rate—but that does not mean the overall cost of the loan is less. If a loan does not have any points or other prepaid finance charges, its annual percentage rate should generally correspond to the interest rate(s) that will apply to that loan. Points and other prepaid finance charges will generally cause the annual percentage rate to be higher than the interest rate(s) that will apply to the loan. Some lenders allow borrowers to add points and other closing costs to the principal amount of the loan (to borrow the points and other closing costs that are due at loan closing), which results in interest being charged on those borrowed points and other closing costs, until the borrowed funds have been repaid. If the borrower wants to pay fewer points (or no points at all), the lender might quote a higher interest rate.

ing. This is called the **right of rescission**. Not all mortgage loans are subject to the right of rescission, however. You should always carefully review all cost-related disclosures that are given to you in connection with your mortgage loan closing (such as your HUD-1 or HUD-1A settlement statement and any updated, final TILA cost disclosures) before you sign any loan contract documents (such as the mortgage deed and promissory note). You should also always review all contract documents very carefully before you sign them.

Consumers should get information from several lenders or brokers. A mortgage broker may offer to shop for the best available mortgage deal with various lenders. Loan applicants usually pay the mortgage broker a fee for this service. It is important to ask a mortgage broker whether the broker only refers applicants to a limited number of specific mortgage lenders (using a "closed list" of lenders) or whether there is a greater range of lenders to whom the broker refers applicants.

In some cases the mortgage broker may also be paid by the lender, and lenders in turn sometimes pay fees known as **yield spread premiums** to mortgage brokers. A yield spread premium is a fee paid by a lender to a mortgage broker if the interest rate on a mortgage loan referred by the broker is higher than a certain minimum interest rate set by the lender. The higher the loan's interest rate, the higher the yield spread premium the lender might pay to the mortgage broker.

Senator Paul S. Sarbanes described the potential positives and negatives of yield spread premiums at a January 2002 Senate committee hearing on predatory lending. He said:

> Yield spread premiums, properly used, can be a tool in helping a homebuyer or homeowner offset all or some of the closing costs associated with buying or refinancing a home. When used properly, the broker discloses his total fee to the consumer. The consumer may then choose to pay that fee, and perhaps other closing costs as well, by accepting a higher interest rate and having the lender pay the fee to the broker. In such cases, where the borrower makes an informed choice, the payment

helps families overcome a barrier to homeownership—namely, the lack of funds for closing costs.

It is very important that this be transparent and that the borrowers know exactly what their options are. But it appears that, in practice, perhaps in widespread practice, yield spread premiums are not used to offset closing costs or broker fees. Instead, these premiums are used to pad the profits of mortgage brokers without any regard to any services they may provide to borrowers.

In HUD's view, yield spread premiums paid to a mortgage broker by a mortgage lender should be used by the mortgage broker to offset broker fees and other closing-related fees that would otherwise be payable by the borrower at or before the loan closing. HUD has revised its RESPA regulations effective January 1, 2010, so that a yield spread premium paid by a mortgage lender to a mortgage broker will be reflected on the GFE and HUD-1 or HUD-1A settlement statement as an amount that is used to offset (reduce) the total closing-related fees that would otherwise have been payable by the borrower.

When loan shopping, consumers should ask about the best available rates, determine whether the rates are fixed or variable (remember the importance of fixed rates versus variable rates in chapter 5 on credit cards), and ask how variable mortgage interest rates are adjusted during the term of the loan.

Besides points, mortgage home loans also contain numerous other fees, including loan origination or underwriting fees, attorney fees, broker fees, recording fees, title insurance fees, appraisal and credit report fees, and other costs. Many of these fees do not have to be included in the annual percentage rate of the loan. It is important to have an accurate idea of the total dollar amount of fees you will be required to pay at or before the loan closing. You should carefully review all cost-related disclosures that are given to you in connection with a mortgage loan application, such as your good faith estimate (GFE) or estimated Truth in Lending cost disclosures. Also, some loan-related fees and other terms and conditions of a mortgage loan may be negotiable. For this reason, many consumers may want a lawyer or other representative on their side during these transactions.

The Federal Trade Commission has a useful publication, "Looking for the Best Mortgage? Shop, Compare, Negotiate." Visit www.ftc.gov/bcp, click on "Consumer Information" and then "Mortgages/Real Estate," and scroll until you see the title.

HOME EQUITY LOANS: AN AREA RIPE FOR ABUSE BY PREDATORY LENDERS AND BROKERS

The largest single asset many of us have is the equity that we have built up in our homes through the years. Many mortgages these days are thirty-year mortgages. If you've owned your home for twenty years, you may have built up a significant amount of **equity** in the home—that is, the current value of your home minus the amount of any existing mortgages, liens, and attachments on the home. Should you encounter tough financial times, you may need to borrow more money, and the equity in your home may be a promising source. A home equity loan may be an option to use the equity in your home for extra financial support. But you need to understand the risk—if you fail to make the scheduled payments on a home equity loan, the lender may be able to foreclose on your home.

The Federal Trade Commission (FTC) has several useful publications related to home equity loans, including: "High-Rate, High-Fee Loans (HOEPA/Section 32 Mortgages)," "Home Equity Credit Lines," and "Home Equity Loans: Borrowers Beware!" These and other mortgage-related FTC publications are available at www.ftc.gov/bcp/menus/consumer/credit/mortgage.shtm. As the Federal Trade Commission has said, "Remember, if you decide to get a home equity loan and can't make the payments, the lender could foreclose and you would lose your home."

It has been widely reported that some predatory lenders and brokers target certain homeowners—elderly widows, people with poor credit, and those with low incomes. Many of the practices identified in the predatory lending chapter (chapter 10) may surface with respect to home equity lending, including:

• **Equity Stripping**: The lender or a broker offers to make or arrange a mortgage loan with a loan repayment schedule at payment amounts the borrower cannot realistically meet. The lender may eventually foreclose on the property after the borrower falls behind on required loan payments. If the property is sold at a foreclosure sale, there may not be any sale proceeds left to be paid to the homeowner after deducting the amounts owed on the mortgage loan and the mortgage lender's foreclosure costs. In such a case the homeowner would lose all of the equity in the home (with the lender having "stripped" the equity away).

• **Loan Flipping**: The lender or a broker calls the borrower to see if they would like to refinance an existing loan to obtain additional monies for home improvements, debt consolidation, or other purposes. The lender or broker makes it sound attractive but, in reality, the lender or broker may be trying to "flip" an existing loan, by charging the borrower points and fees on both the additional monies that would be lent under the new loan as well as the already outstanding unpaid amounts borrowed under the existing loan to be refinanced. If the principal amount of the existing loan to be refinanced included closing costs (such as points or other fees), then refinancing the existing loan could include paying new points and fees on previously borrowed points and fees. In other words, be very careful when refinancing to make sure you don't pay excessive monies.

• **The Big Balloon Payment**: Some lenders include in their loan contracts provisions by which the borrower has to make one huge payment at the end of the loan term—this final payment is sometimes called a **balloon payment**. Sometimes a loan has a final balloon payment because earlier payments on the loan consist primarily of interest and include only a very small amount to be applied to reduce principal. In other cases, the earlier loan payments might not even cover all accrued interest, so that unpaid accrued interest would be added to the unpaid loan balance. This

TALKING TO A LAWYER

Q. Our mortgage loan just got sold to a huge, out-of-state bank. I assume this is legal—but is there anything we can do about it? We'd rather deal with a bank in our community, where we know people and it would be easier to get the answer to our questions.

A. After a mortgage loan is closed (after the borrower has signed the loan agreement or the promissory note, and the mortgage or deed of trust on the real estate securing repayment of the loan has been executed and recorded with the appropriate public official), and provided that the loan has not been rescinded (cancelled) during the first three business days after the closing, the lender who made the loan generally may sell the loan and/or the right to service the loan (in other words, the right to collect the loan payments required to be made by the borrower).

The loan is considered an asset (property) of the lender, and the lender may sell, assign, or even borrow against the loan (by using the loan as a type of collateral or security). The right to service the loan (the right to collect the loan payments required to be made by the borrower) is also an asset of the lender, and the lender may sell or assign this right, with or without selling or assigning the loan itself.

Borrowers do not have the right to stop a lender from selling a loan or from transferring the servicing of a loan to a third party. However, borrowers should receive notice if the servicing of their loan is being transferred (so that they can send their required loan payments to the new servicer of their loan).

—**Answer by Elizabeth C. Yen, Hudson Cook, LLP, New Haven, Connecticut**

is called **negative amortization**. Amortization usually occurs as part of a traditional mortgage repayment schedule and involves applying some aspect of each loan payment toward the principal and the rest toward accrued interest. With negative amortization, no portion of a loan payment is applied toward the principal, and the loan payment is too low to cover all accrued interest, so the unpaid accrued interest is added to the unpaid principal balance of the loan, creating a larger amount owed, with interest being charged on the full amount owed (including the unpaid accrued interest). Negative amortization may in some cases require the borrower to pay close to the entire original principal amount of the loan at the end of the loan term, or even more than the original principal. If the borrower is unable to pay the balloon payment due on a mortgage loan, and also unable to find a lender willing to refinance the balloon payment, the mortgage lender may foreclose on the borrower's home.

• **Credit Insurance Packing**: In this practice, the lender or broker adds in, or packs, credit insurance and other benefits into the terms of the loan, sometimes without fully explaining the benefits to the borrower. The borrower might not realize that adding the cost of insurance and other benefits to the loan amount will increase the fees and payments payable to the lender or broker. Lenders or brokers may also earn a commission when they sell insurance and other benefits to borrowers, further increasing the total fees they may earn in connection with the loan.

REVERSE MORTGAGES

Reverse mortgages are also a potential risk, especially for older people. At their best, they permit older people to take advantage of the equity they have built up in their home, using it for living expenses and other purposes. At their worst, they can have all the downsides of home equity loans.

Here is how they work. A **reverse mortgage** lets you borrow against the equity in your home, without having to repay the loan right away. You can get the money in a lump sum, in monthly cash payments for life, or by drawing on a line of credit (a revolving loan account that a consumer can tap into for loan advances as needed), or you can choose a combination of these options (e.g., monthly payments plus a line of credit for emergencies). The amount you can borrow, and the size of the loan advances, are based on several factors, including: your age, the value of the home and of the equity you hold, the interest rate, and the kind of loan you select. Reverse mortgage loans can be costly, with significant fees due up front at closing, although the overall annualized costs generally lessen over time, and you will generally never owe more than the value of your home.

Most reverse mortgages have very few or no restrictions on how you use the money. The loan usually does not have to be repaid until you sell, die, or move from your home, although some loans must be repaid at the end of a specified number of years. Some lenders offer reverse mortgage loans in combination with an annuity (a type of insurance contract, similar to life insurance) that allows you to receive payments under the annuity even after you sell your home and move.

When you sell your home or move, or at the end of the term of a reverse mortgage loan, you must repay the money you have borrowed plus the accrued interest and fees. The house can be sold to repay the loan, or the funds collected some other way. The lender generally cannot collect more than the appraised value of the house at the time the reverse mortgage loan is repaid, even if the loan exceeds that amount. For example, if the reverse mortgage loan amount is $300,000 but the home is now worth $250,000, the lender generally could collect only $250,000.

The most widely available reverse mortgage product is the federally insured **Home Equity Conversion Mortgage** (or **HECM**). Under this HECM program, the Federal Housing Administration (FHA) provides insurance for reverse mortgages placed through private financial institutions. HECM borrowers are charged FHA insurance fees (these fees are added to the amount borrowed under the HECM). Another reverse mortgage program that has been available nationally through private lenders is **Home Keeper® Mortgage**. A few private companies also offer their own reverse mortgage products. These tend to be more costly, because the lender must charge customers more in order to self-insure against potential losses. Federal law requires all reverse mortgage lenders to inform you, before making the loan, of the total amount you will owe through the course of the loan. This enables you to compare the costs.

Eligibility. Whether a borrower is eligible for a reverse mortgage depends on the individual product, but most have rules similar to the FHA HECM program. The borrower and every other person whose name is on the deed must:

• be at least sixty-two, and

• generally own the property free and clear, except for liens or mortgages that can be paid off with proceeds from the loan (HECMs also may be used to purchase the borrower's primary residence).

In addition, the property must be:

• the borrower's primary residence (that is, not a vacation home), and

• a one- to four-unit family residence,

The decision to take out a reverse mortgage is one that requires careful consideration. Reverse mortgages allow you to spend your home equity while you are alive. However, you should realize that you may end up using all of your equity, and not have any left to pass down to your heirs. Some reverse mortgage plans allow you to set aside some of the equity, so that it is not used by the reverse mortgage lender. This may reduce the total amount you would be allowed to borrow under the reverse mortgage.

The FHA requires all potential HECM borrowers to receive financial and homeownership counseling from an agency certified by the Department of Housing and Urban Development (HUD) before closing a reverse mortgage loan. Some state laws require financial and homeownership counseling for all reverse mortgage loan borrowers, no matter what type of reverse mortgage product is being considered; however, borrowers looking at private (non-FHA) reverse mortgage products generally are not required to have counseling before they obtain a reverse mortgage loan.

Reverse mortgages are very complex and involve difficult financial, legal, and personal decisions. Examine them carefully, and look for alternatives that may suit your needs. You should have professional advice in making this decision. Talk to a lawyer, financial planner, or other qualified housing counselor who is familiar with the issues, and discuss your aims and concerns with family.

Consumer information about reverse mortgages, including booklets, information about loan costs, and an interactive loan guide, is available from AARP at www.aarp.org/money/personal/reverse_mortgages/. Additional information is available from the National Center for Home Equity Conversion at www.reverse.org.

PROTECTIONS AGAINST PREDATORY HOME EQUITY LOANS

In 1994, Congress passed the **Home Ownership and Equity Protection Act (HOEPA)**. This law amends the Truth in Lending Act and establishes requirements for certain high-cost loans secured by the borrower's primary residence. However, HOEPA does not apply to revolving (open-end) lines of credit (such as home equity lines of credit or HELOCs), reverse mortgage loans, and closed-end loans taken for the purpose of financing the purchase or initial construction of the borrower's primary residence. This means that HOEPA generally applies only to those closed-end loans that are intended to help with home renovations or improvements or to provide extra money for the homeowner for other uses (medical care, for example). Furthermore, for HOEPA to apply, the annual percentage rate or the fees paid by the borrower must exceed a certain level.

If a loan falls within the scope of HOEPA, the lender must meet certain requirements, as well as make extra disclosures. Specifically, HOEPA restricts prepayment penalties, post-default interest rate increases, balloon payments, negative amortization, prepaid monthly payments, and due-on-demand clauses, in which the lender has the right to demand that the loan be repaid in full at any time.

HOEPA prohibits lenders from engaging in a pattern or

practice of making high-cost mortgage loans to consumers based on the value of their homes without regard to consumers' ability to repay. The law prohibits creditors from engaging "in a pattern or practice of extending credit . . . based on the consumers' collateral without regard to the consumers' repayment ability, including the consumers' current and expected income, current obligations and employment." (As of October 1, 2009, the Federal Reserve Board's HOEPA regulations will include provisions concerning how lenders making mortgage loans subject to HOEPA should verify a borrower's income, assets, and current obligations.) HOEPA was passed in part to prevent a form of "reverse redlining"—targeting residents in certain low-

 THE GOVERNMENT IS AWARE

The federal government and many state governments are aware of the dangers of predatory mortgage lending and are attempting to respond in whatever ways they can.

For example, in 2008, Congress passed the Mortgage Disclosure Improvement Act of 2008 to generally require Truth in Lending disclosures to be given to residential mortgage loan applicants and borrowers earlier in the application process and several days in advance of loan closing, to enhance the Truth in Lending disclosures required to be provided in connection with variable interest rate residential mortgage loans, and to increase the civil penalties available for certain Truth in Lending disclosure errors. The Federal Reserve Board also recently amended its Truth in Lending regulations to (among other things) add new requirements for certain higher-priced subprime residential mortgage loans, and to enhance pre-existing residential mortgage loan advertising disclosure requirements.

However, government action can only do so much. The best way to protect yourself is to educate yourself. Understand what you can and cannot afford, read any and all disclosures and agreements before you sign them, and when in doubt, ask questions.

TALKING TO A LAWYER

Q. How do you know when you've taken on too much indebtedness on a home equity loan?

A. You've taken on too much debt if you need to resort to credit cards, payday loans or other credit advances to make any payments.

—Answer by Marc S. Stern, Law Offices of Marc S. Stern, Seattle, Washington

Q. I'm older but I've got the credit needs of a younger person. I just got remarried at age 62, and I'd like to buy a new house for us, fix it up, etc. Can I get mortgage loans and a big amount of credit at my age? After all, I don't plan to work forever.

A. Yes, even though you are older, you can still qualify for a mortgage loan. Mortgage loans are often for larger amounts of money and are often for terms as long as thirty years. However, fifteen-and twenty-year terms are also available. In addition to having a generally good credit record, you will need to show the creditor that your income will be sufficient to cover your mortgage payments, homeowners insurance, property taxes, and other expenses. This might require that you be able to show what income you will have (including Social Security and any pension funds) after you retire. As with all mortgage loans, the creditor will also want to ascertain the value of your house and the amount of your equity in the house (the total value of the house minus the amount of any mortgage or other debts secured by the house) to be sure that the equity will support the loan amount requested.

—Answer by Robin K. Warren, formerly with Bank of America, Charlotte, North Carolina

A. Before making these decisions, you need to figure out if you are going to be able to make the payments. As you indicate, you are not going to work forever. If you are not going to work, and if your retirement income will not support the payments, do you want to do this? It seems to me that you might be setting yourself up for a bankruptcy.

—Answer by Marc S. Stern, Law Offices of
Marc S. Stern, Seattle, Washington

or moderate-income areas for mortgage loans at above-market rates, fees, and other terms. As one court has explained, "the legislative history of HOEPA demonstrates that Congress enacted HOEPA to force the high-cost mortgage market to police itself."

REMEMBER THIS

• Shop around for the best deal with respect to credit. Many consumer credit laws, including the federal Truth in Lending Act, require lenders to disclose the terms of the deal to you.

• If a lender or broker is being evasive, avoid that lender or broker at all costs.

• Be especially careful when taking a home equity loan. Carefully research the lender and any mortgage broker you may be using, and the terms of the loan. You don't want to fall victim to a predatory lender or broker.

• Federal law generally gives you three business days to cancel for any reason a non-purchase money loan that is secured by property used as your principal dwelling. That law covers most home equity loans. If something is bothering you about the loan or the lender has engaged in questionable behavior, you may still have time to release yourself from the loan obligations within the first three business days after the loan closing. This is called the right of rescission.

• Carefully review all cost-related disclosures you receive in connection with your mortgage loan. And always review all contract documents very carefully before you sign them.

- Talk to a lawyer, financial planner, or other qualified housing counselor before you take out a mortgage loan.
- Mortgage loans are complicated transactions in which consumers must be informed of myriad costs. As the FTC says, "shop, compare, and negotiate."

CHAPTER 12

Auto Financing and Leasing

The Lowdown on Buying, Financing, and Leasing a Car

Your old clunker just completely clunked and you don't have access to reliable public transportation. You need a new car, but you don't have enough money to pay for one. You'll have to finance or lease your vehicle. You go to a car dealership and they say it would be best for you to obtain financing through the dealership. They also tell you it would be even better to lease a vehicle from them. What should you know about auto financing before taking this plunge?

Buying an automobile may be your biggest financial purchase other than buying a home. Before going to the dealership, you should do some research. You should: (a) know how much you can afford to spend on a monthly basis; (b) identify the price range of the car you wish to buy; and (c) learn the annual percentage rates (APRs) offered by various banks and other alternative sources of credit so that you can compare them with the APR offered by the dealership.

DEALERSHIP FINANCING

The most common type of financing is "dealership financing." In this arrangement, a buyer and a dealership enter into a retail installment sale contract where the buyer agrees to pay the dealership the amount financed, plus an agreed-upon finance charge, over a period of time. The dealership may hold on to the installment sale contract, but usually sells it to an **assignee** (such as a bank, finance company, or credit union), which services the account and collects the payments.

Most dealerships have a Finance and Insurance (F&I) Department, which provides one-stop shopping for financing. If you are getting dealership financing, the F&I Department manager will ask you to complete a credit application. The dealership may obtain a copy of your credit report, which contains information about current and past credit obligations, your payment record, and data from public records (for example, a bankruptcy filing obtained from court documents).

As noted above, if you enter into a retail installment sale contract with a dealership, the dealership typically will sell your retail installment sale contract to an assignee, such as a bank, finance company, or credit union. Accordingly, the dealership submits your credit application to one or more potential assignees to determine their willingness to purchase a retail installment sale contract between you and the dealer. These potential assignees will usually evaluate your credit application using automated techniques such as credit scoring, where a variety of factors, like your credit history, length of employment, income, and expenses may be weighed and scored.

Since the bank, finance company, or credit union does not deal directly with the prospective vehicle purchaser, it bases its evaluation upon what appears on the individual's credit report and score, the completed credit application, and the terms of the sale, such as the amount of the down payment. Each finance company or other potential assignee decides whether it is willing to buy the retail installment sale contract, notifies the dealership of its decision and, if applicable, offers the dealership a wholesale rate at which the assignee would be willing to buy the retail installment sale contract, often called the "buy rate."

Your dealer may be able to offer you manufacturer-sponsored incentives, such as reduced finance rates or cash back on certain models. You may see advertisements for these specials (such specials are usually limited to a specific geographic region). Make sure you ask your dealer if there are any special financing offers or rebates with respect to the model in which you are interested. Generally, these discounted rates are not negotiable and may be limited by a consumer's credit history and are available only for certain models, makes, or model-year vehicles.

DIRECT LOANS

An alternative type of vehicle financing is "direct lending." In the case of direct lending, the buyer obtains a loan directly from a finance company, bank, or credit union. The buyer enters into a loan agreement with the lender and agrees to pay the lender the amount financed, plus an agreed-upon finance charge, over a period of time. Once a buyer and a vehicle dealership enter into a contract of sale and the buyer agrees to a vehicle price, the buyer uses the loan proceeds from the lender to pay the dealership for the vehicle. Consumers also arrange such vehicle loans over the Internet.

DEALER-ASSISTED LOANS

A dealer-assisted loan is a type of direct loan in which the dealership arranges for the buyer to obtain a loan directly from a finance company, bank, or credit union. If the dealership has attempted to arrange a loan for you, each lender to whom the dealer submitted your credit application decides whether it is willing to make you a loan, notifies the dealership of its decision and, if applicable, informs the dealership of the base rate required by the lender.

You may negotiate the annual percentage rate (APR) and the terms for payment with the dealership if the dealership has arranged for your loan, just as you negotiate the price of the vehicle. The APR you negotiate with the dealer is usually higher than the base rate required by a lender with whom the dealer has arranged a loan for you. This negotiation can occur before or after the dealership accepts and processes your credit application. As with any other direct loan, if the dealership succeeds in arranging for a loan, you enter into a loan agreement with the

INCENTIVE FINANCING/LOW-COST FINANCING

Many car dealers offer low-cost financing as a promotion. One example would be **incentive financing** with an APR that is below the rate being offered by, say, your credit union for the same term. How do you decide if these promotions are a good deal? All other things being equal, the incentive financing rate offer is probably a good deal.

Answering the question is more complicated if the auto dealer or manufacturer is offering a cash rebate as an alternative to the incentive financing rate if you buy the car for cash or you arrange your own financing through your bank, credit union, or someone else. In other words, should a consumer attempt to negotiate with the car dealer's finance company or deal directly with the bank and then purchase the car? Keep in mind that as a consumer you may have little bargaining power in lowering an APR. To see whether the incentive financing rate or the cash rebate is the better deal, you need to compare financing through the dealer at the low rate versus financing through your bank or credit union at the rate they will offer you for the same term using the cash rebate as an additional down payment. Generally, the better deal is the one with the lowest monthly payment over the same term. But consider also the convenience of dealership financing and whether you will need your bank/credit union credit lines for other needs. For example, a major car maker once offered a choice of a $1,500 cash rebate or 5.8 percent financing for four years on certain models. Assume that the car you would like to buy costs $16,000. If you have $2,000 for a down payment, you have the following choices:

1. If you finance with the dealer, your $2,000 down payment leaves $14,000 ($16,000 minus $2,000) to be financed over four years at 5.8 percent. The monthly payments would be $327.51.

2. If you finance with your bank, credit union, or another credit grantor, the $1,500 cash rebate from the dealer plus your $2,000 gives you a total down payment of $3,500. This leaves $12,500 to borrow ($16,000 minus

$3,500). If you borrow $12,500 for four years at 11.17 percent, your monthly payments would be $324.10, which, all other things being equal, is a slightly better deal.

If the rebate in the above example were available in combination with the low finance rate, the low finance rate would clearly be the better deal.

lender and agree to pay the lender the amount financed, plus an agreed-upon finance charge, over a period of time.

PRICE OF THE VEHICLE

Buyers should be aware of the terminology used to describe the price of the vehicle. There is the **invoice price**, which refers to the manufacturer's charge to the dealer. Sometimes, you will hear salespeople refer to the price of a car as "five percent above invoice" or "$200 above invoice." The base price refers to the cost of the car without any special options. The base price includes the standard equipment and factory warranty. The **"Monroney" sticker price** is the price that federal law requires be attached to the car window. It includes the base price, manufacturer-installed options and their retail prices, transportation (destination) charges, and the total manufacturer's suggested retail price. It is named after U.S. Senator Michael Monroney, who in 1958 spurred the passage of the law that mandated auto sellers to place this sticker on cars. Finally, the **dealer sticker price** is the regular sticker price plus the suggested retail price with the dealer-installed upgrades and options.

Consumers should carefully do research on base car prices before meeting with the salesperson. Some dealerships will also add dealer markups. These are simply additional fees that the dealership adds to the car price to increase their profit.

This is not to suggest that the auto-buying world is never friendly to consumers. In fact, due to the law of supply and demand, there are often great incentives on the part of dealerships to sell cars at reasonable prices. Consumers may be best served to find out the dealer cost of the vehicle and then negotiate upward with the car dealership, rather than attempt to make the dealer come down in price from the manufacturer's suggested retail price (MSRP). The reality is that the MSRP is always much higher than the dealer's cost price. Consumers should check carefully for special rebates (money paid back to the consumer).

LEASING A VEHICLE

Many consumers lease their vehicles rather than purchase them. Under a lease, you pay a certain amount each month to drive a vehicle over a period of time, normally two to four years. You must return the vehicle at the end of the lease. (Most leases also give you the right to purchase the vehicle at the end of the lease.)

The most common form of consumer lease is a **closed-end lease**. Under a closed-end lease, you may return the vehicle at the scheduled end of the lease term, pay any scheduled end-of-lease costs, and walk away. An **open-end lease** is a lease agreement in which the amount you owe at the end of the scheduled lease term is based on the difference between the residual value of the vehicle (defined as the **estimated** value of the vehicle at the end of the lease) and its actual value at lease end. The remainder of this discussion focuses on closed-end leases because they are much more common than open-end leases, which are riskier and perhaps should be avoided or at least considered very carefully.

There are several reasons people may prefer to lease. Leasing a vehicle allows you to drive a newer automobile more often than if you purchase for a similar monthly payment. Lease payments are smaller per month than installment purchase payments for the same contract term. Leasing may also give you a chance to drive a more expensive vehicle than you could buy. This is possible because the base monthly lease payments do not recoup the estimated residual value of the leased vehicle. Additionally, sometimes dealers will offer consumers a special subsidized, or **sub-**

vented, lease that is favorable to the consumer. These are used when a car dealer really wants to move certain types of cars.

However, there can be several disadvantages to leasing cars. These include the fact that leasing cars leads to never-ending car payments unless you purchase a car at the end of the lease. If you want to own your car free and clear, it can be better to finance a purchase rather than lease a vehicle. When you lease a car, you build up no equity in the car (unless you later purchase it). A lease need not entail a down payment, and you should refuse to pay one. If you have a used car to dispose of, you may be better off selling it on your own rather than trading it in when you lease a car. If for any reason you need to terminate the lease early, you will have to pay the lessor a very large amount of money, typically thousands of dollars. Therefore, it is unwise to lease a car unless you know you will keep it for the full term of the lease. Even so, if the car is totaled before the end of the lease, you will incur this large early termination fee. Beware.

Furthermore, most leases limit the number of miles you may drive (often 12,000 to 15,000 per year). You can negotiate a higher mileage limit and pay a higher monthly payment. You will have to pay charges for exceeding the allowable mileage if you return the vehicle. Most leases also assess a charge if you return the vehicle with excess wear and tear (as defined in the lease).

See chapter 2 for a brief discussion of rights you may have under a federal law governing leases.

PURCHASE CONTRACT AND LEASE AGREEMENT

If you are financing the purchase of a car from the dealer, you will receive a contract that governs the terms and conditions of the sale and financing of your vehicle. The contract is different from the "buyer's order" —a document that contains all the information on the car and is sometimes referred to as a purchase contract— that you will receive if you order a new car. The contents of the sale and finance contract will vary some, depending on the state in which you sign the contract. At a minimum, the contract should include a description of the make and model of the car and its vehicle identification number, or VIN. The contract also should include: whether the car is new or used; the agreed-upon price of the car; details on the value of the trade-in vehicle (if you traded in a vehicle as part of your purchase), including the amount that you still may owe on the traded-in vehicle; and the financing terms. The financing terms should include the vehicle price, amount of the down payment, trade-in value, less any amount owed to another person on the trade-in, cost of any other ancillary products (like an optional service contract, extended warranty, credit insurance), finance charge, annual percentage rate, and the length of the financing.

Read the contract carefully. If there are any terms you disagree with, discuss them with the dealership's representatives before you sign the contract. Do not sign the contract if you don't understand what you are signing or believe that there is a mistake. Do not simply mark through terms you disagree with. That won't eliminate them from the contract unless both you

 LEMON LAWS

Every state and the District of Columbia has a lemon law designed to protect consumers when they purchase a car that simply does not perform well and constantly needs repairs. Under many state laws, if a vehicle's nonconformity or defect is subject to repair three or more times within a certain time period and the defect continues to exist or if the vehicle is inoperable for thirty days or more, the car is deemed a "lemon."

Under many laws, if the car is deemed a lemon, the manufacturer must pay you the full purchase price of the vehicle and all collateral charges (such as license and registration fees) associated with the purchase of the vehicle.

The Better Business Bureau has a section on lemon laws at www.lemonlaw.bbb.org.

and the dealership's authorized representative initial the change to signify that both parties accept it.

If you are leasing a car from the dealer, you will receive a vehicle lease agreement that governs the terms and conditions of the leasing of your vehicle. The lease agreement is different from the "order" that you may receive that describes the features of your leased car. The contents of the lease agreement will vary some, depending on the state you live in or the state in which you sign the lease agreement. At a minimum, the lease agreement should include a description of the make and model of the car and its vehicle identification number, or VIN. The lease agreement should also include:

• whether the car is new or used;

• the agreed-upon price of the car and other amortized (installment-type payments set aside to pay down a mortgage or loan) amounts such as a lease acquisition fee and the cost of a service contract (called the "capitalized cost");

• details on the value of the traded-in vehicle (if you traded in a vehicle as part of your lease), including the amount that you still may owe on the traded-in vehicle;

• the amount of any down payment (called the "capitalized cost reduction");

• the term of the lease;

• the mileage included in the lease and cost to you for excess mileage at the end of the lease term;

• a description of your responsibility for excess wear and tear on the leased vehicle;

• a description of your liability to the lessor in case you or the lessor terminate the lease before the scheduled lease term; and

• whether you have the right to purchase the vehicle at the end of the lease and, if so, the amount or method of determining the amount of the purchase option price. The lease agreement will also include a formula that shows how the dealer calculated your monthly lease payment.

Read the lease agreement carefully. If there are any terms you disagree with, discuss them with the dealership's representatives before you sign the lease agreement. Do not sign the lease agreement if you don't understand what you are signing or believe that there is a mistake. Do not simply mark through terms you disagree with—any changes must be initialed by both parties (and the person initializing for the dealer must be authorized).

MAKING PAYMENTS

You must make your scheduled payments on your contract or lease agreement. If the dealer has assigned (sold) your contract or lease agreement to a finance company, bank, or other financial institution (these companies are called "holders"), you must make your payments to the holder. If you do not make your payments when they are due, the holder may repossess your vehicle. The holder has the right to repossess your vehicle until your contract or lease agreement is paid in full. In most states, the holder can repossess the car without giving you any notice. The only caveat is that they cannot breach the peace in obtaining the car from you, meaning that they probably couldn't break into your garage to get it or take it from you while you were in it.

Repossession rights vary from state to state. Once a holder repossesses your car, it may be able to sell the car to fulfill your obligations under your contract or lease agreement. If the sale doesn't cover everything you owe plus related expenses, like the repossession and sale, the holder may have the right to hold you responsible for the rest of the debt, often referred to as the "deficiency balance." If the sale brings in more than you owed plus the holder's expenses, the creditor should give the extra money, known as the **surplus**, to you. (A lessee is not entitled to any surplus because the lessee has no ownership interest in the leased vehicle.)

In some states, you will be given the option to reclaim the car before it is sold. Reclaiming means that the purchaser pays the entire amount owed, plus additional costs incurred by the holder in repossessing the car. This is called the **right of redemption**.

THE "NEGATIVE EQUITY" PROBLEM

Most consumers do not write a check or pay cash for the entire car purchase. Most people finance their car through monthly payments as discussed earlier. Some payment plans now stretch for five or six years. As a result, a vehicle's value may decline more quickly than the balance owed under a retail installment sale contract or a loan agreement. This leads to a condition where you could owe more on your contract or loan than the vehicle is worth for several years after your purchase. This condition is sometimes called **negative equity**. It is also referred to as being "upside down" or "underwater." This is important at trade-in time.

Edmunds.com, a leading tracker of the auto industry, has reported that more than 30 percent of car buyers end up in negative equity situations.

You can avoid a negative equity situation by making a larger down payment and making your payment plan shorter. If you find yourself in a negative equity situation, a dealer may be willing to finance the negative equity on your trade-in as part of your purchase or lease of a new vehicle. However, this will increase your payments on the new vehicle unless you make a larger down payment on the new transaction.

 TALKING TO A LAWYER

Q. What is spot delivery, and how is it tied in to financing?

A. Spot delivery, also known as a yo-yo sale (because the car may come back to the dealer), is very risky for the buyer. If the dealer cancels the contract, the buyer must return the vehicle and pay for its use during the period—often 3 to 4 weeks—that he or she has had it. The charge for this use may be hundreds of dollars. You should not take possession of the new car until the dealer agrees in writing that the financing is final.

—Answer by Michael M. Greenfield, George Alexander Madill Professor of Contracts and Commercial Law, Washington University in St. Louis, St. Louis, Missouri

Q. We're looking into leasing a car, and trying to compare one offer to another, but we're thoroughly confused by the terms. I know that in theory the law requires dealers to show the terms so that we can make sense of them, but I'm lost. Is there any practical advice you can give? What are the most important terms to look for?

A. Information on leasing is available from the Federal Trade Commission and perhaps from individual state agencies. Careful studying of lease disclosures required by law, which must be made clearly and in standard form, will also help you understand this information.

—Answer by Frederick H. Miller, Of Counsel, Phillips Murrah, P.C. Oklahoma City, Oklahoma

Q. Is there subprime car financing? How does it differ from the financing offered to people with better credit?

A. Subprime financing is the term that is used to describe financing made available to people with a history of credit problems. As a result of credit difficulties (prior bankruptcies, bad payment history, lack of credit history), these individuals pose a greater credit risk for dealers and for finance companies, banks, and other financial institutions that may purchase their contracts from the dealers. Customarily, the increase in risk is reflected in a higher finance charge. In addition, persons with increased credit risk may be required to pay a down payment that is a greater percentage of the amount financed than those with better credit.

—Answer by Mark S. Edelman, McGlinchy Stafford, PLLC, Cleveland, Ohio

REMEMBER THIS

- Before going to the dealership, you should do some research. The Internet is very helpful. You should: (a) know how much you can afford to spend on a monthly basis; (b) identify the price range of the vehicle you wish to buy; (c) ascertain the dealer's cost for the car and its accessories; and (d) compare the finance rates offered by various banks with the finance rate offered by the dealership.

- You must make your monthly payments to the holder of the loan or contract. If you fall far enough behind on your payments, the holder of the loan or contract may repossess your vehicle.

- Read any sales or lease contracts carefully. If there are any terms you disagree with, discuss them with the dealership's representatives before you sign the contract. Do not sign the contract if you don't understand what you are signing or believe that there is a mistake.

CHAPTER 13

Debt Collection
and the Law

*Your Rights Under the Fair Debt
Collection Practices Act*

*You recently moved into a new house, but soon realized that you
didn't have enough furniture to fill the rooms. While shopping
at the local department store, you find a sofa that you know will
go perfectly in your family room. While purchasing, the salesperson convinces you to put the sofa on a store credit card, allowing
you to save 15 percent off the regular sale price. Unfortunately,
during these last two months, you have run into hard times and
have not had the money to pay the department store bill. The
store contracts with a debt collector to attempt to collect the
money. The debt collector is relentless. The collector calls you at
work, early in the morning, and late at night. The collector's
employees use every means of verbal persuasion, including hu-
miliation and outright threats, to shame you into paying the
debt. Do you have any relief from such collection practices? Is
this conduct legal?*

Such conduct may very well violate a federal law known as
the **Fair Debt Collection Practices Act (FDCPA)**. Passed
in 1977, the law amends the Consumer Credit Protection Act to
prohibit certain conduct by "debt collectors." The United States
Congress made findings in 1977 that: "There is abundant evidence of the use of abusive, deceptive, and unfair debt collection
practices by many debt collectors. Abusive debt collection practices contribute to the number of personal bankruptcies, to marital instability, to the loss of jobs, and to invasions of individual
privacy." The FDCPA was last amended in 2006, indicating that
Congress remains concerned about the debt collection practices
used by many debt collectors.

CONSEQUENCES OF NOT PAYING DEBT

Besides constant worry about your financial situation, there are a variety of concrete consequences for not paying debts that you owe, including harm to your credit record, possible court action, garnishment, repossession, and having debt collectors come after you (discussed below). Of course, paying owed debts is the best way to avoid credit problems and having creditors come after you. If you don't pay your debts on time, creditors are likely to report your delinquencies to one or more credit bureaus, thus harming your credit record. Creditors may also file a lawsuit against you seeking a judgment (i.e., a determination by a court that you owe a certain amount to a creditor) or seeking permission to attach property you own (such as bank accounts or wages). You will always have a chance to appear in court to defend yourself.

If the creditor obtains a judgment, and you do not pay that judgment, the creditor will likely be entitled to **garnish** your wages; that is, to direct your employer to pay some portion of

WHAT IF YOU DON'T PAY DEBTS AS PROMISED?

The law allows creditors various ways of collecting unpaid debts, some of which depend upon the law of the state in which you live. They may be able to seize part of your wages or the car or other merchandise that you purchased on credit. Or they may rely on debt collectors to get the money from you. The law attempts to balance the rights of the creditor who provided the credit and the rights of consumers who used the credit but did not fully pay for it. However, even if you have managed your finances successfully, as explained at the start of this book, this chapter may still be useful to you, because the FDCPA also gives rights to people who are not responsible for the debt the debt collector is trying to recover.

your wages directly to the creditor. Federal law sets a limit on what portion may be taken, and many state laws are even more protective. But if you have good employment income, some of it can probably be garnished. If a garnishment is used, the creditor will direct your employer to subtract a given amount from your paycheck each payday and pay that amount to the creditor until the debt is satisfied. Your employer cannot fire you because of garnishment by one creditor, but may be able to if another creditor also garnishes your wages. Check your individual state laws on this issue, as some states prohibit the firing of employees for more than one garnishment. (For example, Connecticut law prohibits employers from disciplining, suspending, or discharging "an employee because of any wage execution against the employee unless the employer is served with more than seven wage executions against the employee in a calendar year." See Conn. Gen. Stat. Section 52-361a[j].)

If you purchased a car, truck, boat, home appliance, or other item on credit, your creditor may have a security interest or **lien** on the item that you purchased. This is especially likely if you signed a "Retail Installment Sale" agreement with the creditor. Having a security interest or lien means that if you fail to pay as agreed, the creditor may **repossess** (recover) the item that you purchased with credit. Some state laws require that the creditor notify you, say ten days or two weeks in advance, that a default has occurred or that the creditor intends to repossess, so that you may have a last chance to pay your outstanding debt on the item before it is repossessed. The creditor may not breach the peace when repossessing items you bought on credit. This means that the creditor may not seize an item by force if you refuse to surrender it or break into your garage to seize a car. Many state laws also require that the creditor give you advance notice before selling any repossessed item.

Remember, most credit agreements specify that if you fail to make payments, the entire debt, not just the past due monthly payments, is immediately due. In the event of a default (for example, if you are behind in payments or have otherwise failed to meet the requirements of the credit agreement), the creditor is usually not required to repossess the property. Rather, the creditor could simply file a suit against you to collect the entire amount due. However, even if the creditor does repossess the property bought on credit, the repossession may not end your obligation to the creditor. If your unpaid balance and accumulated, unpaid finance charges, plus the creditor's costs of repossessing, storing and selling the property, are more than the amount that the creditor obtains from the sale of the property, you may still be legally liable to the creditor for some or all of the shortage. If the creditor thinks that you may be able to pay something toward the shortage, the creditor can ask a court to assess a deficiency judgment against you for the shortage. If you have a **deficiency judgment** against you, the creditor can take your other property (unless it is exempt from creditor process, which depends on state law) or possibly garnish your wages to satisfy the judgment. Laws in a few states prevent or limit deficiency judgments in some cases.

If you are sued on a debt and believe you shouldn't have to pay, consult a lawyer. If you do not contest the case, the court will accept the creditor's version of events. You should also consult a lawyer if you owe a debt but believe that the debt collector's techniques violate the FDCPA or your state's laws (discussed below). In such a case, if you win against the debt collector, you will generally be able to recover some money, but you will not be excused from paying the balance of the debt that you owe.

DEBT COLLECTORS

If you are being contacted by a debt collector, federal and state laws place restrictions on what the collector can say to you and when and how they can contact you. Under the federal Fair Debt Collection Practices Act, a **debt collector** is someone, other than a creditor or its employees, who regularly collects consumer debts on behalf of creditors. This federal law does not cover creditors per se (unless the creditor uses a false name in attempting to collect the debt), although your state laws may govern them. Thus, a retailer who attempts to collect unpaid debts owed to it would not

TALKING TO A LAWYER

Q. What are "time-barred" debts, and how does that time differ from state to state?

A. The statute of limitations says that a lawsuit must be filed within a specified period of time from the last payment or promise of payment. It varies from state to state. More importantly, the agreement that you signed may include a provision or provisions that the law of a specified state applies. That means that even if the lawsuit is time-barred in your state of residence, it may not be time-barred under the law that applies to the agreement.

—Answer by Marc S. Stern, Law Office of
Marc S. Stern, Seattle, Washington

A. After a certain amount of time after you have defaulted on a debt (often between four and ten years), the creditor no longer has the right to bring a lawsuit to recover the debt. When a creditor files a lawsuit after the statute of limitations has expired, the lawsuit is time-barred and may be immediately dismissed.

You should be aware that a debt is not eliminated just because it is time-barred. Courts have held that creditors may still pursue "time-barred" debts as long as they do not threaten to file a lawsuit against you.

—Answer by Bruce Menkes, Mandell
Menkes LLC, Chicago, Illinois

Q. What kinds of debts are covered by the Fair Debt Collection Practices Act?

A. The FDCPA covers communications by debt collectors attempting to collect debts that were incurred by individuals for personal, family, or household purposes. The word "debt" includes any amount a consumer has agreed to pay and has been held to include condominium assessments, student loans, and even NSF (bounced) checks. However, the FDCPA does not apply to attempts to collect taxes owed to governmental entities.

—Answer by Bruce Menkes, Mandell Menkes LLC, Chicago, Illinois

A. All debts being collected by a third-party collector or by a division of a bank that deals solely with bad debts.

—Answer by Marc S. Stern, Law Office of Marc S. Stern, Seattle, Washington

A. Any obligation to pay money involving a loan, or a purchase of property, insurance, or services, for personal, family, or household purposes.

—Answer by Frederick H. Miller, Of Counsel, Phillips Murrah, P.C., Oklahoma City, Oklahoma

be covered by the FDCPA, but may be covered by the debt collection laws of the state where the delinquent consumer resides. These laws are usually similar to the federal FDCPA. The rest of this chapter is based on that federal law.

A debt collector may contact you by mail, in person, or by telephone or telegram, but the debt collector may not contact you at times the debt collector knows are inconvenient for you, unless you agree (or a court specifically grants permission). Unless a debt collector has information to the contrary, the debt collector must assume that times before 8 A.M. or after 9 P.M. are not convenient. Also, a debt collector is not permitted to contact you at work if the collector knows or has reason to know that your employer forbids employees from being contacted by collectors at the workplace. You can tell the debt collector what times and places are inconvenient for you to receive calls.

A debt collector is also forbidden from contacting you if he or she knows that a lawyer represents you in connection with the debt. In a few instances, debtors have been able to sue creditors for intentional infliction of emotional distress (sometimes called outrageous conduct) when debt collectors engage in repeated patterns of harassing behavior. If you believe that legitimate debt collecting has crossed the line into unlawful harassment (for example, calling you repeatedly at work after being told not to and calling late at night), you may wish to mention that to your attorney. The Sixth Circuit U.S. Court of Appeals recently reinstated an outrageous conduct claim by a man who alleged that a credit card company crossed the line when it threatened him with criminal prosecution for fraud when his wife applied for credit cards without his knowledge. Representatives of the card company allegedly said: "if you don't pay up I'll have the district attorney take a little trip to your house." Even though the court in *MacDermid v. Discover Financial Services* (2007) rejected the claim based on the FDCPA, it reinstated the state law outrageous conduct claim. If a creditor hires a debt collector who engages in egregious enough actions to constitute outrageous conduct, not only the debt collector, but also the hiring creditor, could be liable. Because outrageous conduct or intentional infliction of emotional distress claims are state tort-law claims, the law can vary from state to state.

LIMITING CONTACT FROM DEBT COLLECTORS

You can stop a debt collector from contacting you by notifying the collector in writing. (However, the debt collector could still file a lawsuit against you.) After that, the attempts at contacting you must stop. There are two exceptions to this. The debt collector may tell you that there will be no more contact and that some specific legal or other action may be or will be taken. However, debt collectors may state this only if they actually plan to take such action.

Debt collectors must also stop trying to contact you if you notify them, by mail, within thirty days after they send you the notice described in the next paragraph, that you dispute all or part of the debt or that you are requesting the name and address of the original creditor. However, debt collectors are permitted to begin collection activities again if they send you proof of the debt, such as a copy of the bill, or the information you requested about the original creditor. This process is called verification of the debt. Remember that the debt collector must provide you with a copy of the debt verification if you request it within thirty days after you receive the notice described in the next paragraph.

The FDCPA requires debt collectors to give you a notice within five days of first contacting you, containing:

- the name of the creditor to whom you owe the money;
- the amount of money you owe;
- a statement to the effect that the debt collector will assume the debt is genuine unless you challenge all or part of it within thirty days; and
- a statement about what to do if you believe you do not owe the money—for example, if you dispute the validity of the debt in writing within thirty days, the agency will send you verification of the debt.

Debt collectors don't have to send a separate document with this information if they provided it in the initial communication or if you've already paid the debt.

A debt collector may contact any person to locate you. However, in doing so, the collector usually may not talk to anyone more than once or refer to the debt when talking to that person. If debt collectors use the mail to contact you or another person, they may not send letters in envelopes identifying themselves as bill collectors. They may not send a debt collection communication by postcard. Once collectors know that you have hired a lawyer with respect to the debt, they may communicate only with your lawyer about the debt, unless the debt collector cannot find the lawyer's name and address, or the lawyer fails to respond to the debt collector within a reasonable time, or the lawyer agrees to allow the debt collector to communicate directly with you.

GROWTH OF DEBT-BUYING BUSINESSES BAD NEWS FOR DEBTORS

A growing industry has exploded in the past few years that could affect millions of consumers. This industry is the debt-buying industry. Some companies buy up past-due (delinquent) consumer debt from credit card companies, health clubs, and other businesses that give up pursuing past-due consumer debt. The debt-acquiring companies often buy the consumer debt at a very large discounted price (that is, for an amount significantly less than the amount of the debt actually owed), including debt that is not legally enforceable because the statute of limitation bars legal action to collect it. These companies then aggressively pursue the individuals, including suing them in small claims and municipal courts, for the full amount of the debt actually owed. *The Wall Street Journal* reports that this is a "million-dollar industry." One effect of this industry is that consumers can no longer assume that seemingly ignored consumer debts will be forgotten.

Source: Suein Hwang, "Once-Ignored Consumer Debts Are Focus of Booming Industry," *The Wall Street Journal*, 10/15/2004, A1; Arthur Epstein. "Bad Times Are Good for Debt Collectors; the debt collection industry is poised to prosper amid rising levels of bad debt and a souring economy," *Business Week Online*, 4/11/2008.

PROHIBITED CONDUCT

A debt collector may not harass, oppress, or abuse any person. For example, a debt collector may not:

- use threats of violence to harm you, your property, or reputation;
- use obscene or profane language;
- repeatedly use the telephone to annoy you;
- make you accept collect calls or pay for telegrams; or
- publish a "shame list" or other roster of individuals who al-

legedly refuse to pay their debts (though the debt collector can still report you to a credit bureau).

A debt collector may not use false, deceptive, or misleading statements when trying to collect a debt. For example, a debt collector may not:

- misrepresent the amount of the debt;
- falsely imply that the debt collector is a lawyer;
- tell you that your property or wages will be seized, garnished, attached, or sold, unless the debt collector or the creditor intends to do so and it is legal; or
- threaten any action unless the action is lawful and the debt collector (or creditor) intends to take that action.

A debt collector may not use unfair means to collect a debt, such as:

- collecting any amount (including interest or any fee, charge, or expense) unless that amount is authorized by agreement or law;
- taking or threatening to take nonjudicial action to seize property that is exempt by law from legal process; or
- bringing a lawsuit in an inconvenient court or location.

If Debt Collectors Break the Law

There are several steps you can take if you think a debt collector is breaking the law. If a creditor (for example, a retailer or bank) is making the collection effort, check the law with the consumer protection office of your state or your state attorney general's office and write that office a letter detailing your complaint (with a copy to the offending creditor). If the collection effort is by an independent debt collector, write to the nearest office of the Federal Trade Commission (FTC) or the FTC's main office in Washington, D.C. (The addresses can be found in the appendix of this book or at the website: www.ftc.gov.) The FTC has been active in pursuing FDCPA violators and may occasionally fine them heavily or even put them out of business.

In addition, if debt collectors violate the Fair Debt Collection Practices Act, you may sue them in a state or federal court. However, you may do so only within one year from the date they

"NONPROFIT" HOSPITALS AS AGGRESSIVE DEBT COLLECTORS

There are many aggressive debt collectors, including some nonprofit hospitals. A 2003 story by the *Wall Street Journal* showed that some hospitals were taking extreme measures to collect debts from those who had not paid their medical bills and who did not appear in court for certain debt collection hearings. The article described a tactic that some hospitals were using known as "body attachment"—the arrest of a person who fails to show up for a debt collection court hearing. Some debtors who didn't attend a court hearing to determine their assets after a hospital had been awarded a judgment against them found themselves in jail. The article states that one hospital in southern Illinois issued 164 arrest warrants for debtors who missed this kind of court hearing. See Lucette Lagnano, "Hospitals Try Extreme Measures to Collect Their Own Debts," the *Wall Street Journal,* 10/30/2003, pg. 1.

According to a *National Law Journal* article in July 2004, 31 lawsuits have been filed against 300 nonprofit hospitals in 17 states. See Leonard Post, "Hospital hit with plague of lawsuits; Unfair billing practices alleged against nonprofits," *National Law Journal,* 7/19/2004, pg. 1. As of 2008, many of these lawsuits are still in litigation. However, some of the lawsuits have failed, including some that have alleged nonprofit hospitals engaged in unlawful behavior by charging uninsured patients more than insured patients. See Stephanie Potter, "Suit over hospital bills fails," *Chicago Daily Law Bulletin,* 4/14/2008, at p. 10001.

violated the law. You may recover money for the actual damage you suffered. The court may also award you an additional amount up to $1,000. You may also recover court costs and your lawyer's fees. Class action suits can be brought against debt collectors who violate the FDCPA. Through such suits, the class may be able to recover actual damages and can potentially recover an amount up to $500,000 or 1 percent of the debt collector's net worth—whichever is less. There may be a possibility that some creditor debt collection behavior may make the creditor liable for damages under an applicable state law.

Filing Complaints with Your State About Debt Collectors

As noted above, you should file complaints about consumer debt collection agencies with the Federal Trade Commission. You should also consider filing a complaint with the applicable state agency that regulates collection agencies. For instance, if a collection agency located in Tennessee were violating your rights, you could contact the Division of Consumer Affairs at the Department of Commerce and Insurance in Nashville, Tennessee. We list state consumer protection agencies in this book's appendix.

 STATE COMMON-LAW CAUSES OF ACTION

Federal law is not the only source of law available to consumers harmed by the unlawful conduct of debt collectors. A variety of state common-law tort theories may be used against certain overreaching conduct of debt collectors. These include defamation, invasion of privacy, intentional infliction of emotional distress, abuse of process, and malicious prosecution.

Defamation seeks to protect people from false statements that impugn their reputation. Given the importance of credit in today's society, false information regarding someone's credit may give rise to an actionable claim for defamation. If a debt collector engages in overly intrusive conduct in the pursuit of collecting a debt, an **invasion of privacy suit** is possible. The specific privacy tort, called **intrusion**, protects against invasive conduct that would be highly offensive to a reasonable person. Particularly outrageous conduct by debt collectors could give rise to a common-law suit for **intentional infliction of emotional distress** or **outrageous conduct**. Such conduct would have to exceed all bounds of social decency and cause severe mental injury or severe emotional distress.

In addition, some states prohibit nonlicensed collection agencies from collecting debts in their state. To collect a debt in Washington state, for example, the debt collector generally needs to be licensed there, regardless of where the creditor is located. Failure to be licensed also may be an unfair and deceptive trade practice under separate state laws prohibiting such trade

 TALKING TO A LAWYER

Q. How can having a lawyer help you deal with bill collectors?

A. There are a number of ways:

1. They can keep creditors from calling you.

2. They can negotiate a settlement and, more importantly, document it in such a way that it can't come back on you, so that there is no question that there is a settlement.

3. They can provide unbiased advice about what your options are, whether bankruptcy is a good idea, or whether there are other alternatives.

4. They can help you structure your financial situation so that creditors cannot collect from you.

—Answer by Marc S. Stern, Law Office of
Marc S. Stern, Seattle, Washington

Q. I understand that the federal law only protects you against certain debt collectors. How could I find out if my state law gives me greater protections?

A. You need to speak with a lawyer in your state who is familiar with the state laws. You can try to do the research yourself, but, since laws are written for lawyers to read, unless you understand the language, you may miss several things.

—Answer by Marc S. Stern, Law Office of
Marc S. Stern, Seattle, Washington

practices, in which case there could be additional damages available under such separate state laws.

If you believe that you have been the victim of unfair debt collection harassment, you might also consider consulting an attorney. As outlined above, victims of FDCPA abuse can recover actual damages, including attorneys' fees and court costs.

REMEMBER THIS

• Debt collectors can generally contact you at home or at work by mail, in person, or by telephone after 8 A.M or before 9 P.M. If debt collectors are contacting you at other times, they are violating the Fair Debt Collection Practices Act, unless they have reason to know that these times are not inconvenient to you.

• You may notify a debt collector in writing to stop contacting you. You may also inform a debt collector to stop calling you at work.

• Debt collectors may not harass, oppress, or abuse you. They may not repeatedly call you on the telephone to annoy you. The federal law known as the Fair Debt Collection Practices Act regulates the conduct of debt collectors. Read this law and become familiar with it if you believe a debt collector is using improper techniques to collect a debt or is trying to collect a debt that you do not owe. Also check with an attorney about possible state law actions under state statutes or state common law if debt collectors act egregiously toward you or your family. Some egregious debt collection practices may also be tortious or unlawful under state law.

CHAPTER 14

Credit Counselors:
A Potential Pitfall

Know Exactly What You're Getting Into

You've seen the advertisements: "Credit Problems No More!—We Can Erase Bad Credit Records, 100 Percent Guaranteed." Unfortunately, such promises often turn out to be gimmicks that only draw unwitting consumers further into financial trouble. You must be careful when choosing a credit counselor; a bad choice could plunge you further into debt.

Accroding to the Federal Trade Commission (FTC), every day these companies target consumers with poor credit histories. These companies will offer, for a fee, to clean your credit report, allowing you to get a car loan, a home mortgage, insurance, or even a job. However, as the FTC points out, these promises often go unfulfilled. After paying these companies hundreds or sometimes thousands of dollars in fees, the companies many times do nothing, other than vanishing with the money.

MANY ORGANIZATIONS CAN HELP

Despite the FTC's warning, some organizations do provide quality services for debtors and consumers. To find a quality organization, contact the National Foundation for Credit Counseling (NFCC) at www.nfcc.org. Founded in 1951, the NFCC is the nation's largest and longest-serving national nonprofit credit-counseling network. Its members, which typically do business using the name "Consumer Credit Counseling Service," provide counseling services, debt management services, and homeowner counseling and educational services. Such a group could help you negotiate with your creditors and reduce your debt to a more manageable level. In addition, the NFCC has a program called DebtAdvice.org

CREDIT COUNSELING AGENCIES AND CURRENT BANKRUPTCY LAWS

The importance of credit-counseling agencies has arguably increased since the 2005 changes to the bankruptcy laws took effect. The current law provides that a debtor cannot file for bankruptcy unless he or she, in an individual or group setting, has completed mandatory credit counseling within 180 days prior to filing a bankruptcy petition.

The U.S. trustee must approve not-for-profit credit-counseling agencies that can provide such services, and a list of such approved agencies must be provided in a "publicly available list." Agencies will be approved only if they demonstrate that they:

- provide qualified counselors,
- maintain adequate provision for safekeeping and payment of client funds,
- provide adequate credit counseling, and
- deal responsibly and effectively with other matters relating to the services they provide.

Credit-counseling agencies must charge only "reasonable fee[s]" and "provide services without regard to ability to pay the fee." These agencies can help debtors develop debt management plans. Once a debt management plan is developed, it must be filed with the applicable bankruptcy court along with a certificate from the agency that helped developed it.

(www.debtadvice.org) that helps consumers manage a wide variety of credit problems. Debtadvice.org also offers a companion site in Spanish (which can be accessed through their main website).

SOME ORGANIZATIONS MAKE PROBLEMS WORSE

Unfortunately, not every organization operating as a debt consolidator, credit counselor, or credit repair group has altruistic motives. Some engage in the types of actions that caused the Federal Trade Commission to issue the stern warning quoted at the beginning of this chapter.

It was for this very reason that Congress passed the **Credit Repair Organizations Act (CROA)**, which was signed into law by President Bill Clinton in 1996. The CROA amends the Consumer Credit Protection Act to protect consumers from credit repair scams and false promises. Congress passed the measure, in its own words, because "certain advertising and business practices of some companies engaged in the business of credit repair services have worked a financial hardship upon consumers, particularly those of limited economic means and who are inexperienced in credit matters."

The CROA provides that credit repair organizations cannot charge or receive money until a service they provide is fully performed. It also provides a list of disclosures that credit repair organizations (CROs) must make to consumers, including disclosure of the fact that neither a consumer nor a CRO has the right to remove accurate, correct, and verifiable information from a customer's credit report, which contains the consumer's credit history, unless it is old negative information as defined in

 TALKING TO A LAWYER

Q. What are debt management plans and negotiation programs? Are they a good idea?

A. If your self-help efforts have not been successful or you need the assistance of a professional debt counselor to establish a budget and negotiate better credit terms with your creditors, then debt management or debt negotiation plans offered by reputable organizations (like the Consumer Credit Counseling Services, as discussed above) may be a good idea. In many cases, these organizations have established payment plans with major creditors. They may be able to assist you, either by collecting a lump sum from you each month and distributing the funds to your creditors (debt management) or by helping you obtain better credit terms while you continue to make payments directly to your creditors (debt negotiation). In many cases, creditors may be willing to accept payments of outstanding principal and reduce or waive applicable fees and finance charges for as long as you make timely payments under a plan. In other cases, the creditor may be willing to report your debt as "current" as long as you remain in good standing under the plan; this is known as "re-aging." Upon completion of the plan or program, your debt may be reported as "settled," though you may lose future credit privileges. This can be a better outcome than default or bankruptcy, and may permit you to reapply for credit with your creditor at a later date. In the case of the Consumer Credit Counseling Service, your creditor may even pick up part of the cost of such a plan through a "Fair Share" contribution to the service. Importantly, however, such plans typically may be used to manage or negotiate only your unsecured debt.

Firms to be avoided are those that suggest you can stop making payments, refuse to communicate with your creditor, or pay only pennies on the dollar for your outstanding debt. Such strategies can have dire consequences: Your creditors may continue to report you as delinquent in real time (i.e., no re-aging), may refuse to accept any settlement of your account, or may incur collection expenses for which you could ultimately become liable. Such firms may also charge hefty up-front fees that limit your ability to pay your creditors and eliminate your debt as quickly as possible.

Be careful in your selection of advisors. It's your reputation on the line; it's your money. Don't be fooled by promises of a quick fix. A good workout plan could take as long as forty-eight to sixty months to complete.

> —Answer by Michael C. Tomkies, Drecher Langer &
> Tomkies, LLP, Columbus, Ohio

the Fair Credit Reporting Act. (See chapter 7 for more information about credit reports.) Furthermore, the CROA bars CROs from advising consumers to make untrue or misleading statements regarding their credit histories.

Exception for Nonprofit Counseling Groups

When dealing with credit counseling groups, consumers should be aware of an important distinction regarding nonprofit counseling groups. These groups are not covered by the Fair Debt Collection Practices Act. The law does not apply to "any nonprofit organization which, at the request of consumers, performs bona fide consumer credit counseling and assists consumers in the liquidation of their debts by receiving payments from such consumers and distributing such amounts to creditors."

A number of groups have sprung up that purport to be nonprofit, but actually exist to line their own pockets. They operate relatively freely because federal law does not cover them (although some state laws do). However, an organization composed of representatives of the states, called the National Conference of Commissioners on Uniform State Laws, completed work on a uniform law called "the Uniform Debt Management Services Act." This model law, which several states have adopted, is designed to "rein in the excesses while permitting credit-counseling agencies and debt-settlement companies to continue providing services that benefit consumers." To find out more about this law and in which states it has been passed, go to www.nccusl.org, and click on "Final Acts and Legislation."

In late 2003, the Federal Trade Commission filed a lawsuit against Ameridebt, Inc., one of the leading nonprofit consumer debt-counseling organizations, charging that the company had engaged in fraudulent and deceptive practices. "We will not allow consumers to be duped into 'contributing' hundreds of dollars to these so-called 'non-profits,'" said Howard Beales, director of the FTC's Bureau of Consumer Protection. "There was nothing voluntary and nothing charitable about these payments.

TIP-OFFS TO RIP-OFFS

The FTC warns consumers to steer clear of companies that:

- guarantee they can erase your unsecured debt;
- promise that unsecured debts can be paid off for pennies on the dollar;
- claim that using their systems will let you avoid bankruptcy;
- require substantial monthly service fees;
- demand payment of a percentage of your savings;
- tell you to stop making payments to or communicating with your creditors;
- require you to make monthly payments to them, rather than to your creditors;
- claim that creditors never sue consumers for nonpayment of unsecured debt;
- promise that using their systems will have no negative impact on your credit report; or
- claim that they can remove accurate negative information from your credit report.

Consumers' money didn't go to creditors, it just ended up lining the pockets of the defendants." The suit eventually led to a settlement. In September 2008, the FTC announced that as part of the settlement, 287,000 Ameridebt, Inc. customers were mailed "redress checks" that totaled $13 million (see www.ftc.gov/opa/2008/09/ameridebt.shtm). Ameridebt, Inc. is now defunct.

The Federal Trade Commission warns that consumers should pay close attention when choosing any credit counselor, whether the counselor is for-profit or nonprofit, as some such groups may simply create more problems for consumers. (See the "Tip-offs to Rip-offs" sidebar for some specific recommendations.)

FIGHTING BACK AGAINST BAD CREDIT REPAIR ORGANIZATIONS

FACTS

In *Limpert v. Cambridge Counseling Corporation*, two people filed a class action lawsuit against a credit-counseling company under the Fair Debt Collection Practices Act (FDCPA), the Racketeering Influenced and Corrupt Organization Act, and the Credit Repair Organizations Act (CROA). The plaintiffs had enrolled in a debt management plan with the defendants. Under that plan, they gave money to the defendants to pay their unsecured debts, and the defendants then disbursed those payments to the plaintiffs' creditors. However, the plaintiffs later claimed that the company had also falsely promised them lower credit card balances, improved credit ratings, fewer late fees, and lower interest rates.

DECISION

The court rejected the plaintiffs' FDCPA claim because the defendants were credit counselors, not debt collectors: The court found that, "while the distinction between credit counseling and debt collection is finely cut, it is nonetheless controlling. . . . Defendants are not debt collectors as they do not collect debts owed to others; rather, they assume such debts as part of their method, whatever its merits, of credit counseling."

However, the court refused to dismiss the CROA claim, noting that "there is a fine line, in advertising and soliciting for credit-counseling services to an unsophisticated audience of lower-income debtors, between promising future rewards for creditworthiness, and implying that existing bad credit records may be prematurely expunged." (As this book goes to press, the outcome of the *Limpert* case is still pending.)

CREDIT REPAIR ORGANIZATIONS— THEY CAN'T CHANGE THE TRUTH

Credit repair organizations deserve a special word of warning. Such organizations generally advertise that they can help you review and update your credit record and report; their fees are often as high as $1,000. If your credit report has an error or needs updating, however, you can deal directly with a credit bureau on your own, for free or at very little cost. If the negative information in your credit report is accurate, only better management of your debts can offset your negative record, and only the passage of time can remove it. Be very suspicious if a credit repair clinic promises that it can remove accurate records of bankruptcy and bad debts from your credit record or if it promises to get you credit. If a credit program sounds too good to be true, it probably is.

Finally, remember that for-profit credit repair organizations are regulated by federal and some state laws, and federal law prevents a credit repair company from receiving any money from you before it has completed its services. However, you should be aware that not all credit repair groups are subject to the requirements of the Credit Repair Organizations Act; the law does not cover nonprofit organizations that are tax-exempt under Section 501(c)(3) of the Internal Revenue Code.

REMEMBER THIS

• Credit counseling sounds like a good thing, but not all credit-counseling groups are the same. Some are rip-offs for consumers. Be very careful if you decide to selecting one.

• Credit repair organizations are not the same as credit-counseling companies. Be careful in determining whether you wish to consult with a credit repair organization or a credit-counseling organization.

• Credit counseling has become even more important with the passage of the new bankruptcy law. That law requires individuals to undergo mandatory credit counseling 180 days before filing for bankruptcy.

• The current bankruptcy law also requires debtors under Chapters 7 and 13 to complete an "instructional course concerning personal financial management." If you don't complete this course, a discharge of debts will not be granted—you will still owe them.

• The Federal Trade Commission provides a checklist of guarantees that credit repair companies should not make. In particular, such companies should not claim that their systems will let you avoid bankruptcy and should not guarantee that they can erase all of your unsecured debt.

PART II

Bankruptcy

CHAPTER 15

Problem Debt

What to Do When You're Swimming in Red Ink

You notice that your debts far exceed your income. You can barely pay your mortgage and provide enough food for your family. You haven't made a credit card payment in three months, a car payment in two months, or a payment on your doctors' bills in several months. Creditors are calling your house from morning until night and writing aggressive collection letters threatening you with lawsuits. You feel you are running out of options. What should you do? Should you file for bankruptcy?

Many Americans find themselves in the type of situation described above: They are in serious debt trouble. The creditors keep calling, but the debts just keep growing. Sadly, this cycle is escalating with the economic recession that started in 2008, as unemployment and foreclosure rates soar. Bankruptcies in 2008 rose between 30 and 35 percent over the 2007 rates. Some analysts predict an even higher increase in future years. Historically, debtors who failed to pay their debts were sent to prison. But in America, we now have a uniform system of bankruptcy laws that provide relief and a fresh start to many individuals who are in financial trouble and distress.

Bankruptcy is one of the alternatives available for relieving financial distress, but it is a serious legal procedure with long-term consequences. Before you take the step of filing for bankruptcy, you should learn about bankruptcy and how it works, explore other options with a credit counselor, and decide which course of action is best for you.

Some people in financial trouble can improve their situations simply by contacting and negotiating directly with creditors. Others may get help from reputable local financial-counseling programs or reputable consumer credit counseling services, which have experience negotiating with creditors and formulating and establishing repayment plans. Remember, bankruptcy is a last resort, not a first resort. For some people, however, bankruptcy relief may be the only realistic alternative.

The choice of a remedy is not always easy. As a first step, consider the pros and cons of filing for bankruptcy, and compare the two basic types of consumer bankruptcy: **Chapter 7 bankruptcy** ("straight bankruptcy") and **Chapter 13 bankruptcy** (sometimes called "wage-earner bankruptcy"). (These types of bankruptcy are compared and contrasted in chapters 17, 18, and 19 of this book.) Each of these types of bankruptcy is covered by a section of the federal Bankruptcy Code, under which bankruptcies are filed all over America.

In April 2005, President Bush signed into law the **Bankruptcy Abuse Prevention and Consumer Protection Act of 2005**. This law was the first major overhaul of bankruptcy legislation since 1978 and effected major changes in the existing bankruptcy system. One major change is that those who file for bankruptcy are required to consult with an "approved nonprofit budget and credit counseling agency" before filing. Other major changes make it more difficult for people to file for bankruptcy under Chapter 7, which means that more people will have to file under Chapter 13.

If you ultimately decide to seek bankruptcy relief, you should hire a lawyer who is familiar with the federal bankruptcy laws. You will need to make sure you are working with an attorney who has stayed abreast of recent changes in the law. (See the "Working with a Lawyer" section in chapter 16 starting on page 231 for how to find a qualified bankruptcy lawyer.)

ALTERNATIVES TO BANKRUPTCY

Before resorting to bankruptcy, you should explore alternatives for taking care of debts you cannot pay. For example, a creditor might be willing to settle its claim in exchange for a partial cash payment, or it might be willing to stretch out the term of its loan and reduce the size of the payments you owe each month. These concessions would allow you to pay off your debt by making smaller payments over a longer period of time; the creditor would eventually receive full payment. If you pursue this option, you should make sure you do not end up paying too much interest.

You may also find that you are **judgment proof**, in which case you do not need to file for bankruptcy to protect your property and wages. "Judgment proof" simply means that you have so little money, income, and property that you would be unable to pay a court judgment entered against you. In addition, under state and federal exemption laws, creditors are not allowed to seize certain income from judgment-proof debtors, such as Social Security income, wages below certain levels, and certain personal property. If there's no point in creditors going after you in court, there may be less reason for you to declare bankruptcy. If you believe that you may be judgment proof, discuss your situation with a credit counselor.

Keep in mind, however, that if you don't declare bankruptcy, creditors can foreclose on your home, repossess your car, and continue their collection efforts. Creditors will also be able to enforce court judgments against you if your financial situation improves.

Learn What You Owe

When considering filing for bankruptcy, a good first step is to assess your debt level as compared to your income level. Before you can make a plan as to your financial future, you need to determine what debts you owe and whether you can live within a strict budget. Many people can reduce their debt significantly simply by living within a self-imposed budget and not spending money on unnecessary items. They can learn to take charge of their lives and begin to reclaim their financial futures. For others, bankruptcy might be the only realistic option. But you can't make this decision until you figure out and carefully examine your income and debt.

Contacting Creditors

If you are behind on your payments, the debt collectors for each of your creditors may already be calling or writing you. You might be more successful if, acting on your own behalf without a lawyer, you phone each creditor, ask for the credit department, explain your sincere intent to repay the account, and express your need to stretch out the number of monthly payments and reduce the dollar amount of each payment. You might also offer to come to the collection department's office to further discuss your situation. Make sure you always ask for and write down the name of each person you talk to. Ask each creditor to agree to a voluntary plan for the repayment of your debts. This may help you avoid bankruptcy.

In dealing with creditors, ask them to reduce or drop late fees and interest, and get all agreements in writing before making payment. If you reach a settlement for a single payment, when making the full and final payment be sure to include the language "paid in full, final, and complete satisfaction of [your account, including account number]" on the face and back of your check. Never give creditors information that would enable them to directly access your checking account; maintain control over your payments.

One problem that often arises when dealing with multiple creditors is that some creditors may be unwilling to give you more time to pay without knowing what your other creditors are willing to do. In such cases, it may be difficult for you to arrange a meeting of your creditors to negotiate a collective reduction in your monthly payments or the amount of your debt. If this is the case, you can also seek the help of a lawyer to negotiate such an arrangement. Some universities, local courts, military bases, credit unions, and housing authorities have credit-counseling programs, but counselors affiliated with such programs may not have the ability or experience to meaningfully negotiate with your creditors to reduce your monthly payments.

Your best bet may be to seek the help of a reputable nonprofit consumer credit counseling service (CCCS). You can find the nearest CCCS by calling 800-388-2227 or by visiting www.nfcc.org. There is a section on the left side of the website called "Find a Counselor Now." Click on that and it will take you to a site that allows you to find a credit counselor by ZIP code. Some CCCS establishments charge a small monthly service fee. In addition, you should be aware that creditors frequently provide most of the support for financial-counseling services. As a result, some observers believe that they tend to downplay bankruptcy as an option—though this is not necessarily a bad thing, since you are generally better off if you can avoid bankruptcy by reducing your debt to a manageable level.

In the repayment plans arranged through credit-counseling centers, you generally make monthly payments that are distributed among your creditors until your debts are paid in full. Creditors usually prefer this kind of plan, since it eventually allows them to get more of their money than they would if you filed for Chapter 7 bankruptcy. This approach may also benefit you, to the extent that it prevents you from having to file for bankruptcy.

Under a repayment plan arranged through a financial-counseling service, you still might have to pay interest charges on some or all of your debts. However, in these types of situations, many creditors will agree to waive or reduce interest charges and delinquency fees if you ask them to do so.

 A WORD OF WARNING

Be cautious when seeking out a for-profit counseling service. If you choose such a service, be sure you understand its fees and what it will do for you. Some services require long-term commitments. Investigate the service and its credentials carefully; consider calling the local Better Business Bureau for information. And always be on the lookout for predatory debt counselors. (See chapter 14 for more information and advice about choosing a credit counselor.)

⟨⟩ TALKING TO A LAWYER

Q. I'm considering debt consolidation, but it sounds too good to be true. What should I be wary of? How can I protect myself in this process?

A. If it seems too good to be true, it probably is. What fees are there to obtain the loan? What will your payments be? What is the interest rate? Is there a prepayment penalty? What would you have to give up? If you do consolidate, cut up your credit cards—or put them in a safe-deposit box, or even in the freezer in a plastic bag filled with water. If you lower your payments by consolidating, you will not accomplish anything if you continue to use your cards and run up more debt.

—Answer by Marc S. Stern, Law Offices of
Marc S. Stern, Seattle, Washington

A. You might first consider meeting with a not-for-profit financial-counseling service or a bankruptcy lawyer about the pros and cons of debt consolidation, especially if your home is involved. Compare the interest rate to be paid if you consolidate your debts with your current interest rate. After the debt consolidation, do not abuse credit cards. Otherwise, you will find yourself in the same position that you were in before—but the second time around, there will be no equity in your home to justify consolidation. Be careful: You could lose your home if you use it as collateral for the consolidated debt. Remember that with debt consolidation you are trading in your unsecured credit card debt for a secured lien against your home—that's the trade-off for a lower interest rate! Maybe a Chapter 7 or Chapter 13 bankruptcy would be best for you instead of debt consolidation if the risks of relapsing into financial trouble are too high.

—Answer by Judge David S. Kennedy, U.S. Bankruptcy
Court, Western District of Tennessee

A. You can try to consolidate your debts on your own, or through an agency. If you use an agency, be sure to check its references with the

Better Business Bureau and ensure that it is approved by the U.S. trustee for credit counseling in the bankruptcy system. It is important to understand the fees, both up front and during the payment period, and what happens if you can't make a payment—for example, a drastic increase in your interest rate. Be careful if you take a second mortgage or a home equity loan: In either case, you place your home at risk, and your interest payments may not always be deductible in full.

—Answer by David Greer, Williams Mullen Hofheimer, Nusbaum, Norfolk, Virginia

Consolidating Debt

Occasionally, you may buy time and avoid bankruptcy by consolidating your debts—that is, by taking out a big loan to pay off your smaller debts. However, the primary danger of consolidation is that you may find it very easy to use your credit cards to borrow even more money, which could leave you with even more total debt and no additional income to make the monthly payments. Indeed, if you have taken a second mortgage on your home to get a consolidation loan, failure to make payments on the loan could even put you at risk for losing your home. You should also analyze thoroughly the interest rates and up-front fees on such loans: Make sure a loan's interest rate is lower than that of your credit cards.

There are many places on the Internet that provide more information on credit counseling and bankruptcy. Some of the more helpful resources can be found in appendix B, "The World at Your Fingertips."

REMEMBER THIS

• Bankruptcy is one of many alternatives available for relieving financial distress. Examine all the options available to you for dealing with your financial problems and decide which course of action is best for you. These days, Chapter 7 is not an automatic option for everyone; you may wish to speak to an attorney about the different types of bankruptcy available to you.

• Try negotiating directly with creditors to obtain some financial relief. Creditors may be willing to reduce their interest rates or allow a longer payment plan.

• You may also seek help from a reputable local financial-counseling program or a reputable consumer credit-counseling service. Such services may be able to help you consolidate—and reduce—your debt.

• If you do decide to file for bankruptcy, you must undergo credit counseling through a nonprofit credit-counseling agency that has been approved by the local U.S. trustee in the six months before you file. You have nothing to lose by exploring this option, whether you eventually file for bankruptcy or not.

• Remember that not all for-profit and nonprofit credit-counseling services are equal; some are better than others. Contact the Better Business Bureau before dealing with such a service.

• In dealing with creditors, ask them to reduce or forgive late fees and reduce interest. Get all agreements in writing before making payment. Never give creditors information that would enable them to directly access your checking account; maintain control over your payments.

• Occasionally, you may buy time by consolidating your debts—that is, by taking out a big loan to pay off your smaller debts. However, the primary danger of consolidation is that you may find it very easy to use your credit cards to borrow even more money, which could make the total amount of your debt even larger. Consolidating credit card debts by taking out a second mortgage can also put you at risk of losing your home if you can't make the payments.

CHAPTER 16

Bankruptcy Defined

Your Guide to a Complicated Area of Law

You are mired in debt. You are essentially broke. You've assessed your income as compared to your debt level, you've tried to negotiate with creditors, you've tried to work with a nonprofit credit-counseling center, and you've tried to develop a workable budget. But your debt level is simply too high. You probably need to consult a lawyer and file bankruptcy. You need a fresh start.

Bankruptcy is a legal process through which people and businesses can seek to obtain fresh financial starts when they are in such financial difficulty that they cannot repay their debts as agreed. When a person files bankruptcy, a court eliminates all or a portion of that person's or business's existing debts under Chapter 7, or stretches out the monthly payments on those debts under the court's protection and supervision under Chapter 13.

The bankruptcy process is also designed to provide a measure of protection to creditors. Secured creditors are often in a better position than unsecured creditors because they hold a lien—an interest in the property of the debtor that backs up the right to payment—on the debtor's assets. (Secured debts are those for which the creditor is entitled to collect by repossessing some of your property; unsecured debt is that which is not backed by any property. See the discussion below for more information on this difference.) But sometimes even general unsecured creditors can obtain some money from a debtor's estate, and will share equally in whatever payments the debtor can afford to make.

While your bankruptcy case is pending, most creditors cannot try to collect their debts from you directly. (See below for an

WHAT CAUSES BANKRUPTCY?

There can be many causes of bankruptcy. Approximately 90 percent of bankruptcies are the result of unemployment, medical bills, or divorce. The remaining 10 percent are caused by a variety of factors—including the failure of a business or overuse of credit cards. Every individual situation is different, though a common feature of many bankruptcies is a large amount of debt on credit cards with high interest rates, and it is often a dramatic downward shift in financial circumstances that triggers the bankruptcy process.

explanation of this automatic stay.) Nor can they try to collect from you after the conclusion of the case for any and all discharged debts—that is, debts that the court has excused you from paying. It is important to note, however, that not all debts will be discharged. There may still be debts for which you are liable after the conclusion of your bankruptcy case.

LEGAL FOUNDATIONS OF BANKRUPTCY

Article I, Section 8, Clause 4 of the Constitution authorizes the U.S. Congress to pass "uniform laws on the subject of bankruptcies throughout the United States." In keeping with this authorization, Congress has created an intricate body of law that governs bankruptcy, most recently the Bankruptcy Abuse Prevention and Consumer Protection Act of 2005. This law builds upon the Bankruptcy Code that Congress passed in 1978, which was generally effective on October 1, 1979. The Federal Rules of Bankruptcy govern the procedure used in bankruptcy cases and proceedings. Federal bankruptcy judges hear such cases and proceedings, and every federal judicial district has a bankruptcy court; there are ninety such courts in the United States.

◖◗ TALKING TO A LAWYER

Q. I'm pretty desperate and seriously considering bankruptcy, but I'm worried about the effect of bankruptcy on the rest of my life. What will happen to my credit cards? Will my neighbors and coworkers know I'm bankrupt?

A. It depends. If you are current on one or more credit cards at the time you file a bankruptcy case, the likelihood is that you may keep them. If you owe debts on your credit cards, however, the likelihood is that the cards will be cancelled—although you can try to negotiate terms with the credit card companies. It is true that bankruptcy filing are a matter of public record; however, unless you owe debts to your neighbors and coworkers, they may not find out about it. If you owe them money, you will have to include them in your list of creditors, in which case, they will receive formal notice of your bankruptcy filing. If a prospective landlord or employer asks about your bankruptcy, he or she may be sympathetic if you explain your reasons for filing—for example, medical problems, loss of a job, or divorce.

> —Answer by Judge David S. Kennedy, U.S. Bankruptcy
> Court, Western District of Tennessee

A. Bankruptcy is a serious measure to be utilized only as a last resort for serious debt problems. The bankruptcy will be a matter of public record, meaning that a record of the filing will be available for anyone to find if they want to look for it, including neighbors, mortgage companies, landlords, and future employers. If you file a Chapter 13 case, your credit cards should be torn up and will no longer be available to you. (This could be changed with court permission and the approval of the credit card companies, but don't count on it.) In a Chapter 7 case, you may be allowed to keep a credit card that has a zero balance, or one that you agree to reaffirm (continue to pay after the filing), but the interest rate may be significantly higher than it was before, and the company may wish to cancel your card in response to the bankruptcy filing. You need to be prepared to pay your monthly balances in full should you decide to keep an active credit card following a Chapter 7 filing. This will prevent you from getting back into the same situation that caused you to file in the first place. Finally, an employer isn't allowed to discriminate against you for filing bankruptcy, but keep in mind that bankruptcy may nonetheless impact your employment in situations where financial stability is an issue—for example, if you seek to attain a new position or license.

—Answer by Shayna M. Steinfeld, Steinfeld & Steinfeld, P.C., Atlanta, Georgia

FILING FOR BANKRUPTCY

Filing for bankruptcy is a very personal, very serious decision. Most people file when they have made a good-faith effort to repay their debts, but see no other way out of debt. Once the decision has been made, a person or business may declare bankruptcy by filing a petition with the U.S. Bankruptcy Court—that is, a request that the court provide protection and relief under the Bankruptcy Code. The person filing for bankruptcy—the debtor—must provide information about his or her assets, liabilities, income, and expenditures, a certificate to prove that he or she has undergone credit counseling within 180 days of filing, tax returns, a photo ID, and evidence of recent payments from employers. Complete disclosure, candor, and honesty are required. Often, debtors have a lawyer prepare and file their bankruptcy petitions and other information for them, although some debtors do represent themselves.

There are two important aspects of your right to file for bankruptcy that are important to note. First, there is no guarantee that you will receive the relief that you seek when you file bankruptcy. Second, federal law protects your right to file for bankruptcy—for example, you cannot be fired from your job solely because you have filed.

Secured and Unsecured Debts

A **secured debt**, such as a home mortgage or a car loan, is a debt that a creditor is entitled to collect by repossessing and selling certain assets of the debtor if payments are missed. With a secured loan, the creditor extends credit but requires the debtor to put up certain collateral to guarantee the loan, such as a house, a car, or household goods. In other words, the creditor has "secured" the loan. Most consumer debts are **unsecured**, and cred-

---

 ## USE BANKRUPTCY WITH CAUTION

Bankruptcy may be the best, or only, solution for extreme financial hardship. But as noted earlier, it should be used only as a last resort, since it always has long-lasting consequences. The record of a bankruptcy can remain in your credit files for as long as ten years; this is a long time in today's economic system, in which so much depends on having good credit. Moreover, there are limits on how often you can fully benefit from certain forms of bankruptcy. Moreover, you may lose any equity you have in your home or car, since that property might be sold and the equity realized for the benefit of your creditors.

Study the pros and cons carefully before resorting to bankruptcy as a means of solving your economic troubles, and be sure you understand the types of bankruptcy cases you can file. Do not wait until the last minute to seek help—the day before a foreclosure or court hearing may be too late to get good advice or to take advantage of nonbankruptcy options. Get advice when you find you cannot pay your monthly expenses in full for more than three months, or if you face a sudden large debt, such as a medical bill, for which you cannot make payment arrangements. Making a decision about filing for bankruptcy is extremely complicated and the decision has lasting consequences. You should seek professional help with the decision if you can. (See the "Working With a Lawyer" section later in this chapter starting on page 231 for help in finding a qualified bankruptcy attorney.)

itors of such debts are not allowed to seize your assets if you miss payments.

Examples of secured debt include home loans, car loans, judgment liens (in which someone obtains a court judgment against you for failing to pay a debt), tax liens (in which the county, state, or federal government has a lien on your property because of failure to pay taxes), and second mortgages. Examples of unsecured debt include most credit card debt, doctors' bills, legal bills, utility bills, and bills for various other miscellaneous purchases.

Advantages of Filing for Bankruptcy

There are several advantages to filing for bankruptcy. By far the most important advantage is that filing for bankruptcy allows the vast majority of filers a fresh financial start. As we shall see below, if you file for Chapter 7 bankruptcy, you may be **discharged from** (forgiven from paying) most unsecured debts. You may be able to **exempt** (that is, keep) many of your assets, although state exemption laws vary widely in their descriptions of which assets you may keep. Bear in mind that in some cases, the current bankruptcy law makes it harder to obtain a Chapter 7 bankruptcy discharge. Consumers must meet a "means" test that will be discussed in greater detail in chapter 17.

Another big advantage of filing for bankruptcy is that the moment you file, most collection efforts must stop immediately. As soon as your bankruptcy petition is filed, there is by law an **automatic stay**, which stops most collection activity immediately, including home foreclosures and car repossessions. If a creditor continues to try to collect a debt, that creditor may be held in contempt of court or ordered to pay damages. The automatic stay applies even to the loan that you may have obtained to buy your car. If you are reasonably current on the payments and continue to make payments on that secured debt, it is unlikely that your creditor will do anything to collect. If you miss payments, however, your creditor will probably petition the bankruptcy court to have the stay terminated in order either to repossess the car or to renegotiate the loan.

TALKING TO A LAWYER

Q. I'm way behind in my rent and my residential landlord is threatening to evict me. Can I stop him from doing so if I file for bankruptcy?

A. Not necessarily. The answer depends upon whether your residential landlord has only threatened to evict you, or has actually begun eviction proceedings before you file for bankruptcy.

Under the law, if your residential landlord has already begun eviction proceedings in state court and has obtained a judgment for possession of the residential premises before you file for bankruptcy, the landlord can evict you unless you, the debtor, do two things: 1) file a certification with the bankruptcy court, along with your bankruptcy petition, that there are circumstances under applicable nonbankruptcy laws that would allow you to reinstate the residential lease and cure the monetary default; and 2) pay thirty days' rent to the bankruptcy court clerk to be transmitted to the landlord. The landlord can still object, in which case the bankruptcy court must decide within ten days of the filing of the objection whether the landlord can proceed with the eviction in order to gain possession of the rental property. Then you must also file a second certification with the bankruptcy court within thirty days of filing your bankruptcy petition, stating that the pre-petition default that gave rise to the landlord's judgment for possession in state court has been cured—in other words, that you have paid all back rent. Even after you file this second certification, however, the landlord may still object, in which case the court must determine within ten days of the objection whether the landlord can proceed with the eviction action.

The law also provides that, if the residential landlord has begun eviction proceedings before you file for bankruptcy on the grounds that you have endangered the rental property or have used or allowed others to use illegal substances on the property, all the landlord has to do is file a certification to this effect with the bankruptcy court clerk. The landlord can then proceed with the eviction process fifteen days later if you do not object. Note that the law does allow you to object within fifteen days and, at a hearing, show the bankruptcy court that the situation has been remedied or never existed in the first place. At that point, it will be up to the bankruptcy court to decide whether your landlord can proceed or not. Bear in mind that the deadlines for these types of situations are very short. An experienced and qualified lawyer will be able to help you better understand your particular position.

> —Answer by Judge David S. Kennedy, U.S. Bankruptcy
> Court, Western District of Tennessee

Q. I'm being sued by one of my creditors. If I file for bankruptcy, will filing stop the suit from proceeding? If so, how long in advance of the court date should I file?

A. Yes, the filing of the bankruptcy will automatically stop the suit. Rely upon the advice of your lawyer regarding when your bankruptcy case is to be filed. Most, but not all, lawsuits will "go away" after a bankruptcy filing, as the defendant's debts will be subject to discharge in bankruptcy. If possible, file the bankruptcy case before a judgment is rendered against you in state court.

> —Answer by Judge David S. Kennedy, U.S. Bankruptcy
> Court, Western District of Tennessee

A. Yes. There is an automatic stay in bankruptcy cases that immediately prohibits creditors from continuing such actions without getting the bankruptcy court's permission. You can file at any time before the date of the applicable hearing in order to stop a proceeding, even moments before if necessary, but the situation becomes much more complicated after a hearing has occurred.

> —Answer by Shayna M. Steinfeld, Steinfeld &
> Steinfeld, P.C., Atlanta, Georgia

Q. My spouse and I are getting divorced. If I file a bankruptcy, will the automatic stay affect my divorce?

A. Yes. While some narrow exceptions to the automatic stay do apply to divorces involving a party to a bankruptcy, in most cases the stay will, as a practical matter, prevent completion of the divorce until the stay is lifted, expires, or is terminated. However, a spouse can file a motion with the bankruptcy court asking for relief from the state so that certain aspects of the divorce and a division of the marital assets can proceed. Failure to obtain relief from the stay before proceeding with certain aspects of a divorce that are not exempt from the stay can lead to sanctions being entered for violations of the stay. The interaction of bankruptcy and divorce law is very complicated. You should consult with a lawyer who is knowledgeable in both areas of the law if you are contemplating filing for bankruptcy while your divorce is ongoing, or vice versa.

—Answer by Gregory S. Mager, Ansay, O'Neil, Cannon, Hollman, DeJong, S.C., Port Washington, Wisconsin

Disadvantages of Filing for Bankruptcy

Perhaps the major disadvantage of filing for bankruptcy is that a record of the filing remains on your credit report for as long as ten years. Filing for bankruptcy will thus make it more difficult for you to obtain credit in the future. Another disadvantage of bankruptcy is that you might have to surrender some of your nonexempt personal property or your home to a bankruptcy trustee, who will then liquidate (sell) the assets and apply the money to debts you have with your creditors. Finally, there is still a stigma associated with bankruptcy in some circles, though that stigma has been reduced over the years as many people—including celebrities—have filed.

Getting Credit After Bankruptcy

A 2007 study by University of Iowa law professor Katy Porter determined that many consumers are able to receive credit even after filing for bankruptcy. Ninety-six percent of those who filed bankruptcy received credit card solicitations one year after filing for bankruptcy.

However, the terms of the new credit may be affected by the fact that a bankruptcy filing has occurred. For example, if you might have been eligible for a bank card with a 14 percent interest rate before bankruptcy, the best card that you can get after bankruptcy might carry a rate of 20 or 25 percent—or you might have to rely on a card secured by a deposit that you make with the credit card issuer. Use your cards only when absolutely necessary, and pay them off in full each month if possible.

TYPES OF BANKRUPTCY

There are several types of bankruptcy, each addressed in a separate chapter of the federal Bankruptcy Code: Chapter 7, Chapter 9, Chapter 11, Chapter 12, and Chapter 13. Chapter 7 and Chapter 13 are the types of bankruptcies available for individual consumers. Chapter 9 involves bankruptcies filed by cities and towns. Chapter 12 deals with the special cases of family farmers. Chapter 11 bankruptcy, called **reorganization**, is used primarily by commercial businesses that are restructuring or liquidating while continuing their operations. While an individual not engaged in business may file for Chapter 11 bankruptcy under some circumstances, such proceedings are expensive and complex, and consumer debtors normally use Chapter 7 or Chapter 13. This

 KEEP UP INSURANCE PAYMENTS

You should be sure to maintain adequate insurance coverage on your home and/or automobile during your bankruptcy case. If you don't maintain insurance coverage, a creditor may be able to get the automatic stay lifted and repossess your car or foreclose on your home.

book focuses on Chapter 7 and 13 bankruptcies, though we will also take a quick look at bankruptcy options for family farmers and family fishermen available under Chapter 12.

Proceedings under **Chapter 7** (straight bankruptcy) involve the debtor surrendering most of his or her nonexempt assets. A bankruptcy trustee is appointed in every Chapter 7 case to administer nonexempt assets (if any) and distribute to the creditors either the assets themselves or the proceeds from **liquidating** (selling) them. Some assets are exempt under Chapter 7 and cannot be sold to satisfy debts. The assets that are exempt depend on specific federal laws and on state laws that vary significantly around the country.

It used to be the case that all consumers were eligible to file for bankruptcy under Chapter 7. This is no longer the case. An individual debtor who earns more than the median income in his or her state may, depending on the particular circumstances, be denied a Chapter 7 discharge. (You can find more information about Chapter 7 bankruptcy in the next chapter.)

Proceedings under **Chapter 13** (so-called wage-earner bankruptcy) require the debtor to propose a repayment plan for repaying all or a portion of his or her debt in installments from his or her future income. Chapter 13 plans can last for anywhere from three to five years depending on the input of the creditors and other factors. Of course, if a person can pay off all of his or her unsecured claims in less than three years, the repayment period can be shorter. The timing of Chapter 13 plans is discussed in more detail in chapter 18.

Under any bankruptcy chapter, once the bankruptcy case ends, most borrowers are discharged from—that is, no longer liable for—most of the debts they incurred before filing their bankruptcy petitions, called **pre-petition debts**. In other words, the court excuses such borrowers from having to repay most debts. The borrowers then start over again with substantially clean financial slates, except that a record of the bankruptcies will generally remain on their credit records for ten years.

You should understand, however, that with both Chapter 7

YOU'LL STILL HAVE TO PAY THESE DEBTS

Ordinarily, after a bankruptcy discharge you must still repay:

- fines and penalties imposed for violating the law, such as criminal court fines and criminal restitution;

- debts your forget to list in your bankruptcy papers, unless the creditor learns of your bankruptcy case or the creditor could no longer file a claim after learning of the bankruptcy;

- student loans, unless it would be an undue hardship for you to repay;

- child support and alimony;

- many property settlement obligations from a divorce or separation, including past due amounts;

- fraudulent debts (last-minute credit binges and/or cash advances);

- debts for personal injury or death caused by your intoxicated driving; and

- recent income tax debts and most other tax debts.

and Chapter 13 bankruptcies, a discharge does not automatically wipe out secured creditors' liens, most student loans, support payments to children, alimony payments, most recent taxes, debts for personal injury due to driving while intoxicated, some fines and penalties, or debts you forgot to list in your bankruptcy petition. Such debts will remain due and payable—along with, perhaps, certain other specifically nondischarged debts. In some cases, the court may deny a discharge altogether.

When Are Debts Discharged?

The bankruptcy court enters a discharge order relatively early in most Chapter 7 cases, usually from four to six months after you file your petition. In Chapter 13 cases, you make full or partial payment to creditors under a court-confirmed plan over a period of time, which can be as long as five years, and then receive a discharge. However, remember that debtors cannot obtain a discharge under Chapter 7 or 13 until they have taken an approved course in personal financial management. (See chapter 15 for information on these credit courses.)

 TOUGH STANCE ON STUDENT LOANS

Whether it's because college seems so long ago, or because the money wasn't spent on anything tangible, many people forget that they have an obligation to repay student loans. However, student loans are one of the most difficult types of debt to escape: Most student loans survive bankruptcy and can still be collected decades after college because there is no statute of limitations on the repayment of such debts. This means that a creditor could institute legal actions to collect a debt years later.

Most student loans are made by private banks, but are subsidized by the federal government so they have relatively low interest rates. According to the American Council on Education, two-thirds of students at private four-year colleges have student loans, which average $17,000 per student by graduation day. Students must start paying off their loans six months after graduation and generally must repay over ten years.

The Department of Education has been pursuing student loan debtors aggressively over the last decade. It has the power to garnish paychecks and seize tax refunds and Social Security payments without a court order.

No student loan is dischargeable (from the government or from a private bank) unless the debtor can show an "undue hardship," which is a difficult standard to meet. The burden is on the debtor to show, by a preponderance of the evidence, that it would constitute an "undue hardship" if the loan is not discharged.

The lesson: Don't forget about your student loans and assume you won't have to pay them. More than likely you'll be repaying what you owe for ten years or more after the golden days of college are over.

AN ALTERNATIVE FOR FARMERS AND FISHERMEN: CHAPTER 12

Family farmers and family fishermen have the option of a special type of bankruptcy under Chapter 12 of the Bankruptcy Code. It is one of a series of special farm aid provisions enacted to help farmers and fishermen survive periodic economic slumps and save their family farms or commercial fishing operations.

Chapter 12 is for family farmers and fishermen who have regular incomes. It allows family farmers and fishermen with commercial fishing operations to avoid foreclosure on their farms or fishing operations by pledging part of the profits from their future crops or commercial fishing vessel.

Only farmers and fishermen acting in good faith have the right to adjust their debts under Chapter 12. In order for a petition to proceed quickly, as in other chapter filings, the debtor must submit to the bankruptcy court a list of creditors, a list of assets and liabilities, and a statement of financial affairs. The debtor usually will require legal help. The process is similar to that of a Chapter 13 case, but the discharge is the same as in a Chapter 7 case (subject to some exceptions).

Chapter 12 of the Bankruptcy Code specifically defines "family farmer" and "family fisherman," and a debtor must fit this definition in order to file.

How Long Will Bankruptcy Remain on a Credit Record?

Most Chapter 7 and Chapter 13 bankruptcies stay on your credit record for ten years from the date you file for bankruptcy. In some states, a Chapter 13 bankruptcy will remain on your record for only seven years, as an incentive for people to use Chapter 13 bankruptcy and pay off part of their debts instead of using Chapter 7 bankruptcy.

The consequences of having a bankruptcy on your credit

record can be severe. Creditors may deny you credit in the future or charge you significantly higher interest rates. So long as your credit record includes unfavorable information, you may have credit problems. This means that you may have trouble renting an apartment, getting a loan to buy a car, or obtaining a mortgage to buy a house.

In one respect, however, bankruptcy may improve your chance for credit. Because Chapter 7 provides for a discharge of debts no more than once every eight years, lenders know that a credit applicant who has just emerged from Chapter 7 cannot soon repeat the process.

WORKING WITH A LAWYER

There are a number of ways for debtors to find bankruptcy attorneys to represent them:

• The American Board of Certification certifies lawyers specializing in bankruptcy. They divide specializations into consumer bankruptcy, business bankruptcy and creditors' rights. You can search for such attorneys at www.abcworld.org/search.

• You can find attorneys who specialize in bankruptcy (and virtually every other legal field) at lawyers.com. There is a section titled "Search by Practice Area." The first entry listed is "Bankruptcy." See www.lawyers.com/Bankruptcy/browse-by-location.html.

• In addition, some states certify lawyers as bankruptcy specialists when they have had significant experience in the field. Access the ABA Web page at www.abanet.org/legalservices/specialization/source.html for a list of state certification programs, some of which encompass bankruptcy law.

• You could also ask a lawyer whom you know well to recommend a specialist.

• Suggestions from a friend, a relative, a neighbor, or an associate who has had a good experience with a particular lawyer may also help.

• Bar associations and groups operated for people with special needs, such as the elderly or persons with disabilities, often provide referral services. For a list of bar association referral programs, access the ABA Web page at www.abanet.org/legalservices/lris/directory/.

- You might also find a lawyer by looking in the yellow pages of your telephone directory or at advertisements in your local newspaper. If you hire a lawyer from the phone book or a direct-mail solicitation, be sure to check his or her references. Remember that phone book ads and direct-solicitation ads do not ensure that you will receive good service.

Be careful in your selection of a lawyer, and make sure your lawyer is familiar with bankruptcy laws and procedures and has a good reputation. When you have an initial talk with a prospective lawyer, ask yourself: Does he or she seem to understand your financial (and emotional) problems and offer solutions, or is he or she simply affiliated with a "factory" that does little more than process paper?

You can, and should, discuss your lawyer's professional fees in advance and understand what procedures are covered by these fees. This will give you as clear an idea as possible of what the bankruptcy procedure will cost. You do not need to be surprised later on.

In addition, discuss with your lawyer whether he or she will charge additional fees if there are proceedings required other than the filing of the case. Your lawyer's responsibilities in a basic case will include preparing and filing the petitions and additional schedules and attending the creditors' meeting. In some states, filing for bankruptcy may also include preparing and filing a homestead deed. A Chapter 7 bankruptcy may also include reaffirmation agreements to negotiate, sign, and file; objections to exemptions; homestead declarations to complete; or objections to the discharge of some or all of your debts. In a Chapter 13 case, your lawyer may have to deal with objections to approval of your repayment plan or the way you have valued your assets. In either chapter, your lawyer may have to respond to your creditors' **motions for relief from the automatic stay**, which seek court approval to repossess property or foreclose on real estate. Once again, make sure you understand what the lawyer's fees will cover and what will cost extra.

In some Chapter 13 cases, you can pay your lawyer from the assets of your estate, which is administered by the court in a bankruptcy case. This is not the case, however, with lawyer fees under Chapter 7. In 2004, the Supreme Court decided in the case of *Lamie v. United States Trustee* that bankruptcy attorneys are not entitled to receive compensation from the bankruptcy estate in Chapter 7 cases. Depending upon the complexity of your case, your legal fees might range from $400 to $5,000. Chapter 13 cases are usually more expensive than Chapter 7 cases, though it helps that such fees may be included in your repayment plan. To understand more about bankruptcy, access the U.S. Bankruptcy Code and bankruptcy rules at www.thebankruptcysite.com/bankruptcy_law.htm.

FILING ON YOUR OWN

It is perfectly legal to file your own bankruptcy petition without a lawyer; however, the more complicated your debt situation, the riskier it is to represent yourself. If you do decide to file for bankruptcy on your own, make sure that the information you rely upon is up to date. It is not advisable to hire a nonlawyer to help you file bankruptcy.

REMEMBER THIS

• Bankruptcy is a legal process through which people and businesses can obtain fresh financial starts. It is for people who are not in a financial position to repay their debts.

• In many cases, bankruptcy could be your only realistic option. If you think this may be the case, consult a lawyer for advice.

• There are different types of bankruptcy. Two major types for consumers are Chapter 7 (straight/liquidation bankruptcies) and

Chapter 13 ("wage-earner" bankruptcies). Your lawyer will help you decide under which chapters you are eligible to file, and which one is best for you.

- Select a bankruptcy lawyer with care. Do not rely solely on advertisements. You may contact your local bar association, refer to the American Board of Certification, or take one of the other steps recommended in this chapter. Do not hire a nonlawyer to file your bankruptcy.

- Bankruptcy cases begin with the filing of a petition with the U.S. Bankruptcy Court.

- During bankruptcy, creditors cannot call you to collect debts. Once a bankruptcy petition is filed, an automatic stay prohibits most collection activities.

- Most consumer debts are unsecured. Some creditors are called "secured creditors" because they have the right to seize and sell the collateral for a loan, such as a car or your home, if payments are missed. Secured creditors have more protection in a bankruptcy than unsecured creditors.

- Use bankruptcy with caution; a record of the filing remains in your credit record for as long as ten years.

- Your bankruptcy must include all of your debts and property; you cannot file bankruptcy only for a certain debt or type of debt. If you have your own business as a sole proprietor, it must be included in the filing. However, if your business is incorporated, it is considered a separate entity and does not have to be included.

CHAPTER 17

Straight Bankruptcy: Chapter 7

The Most Common Form of Bankruptcy

Mr. Smith makes a modest income and has few significant assets. He rents an apartment. He is struggling to pay his rent because of his mounting credit card bills and other debts. He defaults on payments to many creditors and receives collection letters and phone calls every day at home and on the job. He has consulted with a credit-counseling service, and they have told him his best option is to file bankruptcy. What type should he file?

Bankruptcy law, like many aspects of the legal system, can be quite complicated. It is intimidating to the average consumer, who simply knows that he or she cannot pay the bills. You hear lawyers talk in legal jargon about Chapter 7, Chapter 11, and Chapter 13. What do they mean? The following section explains the most common type of bankruptcy available to the average consumer: Chapter 7. This is the type of bankruptcy usually best suited to a person who has a modest income, few assets, and comparatively high debts.

Straight bankruptcy under Chapter 7 is available if less drastic remedies will not solve your financial problems. It allows you to discharge (eliminate) most of your debts. About 64 percent of all consumer bankruptcy filings nationwide are Chapter 7 cases. In the 12-month period ending on March 31, 2008, there were 871,186 consumer bankruptcies and approximately 560,000 were Chapter 7 filings. The percentage used to be even higher (closer to 70 percent), but the Bankruptcy Abuse Prevention and Consumer Protection Act of 2005 imposes more restrictions on consumers filing for Chapter 7. The 2005 law has increased the number of Chapter 13 filings.

THE CASE OF STUDENT LOANS

In most bankruptcy cases, student loans are not dischargeable, which means that the debtor still has to pay them. They may be discharged, however, if a debtor can show that his or her student loan debt would constitute an **undue hardship** if the loans are not discharged.

Because the Bankruptcy Code does not define "undue hardship," various courts have developed tests aimed at determining what does and does not constitute undue hardship for bankruptcy purposes. For example, the U.S. Court of Appeals for the Seventh Circuit has developed a three-part test. Under this test, a debtor must show: 1) that he or she cannot maintain, based on his or her current financial situation, a minimal standard of living for herself or himself and his or her dependents if forced to repay the loans; 2) that other circumstances exist indicating that the debtor will remain in the same financial situation for a significant period of time; and 3) that the debtor has made good-faith efforts to repay the loans.

The debtor carries the burden of proof to establish these factors demonstrating undue hardship. In *Goulet v. Educational Credit Management Corp.*, the Seventh Circuit rejected the claims of a fifty-five-year-old debtor that he had an undue hardship defense to paying his student loans. The debtor argued that his substantial debt, a prior felony conviction, and a substance-abuse problem constituted extraordinary circumstances sufficient for a finding of undue hardship. The Seventh Circuit disagreed, focusing on the fact that the debtor had obtained a quality education with the money borrowed through his student loans. "The natural conclusion, when considering this exemplar educational record and nearly-completed graduate work, is that Goulet can apply himself when he desires to do so," the court wrote. "The record does not demonstrate that he lacks the capacity to work, only that he does not seem anxious to do so" (284 F.3d 773 [7th Cir. 2002]).

A federal district court in Florida reached a similar result in *In Re Mallinckrodt*, which involved a forty-two-year-old debtor who had more than

$70,000 in student loans. The debtor had a master's degree in psychology and had worked as a tennis instructor, but had a very small income. The court determined that the debtor failed the "other circumstances" prong of the undue-hardship test on account of the fact that the debtor "has nothing but opportunities to earn more income" (274 B.R. 560 [S.D. Fla. 2002]).

(Chapter 13 is discussed in the next chapter.) For figures related to 2008 bankruptcies, see http://www.uscourts.gov/Press_Releases/2008/BankruptcyFilingsMar2008.cfm

As noted in the previous chapter of this book, Chapter 7 bankruptcy does not result in a discharge of all types of debt. If a debt is not discharged (meaning the debt is not excused), you remain legally responsible for it.

 TALKING TO A LAWYER

Q. Will I be able to get out of the obligations I was socked with during my divorce last year?

A. Not in a Chapter 7 case. Any and all support-related debts—for example, child support, alimony, medical expenses for a child or ex-spouse, ex-spouse's attorney's fees, guardian ad litem fees, and possibly the debt for your ex-spouse's car, credit cards, or mortgage, depending on the specific facts of your case—are never dischargeable in bankruptcy. Even nonsupport debts (e.g., some credit cards or a property settlement debt) will not be discharged in Chapter 7. In Chapter 13 cases, you may be able to discharge nonsupport debt.

—Answer by Marianne Culhane, Creighton
University School of Law, Omaha, Nebraska

CHAPTER 7 EXPLAINED

The Beginning of a Chapter 7 Case

The first step to any Chapter 7 case is a requirement that the debtor receive credit counseling within 180 days before filing for bankruptcy. (This requirement did not exist prior to 2005.) Debtors must present to the bankruptcy court a certificate that they received such credit counseling. The counseling must be "from an approved nonprofit budget and credit counseling agency." Such agencies must be "approved" or accredited by the U.S. bankruptcy trustee or bankruptcy administrator. (In North Carolina and Alabama, such officials are known as "administrators" rather than "trustees.")

 HOW TO FIND OUT IF A CREDIT COUNSELING AGENCY IS "APPROVED"

Section 111 of the bankruptcy law provides that the bankruptcy court clerk shall "maintain a publicly available list" of approved agencies and "instructional courses" for would-be bankruptcy filers. The U.S. trustee or bankruptcy administrator must review the qualifications of nonprofit credit agencies to ensure that they meet certain standards. For example, the law requires that an agency be approved only if it can demonstrate that it:

> will provide qualified counselors, maintain adequate provision for safekeeping and payment of client funds, provide adequate counseling with respect to client credit problems, and deal effectively with other matters relating to the quality, effectiveness, and financial security of the services it provides.

The law also gives federal district courts the power to review the qualifications of these agencies to ensure they are meeting the applicable standard.

Credit counseling can take place individually or in a group, in person, on the telephone, or on the Internet. Such counseling assists individuals by "outlining the opportunities for available credit counseling and assisting such individuals in performing a related budget analysis." The theory behind this requirement is that individuals will know what they are getting into by filing for bankruptcy and better understanding their financial situation.

A Chapter 7 bankruptcy case officially begins when you file a petition with the U.S. Bankruptcy Court asking it to relieve you (or you and your spouse, if you are both filing) from your dischargeable debts. You will file with the bankruptcy court where you live. The bankruptcy court clerk or the Bankruptcy Noticing Center will notify your listed creditors that you have filed a bankruptcy petition, and creditors must immediately stop most efforts to collect the debts you owe. A bankruptcy trustee will be appointed, usually a local private lawyer approved by the Justice Department who performs bankruptcy work in the normal course of his or her legal practice. Your bankruptcy case is a federal court action (although state laws play a role in bankruptcy cases).

As of the date you file your bankruptcy petition, your assets will be under the protection of the court. In addition, as noted above, the law imposes an automatic stay, which immediately prohibits most creditor collection efforts against you. Note, however, that if someone has co-signed a loan for you, the automatic stay does not stop creditors from seeking payment from the cosigner in a Chapter 7 or Chapter 11 case.

When you file a petition for bankruptcy, you have to fill out and file many forms. Under Section 521 of the bankruptcy law, these forms include:
- A list of creditors;
- A schedule of assets and liabilities;
- A schedule of current income and expenditures;
- A statement of your financial affairs;
- Copies of all payment advances or other evidence of payment received within sixty days before the date of the bankruptcy filing;

- A statement of your monthly net income, itemized to show how the amount is calculated;
- A statement disclosing any reasonably anticipated increase in your income or expenditures over the twelve-month period following the date of the bankruptcy filing; and
- A certificate from an approved nonprofit credit-counseling agency.

These forms can be obtained at www.uscourts.gov/bkforms/index.html.

If requested by a creditor or the trustee, you will also have to provide tax returns and a photo ID. If you are self-employed, a statement of your business affairs must also be included. The re-

---

 ## A BREAK FOR DISABLED VETERANS

A section of the bankruptcy law deals with dismissal of Chapter 7 cases or conversion of such cases to Chapter 13 cases upon a finding of abuse—that is, a finding that a debtor has too much income to qualify for Chapter 7 bankruptcy under the means test. However, an exception exists for disabled veterans whose indebtedness arose during active duty or while such debtors were "performing a homeland defense activity."

The law (38 U.S.C § 3741) defines a "disabled veteran" as follows:

> The term "disabled veteran" means (A) a veteran who is entitled to compensation under laws administered by the Secretary for a disability rated at 30 percent or more, or (B) a veteran whose discharge or release from active duty was for a disability incurred or aggravated in the line of duty.

This means that if you are a disabled veteran, it is likely that your bankruptcy case will remain a Chapter 7 case and will not be converted to a Chapter 13 case. You may, however, need the help of an experienced bankruptcy attorney to determine whether you fit within this exception.

---

quired schedules are quite detailed, and the information you provide must be complete and accurate.

All of these forms will provide the bankruptcy court and parties in interest—that is, your creditors and the trustee—with a complete picture of what is called your bankruptcy estate. Specifically, the information contained on these forms should include a list of all your creditors and the amounts of their claims, the sources and amounts of your income, a list of all your property (both real [land and real estate] and personal), and a detailed list of your monthly expenses. In essence, these forms describe your financial history, listing all of your income, all of your debts, and all of your assets.

Currently, in order to file the necessary forms, debtors must pay a Chapter 7 statutory case-filing fee of $245, an administrative fee of $39, and a trustee surcharge fee of $15, for a total of $299 in fees. You may pay the $299 in installments within 120 days after the Chapter 7 case is filed; in certain circumstances, the court may also extend the length of this period to 180 days. These fees change (and usually increase) over time. For example, the filing fee for a Chapter 7 case in 1979 was only $60. Failure to pay the necessary fees could result in the dismissal of a bankruptcy petition, unless the court waives the fees, which it may do if your income is less than 150 percent of the poverty level and you cannot pay the fees in installments. The form needed to request the waiver of the Chapter 7 filing fee can be found at www.uscourts.gov/rules/BK_Forms_1207/B_003B_1207f .pdf.

 ## LIST ALL OF YOUR ASSETS!

When filing for bankruptcy, don't engage in fraud by failing to list an asset or by giving an asset away to someone just before filing. Such behavior could lead to the denial of the bankruptcy discharge, perjury charges, or possibly even jail time for bankruptcy fraud.

Liabilities and Schedules

For purposes of a bankruptcy filing, your liabilities typically include:

- your priority debts (such as taxes and past-due support payments);
- your debts to secured creditors (bills from auto and furniture dealers, home mortgages, and so on); and
- your debts to unsecured creditors (bills for department store credit cards, medical bills, and the like).

Be sure to list all of your creditors and their correct names and addresses. Remember, liabilities can also include any lawsuits in which you are a defendant or a potential defendant—for example, a personal injury claim against you arising out of a car accident. Even if you are current with your bills, if you omit some creditors from your filing or provide incorrect addresses for them, you might not be discharged from those debts. It may be very helpful to access your credit report before filing to ensure that you have listed all of your outstanding debts. (Chapter 7, Credit Records, explains how to access your credit report.) Also, make sure to give your lawyer copies of all your bills and collection letters.

Don't worry if you do forget to list a creditor—all may not be lost. The Federal Rules of Bankruptcy Procedure typically allow debtors to amend their petitions. If this happens, you should consult with your attorney to determine what steps you need to take.

"Means" Test

A primary purpose of the Bankruptcy Abuse Prevention and Consumer Protection Act of 2005 was to reduce the number of individuals filing for Chapter 7 who really should not be. In other words, some individuals were receiving Chapter 7 discharges under the old law even when they had the "means" to repay some of their creditors.

These days, Chapter 7 includes a "means" test, which compares a debtor's debts with his or her aggregate current monthly income. If the debtor's current monthly income (which can be reduced by necessary expenses) over a period of five years is more than $10,950 or 25 percent of the debtor's nonpriority, unsecured debt, then the debtor may not qualify for Chapter 7. Debtors must fill out a form that calculates their monthly income and the "means-test calculation." The form is accessible at www.uscourts.gov/rules/BK_Forms_08_Official/B_022A_1208 .pdf. You can get around this limitation if you can show "special circumstances," but this is generally not an easy process.

Assets

When filing for bankruptcy, you should list all of your assets, which generally include:

• all of your real property (for example, your home), including any real property you own together with your spouse or other persons;

• all of your personal property (such as household goods, cars, clothing, cash, retirement funds, bank accounts, accrued net wages, and tax refunds to which you may be entitled); and

• any lawsuits in which you are a plaintiff or a potential plaintiff (e.g., workers' compensation claims and/or personal injury claims).

In addition, you will need to designate which of the real or personal property listed above you want to exempt from creditors.

Note that your post-petition earnings from your job are not part of the Chapter 7 bankruptcy estate. Also note that, under Chapter 7, you might well have to turn over many, if not all, of your nonexempt assets to the trustee who is appointed to supervise your case, depending upon the classification (value) of such assets, and on state or federal law exemptions.

Encumbered Assets

Assets pledged as collateral on a loan are known as **encumbered assets**. When you borrow money to buy, for example, a car, a boat, household furniture, or an appliance, the lender commonly has a **lien** (legal claim) on that property to secure the debt until the loan is fully repaid. For other loans, you may also have to give a creditor a lien on property you already own, as in the case of a second mortgage obtained to finance home improvements. Some creditors may obtain liens without your agreement, either because they have won a lawsuit against you or because the law automatically provides a lien for certain claims, such as for duly assessed taxes or purchases that haven't been paid for in full.

In bankruptcy, a claim generally is secured to the extent that it is backed up by collateral. Often the collateral is worth less than the amount of the debt it secures, such as a $1,200 item of collateral securing a loan balance of $3,000. In that case, the lender is **undersecured** and is treated as holding two claims: a $1,200 secured claim and an $1,800 unsecured claim. On the other hand, sometimes a debt is secured by collateral having a value that exceeds the loan balance at the time of bankruptcy, such as a $65,000 home subject to a $30,000 mortgage. In that case, the lender is **oversecured**. In this example, the oversecured lender is entitled to no more than the $30,000 it is owed. The excess value of $35,000 is referred to as the **debtor's equity**.

If you cannot make the required payments on a secured claim (and also cannot catch up on any overdue back payments), the creditor ordinarily has a right to take back the collateral after having the automatic stay lifted or after the discharge. However, you may be able to keep your car, boat, or other encumbered item by redeeming it or reaffirming your debt. These concepts are explained later in this chapter.

Unencumbered Assets

Unencumbered assets include (1) assets on which there is no lien at all; and (2) the debtor's equity in assets that are collateral for oversecured claims. You retain unencumbered assets to the extent that they are exempt from the bankruptcy process (this concept is discussed below); otherwise, they must be surrendered for distribution among those creditors holding unsecured claims, or the equivalent value of the unencumbered assets must be paid to the trustee. However, if your unencumbered assets are worth less than a certain amount, or would be difficult to sell, the trustee might return them to you (i.e. abandon them) if he or she decides it would not be cost-effective to sell them and distribute the money to the creditors.

Exempt Assets

Some of your property may be exempt from the reach of the bankruptcy trustee and your creditors—in other words, the law may allow you to keep it. You must list your **exempt assets** on your schedules (specifically Schedule C). If you do this correctly, then you may shield them from your unsecured creditors. Federal and state laws dictate which assets are considered "exempt." For the most part, state law determines what you can exempt; however, some states do allow you to follow the federal exemptions if you prefer them to the state exemptions. (Remember that your state's exemptions may differ widely from federal exemptions, and from exemptions allowed by other states, and that federal exemptions are not available in all states.) Section 522 of the Bankruptcy Code provides a detailed list of exemptions available to debtors under federal law. In brief, these exemptions include:

(1) $20,200 in your home or burial plot.

(2) $3,225 in one motor vehicle.

(3) $525 per item, up to $9,850 total, in household furnishings, household goods, apparel, appliances, etc.

(4) Jewelry with a fair market value of up to $1,350.

(5) $1,075 in any property, plus up to $10,125 of any unused amount of the exemption for your home/burial plot.

(6) $2,025 in any implements, professional books, or tools of your trade.

(7) Any unmatured life insurance contract you own, other than a credit life insurance contract.

(8) Professionally prescribed health aids.

(9) Your right to receive:

- a Social Security benefit, unemployment compensation, or a local public assistance benefit;
- a veterans' benefit;
- a disability, illness, or unemployment benefit;
- alimony, support, or separate maintenance, to the extent reasonably necessary for your support and the support of your dependents; or
- a payment under a stock bonus, pension, profit-sharing, annuity, or similar plan or contract on account of illness, disability, death, age, or length of service, to the extent reasonably necessary for your support and the support of any of your dependents. Based on a recent ruling by the U.S. Supreme Court, this includes individual retirement accounts (IRAs). The new law also codifies this ruling—that is, writes it into the statute—by exempting retirement funds in a tax-exempt fund or account.

(10) Your right to receive property that is traceable to:

- an award under a crime victim's reparation law;
- a payment for the wrongful death of an individual of whom you were a dependent;
- a payment under a life insurance contract that insured the life of an individual of whom you were a dependent on the date of such individual's death;
- a payment, not to exceed $20,200, on account of personal bodily injury of you or an individual of whom you are a dependent; or
- a payment in compensation for the loss of future earnings of you or an individual of whom you are or were a dependent.

Let's use the example of your home to see how this works. As noted above, under the federal statute you can exempt from bankruptcy up to $20,200 of the equity in your home. A couple filing a joint Chapter 7 case may exempt twice this much—a total of $40,400 worth of equity in their home. This is called their **homestead exemption**. If the home is worth $70,000 and has a $25,000 mortgage, then the couple has $45,000 worth

WHICH LAW APPLIES?

In a number of states, you may elect to exempt assets under either federal or state law. In most states, however, you may use only the state exemptions. Federal law is actually rather complicated as to which state exemptions are available to debtors. The law provides that debtors can choose state exemptions in a state in which they lived for 730 days prior to filing for bankruptcy. If the debtor has lived in more than one state during that 730-day period, then the debtor can choose the exemptions of the state in which he or she lived during the majority of the 180 days before the 730-day period. These exemptions, particularly the homestead exemption, are subject to ultimate limits under federal law.

of equity in their home ($70,000 − $25,000 = $45,000). Since $40,400 is exempt by federal law, the couple's creditors can claim only $4,600 (the difference between the couple's equity of $45,000 and the $40,400 exemption). As a matter of practice, the couple would probably keep their home—perhaps at the cost of paying that $4,600 in nonexempt equity to the bankruptcy trustee—rather than have it sold for the benefit of their creditors. (Note that the couple may also be able to exempt the equity in their home under another statutory category or under applicable state law.)

Note: These figures are adjusted for inflation every three years pursuant to another provision of the Bankruptcy Code. They should change again sometime in 2010.

State-by-State Exemptions

Allowable asset exemptions vary widely from state to state. For example, variations among the states are found with respect to a broad array of exempt assets such as cars, jewelry, household furnishings, books, and tools of the debtor's trade.

Home exemptions also vary by state. The federal exemption for a home is $20,200, but Florida, along with six other states, has no dollar cap on homestead exemptions. Florida allows a homestead exemption that protects from creditors a debtor's home and property so long as the size of that property does not exceed half an acre in a municipality or 160 acres elsewhere. This in theory could mean that investment bankers and Hollywood stars who file for bankruptcy could retain beachfront homes in Florida worth millions of dollars. A number of other states have high caps on homesteads. In Georgia, in contrast, the homestead exemption is limited to $5,000.

It is important to note that it is actually harder to shield money than it may appear, even in those states with high homestead exemptions. Under the federal bankruptcy law, regardless of state law, debtors may exempt no more than $125,000 of interest in a homestead that was purchased within forty months (1,215 days) of a bankruptcy filing. However, you may be able to shelter more than $125,000 (if state law permits) if you bought your home (or a prior home) more than forty months before filing.

Married Debtors

In cases involving an individual married debtor or joint debtors, several specific points about exemptions are worth noting.

First, in joint cases, each spouse must claim exemptions under the same law, with both relying either on state law or on federal law. If they each want to claim exemptions under different law, they need to file separate cases.

Second, when married debtors elect to apply federal exemptions (and often when they elect to apply state exemptions), each spouse can claim the full exempt amount on his or her own behalf, in effect doubling the amount of exemptions to which a single person would be entitled.

Third, in some cases, such as when one spouse has debts and the other is debt-free and has assets, it might be preferable for only the spouse with debts to file for bankruptcy. In about a

WHAT THE TRUSTEE CAN LIQUIDATE

The Bankruptcy Code requires that you give all nonexempt unencumbered assets to the bankruptcy trustee—that is, all the assets that aren't exempted by law and aren't secured as collateral to a loan. Unless it would be too costly, the trustee will then liquidate (sell off) these nonexempt assets to help pay your creditors.

In actual practice, the vast majority of Chapter 7 filings are **no-asset filings**—that is, filings in which there are no nonexempt assets with value left for unsecured creditors after the exempt assets have been claimed and the secured assets returned to the creditors. No-asset filings are often the result of careful planning by an experienced bankruptcy attorney.

---

third of the states, creditors of only one spouse are barred either completely or in large part from reaching real and/or personal property owned by a debtor and nondebtor spouse as joint tenants or tenants by the entirety. Such prohibitions generally apply in any bankruptcy case in which state law exemptions govern. The way your property is titled may determine the appropriate exemption; give your lawyer copies of your deeds, bank account statements, and car titles to find out whether your creditors can reach your assets.

The Case of Secured Lenders and Exemptions

As mentioned above, exempt assets are beyond the reach of unsecured creditors and the bankruptcy trustee. However, exemptions do not ordinarily affect the rights of creditors to assets on which they have liens. For example, a homestead exemption generally does not affect the right of a mortgage lender to foreclose on your home. Similarly, furniture bought on store credit may be subject to a **purchase money security interest** (interest created when a buyer uses a lender's money to make a purchase and then gives the lender a security interest in the property that was purchased), and some credit card companies may attempt to create liens on items you purchase with their cards, in which case such creditors may have rights to your assets even in bankruptcy. Under some specific circumstances, the Bankruptcy Code may permit you to undo a lien and then assert exemption rights. This is a matter about which it is best to consult a lawyer.

CHAPTER 7 IN ACTION

Keeping Assets

If you are required to surrender some nonexempt property that you wish to keep—for example, a car—you may under certain circumstances arrange to **redeem** it (buy it back) for a price no greater than its current **redemption value**. Redemption value is the amount for which a retailer could sell the item, taking into consideration the item's age and condition. For example, if you owe $3,000 on your car, but its redemption value is only $1,200, you can recover the car by paying a lump sum of $1,200 to the creditor who has a lien on it at the time of redemption. Redemption should occur within forty-five days of the first creditors' meeting. The redemption price must be paid in full; this differs from past practice, which allowed a lender to accept the redemption price in installments over an extended period of time.

In the real world, of course, it may be very hard to come up with $1,200, which must be paid from your personal assets, and not from property that has been set aside for distribution to creditors. Possible sources of funds would include your post-petition salary, proceeds from the voluntary sale of exempt assets, or loans from relatives or friends. Some companies specialize in making redemption loans on automobiles. Sometimes you can negotiate a short payment plan, but it is up to the creditor whether or not to allow this.

Another Way to Keep Your Property: Reaffirming Debt

You may **reaffirm** a debt, if the applicable creditor is willing to allow it. By reaffirming a debt, you promise to pay the creditor (usually, but not always, in full), and you may keep the property involved, so long as you keep your promise. But if you later default, the creditor can repossess the property and the remaining balance will not be discharged.

The bankruptcy law provides some protections for consumers considering reaffirmation of their debts. It imposes certain obligations on creditors. The law requires that creditors provide extensive disclosures to debtors, including the following statements:

• "Reaffirming a debt is a serious financial decision. The law requires you to take certain steps to make sure the decision is in your best interest. If these steps are not completed, the reaffirmation agreement is not effective, even though you have signed it."

• "You may rescind (cancel) your reaffirmation agreement at any time before the bankruptcy court enters a discharge order, or before the expiration of the 60-day period that begins on the date your reaffirmation is filed with the court, whichever occurs later."

If a debtor reaffirms a debt, the creditor must inform the debtor as to the amount of debt reaffirmed, the applicable interest rates, when payments will begin, and filing requirements with the court.

There are time constraints on when you can reaffirm a debt. You must reaffirm after the petition for bankruptcy has been filed *but* before the bankruptcy discharge is completed. Thus, there is a narrow gap of time for reaffirmations to take place.

Important Considerations When Redeeming or Reaffirming

If you want to keep some property (either through redemption or reaffirmation), there are a couple of important considerations.

TALKING TO A LAWYER

Q. I think I've got a tax refund coming. What happens to that refund in bankruptcy?

A. The tax refund will have to be disclosed in your list of assets. Depending on the amount of the refund, you may be able to claim all or a substantial portion of it as part of the exemptions to which you are entitled. To the extent you are unable to claim all of the tax refund as an exemption, the excess amount will be turned over to the bankruptcy trustee for distribution to creditors after payment of administrative costs.

—**Answer by Judge David S. Kennedy, U.S. Bankruptcy Court, Western District of Tennessee**

A. Under state and federal law, you are entitled to exemption of certain assets. (Exemptions are a way to "shield" certain amounts and types of assets from liquidation, and vary tremendously by state.) The Chapter 7 trustee will be entitled to any portion of the refund that is not exempt under applicable state or federal law. The issue becomes slightly more complicated if the refund is in two names, and if only one of you files the bankruptcy case. In that case, it is possible that the trustee would get only a portion of the nonexempt refund. Courts in different states rule in very different ways on this issue, so it is best to assume that the trustee would get all or most of the refund.

—**Answer by Shayna M. Steinfeld, Steinfeld & Steinfeld, P.C., Atlanta, Georgia**

Q. I'm behind in my car payments. Can a bankruptcy stop the dealer from repossessing my car?

A. Yes. Upon the filing of a bankruptcy case, an automatic stay takes effect that will stop the dealer from repossessing the car. But unless you can work out an agreement with the creditor or redeem the car (pay it off) for the redemption amount, in a Chapter 7 case the likelihood is that you will eventually lose the car. In a Chapter 13 case, you may be able to keep the car under a repayment plan. Chapter 13 offers broader relief and more options for debtors than does Chapter 7 when dealing with secured claims.

—Answer by Judge David S. Kennedy, U.S. Bankruptcy Court, Western District of Tennessee

First, you cannot simply keep the property by making installment payments and not redeeming or reaffirming the debt. In other words, even if you are current on, say, your car loan, you still must reaffirm or redeem that loan in order to keep the car. This is a change from what used to be permissible in some parts of the country.

Second, Chapter 7 debtors must redeem or reaffirm promptly, within 45 days of the first creditors' meeting. If they don't meet this deadline, they can lose the property: The automatic stay will end, and the creditor could repossess the collateral.

Third, it is also important to note that reaffirmation is not always in your best interest, especially when the reaffirmed debt relates to property worth far less than the debt being reaffirmed. Most reaffirmations relate to mortgage loans and loans for personal property that is especially valued by the debtor—for example, a car or a boat.

Fourth, if you can, it is a good idea to use a reaffirmation negotiation as an opportunity to renegotiate the loan, especially on personal property that has **depreciated** (i.e., decreased in

 YOUR INTENTIONS

Within thirty days of filing for bankruptcy, and usually as part of the papers you file, you must use a court form to advise your secured creditors whether you intend to surrender or redeem any collateral or reaffirm any debt. You can address the issue of reaffirmation at the creditors' meeting.

value). If you want to retain items that are worth less than the secured debt against them, then either redemption or a Chapter 13 reorganization may make more sense.

Lastly, after discharge, it is too late to reaffirm, and the creditor may repossess the property, but cannot collect the balance due.

Other Ways to Keep Property

In the case of a loan securing personal property—for example, a loan for a computer or furniture—you may be able to keep the item and simply continue making payments rather than attempting the reaffirmation path. Creditors cannot be forced to allow this, but some creditors may decide not to repossess if they continue to receive full payment and if you were current with your payments when your bankruptcy case was filed. Again, this is different from reaffirmation.

Leased Automobiles

If you are leasing a car and wish to retain it during and after a Chapter 7 bankruptcy, you must notify the lessor in writing that you want to assume the lease. The lessor will then tell you whether it is willing to let you keep the car, and on what conditions—for example, the lessor may require that you make up back payments. In order to keep the car, you must then agree to the lessor's offer within thirty days. Your liability under the lease will not be discharged if you assume it, so the effect is like that of a reaffirmation, but without the requirement of attorney or court approval.

Transferring Property Prior to Filing Bankruptcy

Bankruptcy trustees will look carefully at any attempts to hide assets or to avoid disclosing the true identity and value of your assets. In particular, they will look at transfers of property and won't allow transfers of property in return for nothing or in return for far less than the property was worth. You will be asked whether you have transferred property within one year prior to filing. If you have transferred property without getting enough in return, a trustee can cancel the transfer and recover the property for your bankruptcy estate and creditors. Moreover, if the trustee discovers that you made the transfer with the intention of defrauding any creditor, you may be denied discharge and also face federal criminal charges for committing a fraudulent transfer. The greater the period of time between a transfer and your bankruptcy filing, the less likely it is that the transfer will be perceived as fraudulent.

The bottom line is that you cannot keep any debts or assets out of bankruptcy, and failing to disclose all of your assets may expose you to criminal charges or the denial of discharge, even after liquidation.

Other Steps for Filing Bankruptcy

Procedures for filing bankruptcy vary greatly by state, but you may be required to take the following steps:

• In some states, you may have to file a **homestead deed** in the appropriate state court; such a filing must generally be made by a specific deadline. A homestead deed, also called a **declaration of homestead**, is a document intended to protect your property from creditors. Generally, it describes the property and assigns an approximate value to it. The document may also have to be recorded in the appropriate office (such as a land record office) in the county in which you live. (In some states, you may be required to take this step before you file for bankruptcy.)

• You will be required to appear at a first meeting of creditors, where the trustee will examine you under oath about your petition, statement of financial affairs, and schedules. Creditors can also question you about your debts and assets and will often attend this meeting to discuss reaffirmation, surrender of property, and related issues. Later, the trustee will determine whether to challenge any of your claimed exemptions or your right to a discharge.

• If you disagree with the trustee's decision, you may protest to the court, which will make the final decision.

TALKING TO A LAWYER

Q. *I'm confused. I hear people who've been in bankruptcy referring to a "341 meeting." What is that? If I file for bankruptcy, is it a big deal?*

A. A 341 hearing is a hearing required by Section 341 of the Bankruptcy Code. It is known as a "first meeting of creditors," a name first used in the Bankruptcy Act of 1898. (For lawyers, old nicknames die hard!)

At a 341 hearing, the trustee and any creditor who wishes to attend (most don't) will question you about your assets, liabilities, and problematic financial situation. Though the hearing is not a big deal for most debtors, there can be exceptions; your lawyer should be able to prepare and warn you if anything extraordinary is expected.

—Answer by Marc S. Stern, Law Offices of
Marc S. Stern, Seattle, Washington

A. This is a question-and-answer session, conducted under oath and subject to the penalty of perjury, before the trustee (not a judge). In a Chapter 7 case, the hearing is conducted by the Chapter 7 trustee; in a Chapter 13 case, it is conducted by the Chapter 13 trustee. Creditors have an opportunity to ask you questions about the debts you owe them and their collateral—for example, they might request insurance information, ask you to specifically identify components of your case, or inquire about the purchase of your home or other property. These questions will generally be formulated based on your bankruptcy paperwork; thus, it is critical that the paperwork contain accurate and complete information. The meeting will usually last less than ten minutes, and there will usually be a waiting room full of other debtors who are there for their own meetings. If you haven't participated in any fraudulent or other "shady" activity, the 341 meeting of creditors really should not be a big deal—though an exception may exist if a creditor or ex-spouse is very angry at you, in which case the meeting may be more complicated.

—Answer by Shayna M. Steinfeld, Steinfeld &
Steinfeld, P.C., Atlanta, Georgia

Q. What happens at the end of a bankruptcy case? Do I go to court? How do I know which debts have been discharged and which have not?

A. The 2005 changes to the law require you to complete a personal-financial-management instructional course before you can obtain a discharge in either a Chapter 7 or Chapter 13 case. The clerk of court will have a list of approved courses. At the conclusion of your case, you will receive a piece of paper called a "discharge," which will state that all pre-petition debts are discharged except for a generic statutory list of debts that are excluded. This will mean that your creditors may no longer collect the discharged debts from you personally—though if they have a lien on your property, such as your house or car or stereo, they may take back their collateral if you still owe them money. Your attorney should be able to tell you which specific debts were or were not discharged. In general, if no creditor files an adversary proceeding seeking to challenge your discharge, and your case is seen through to conclusion—in a Chapter 13 case, for example, this means that your case is not dismissed for nonpayment of monthly trustee fees—you will be discharged from most debts that you incurred prior to filing. (Keep in mind, however, that if you fail to list a creditor in your bankruptcy paperwork, that creditor's debt may be excluded from the discharge.) Debts that automatically remain due include support obligations to a child or ex-spouse, student loans, certain taxes, and restitution and debts incurred while driving intoxicated. There may be other exceptions to the discharge, which also vary by bankruptcy chapter, but most of those require the filing of a lawsuit. Finally, student loans may be discharged if you file a complaint and prove that their repayment will be an "undue hardship" on you and your family. This is a difficult thing to prove.

> —Answer by Shayna M. Steinfeld, Steinfeld &
> Steinfeld, P.C., Atlanta, Georgia

A. In most Chapter 7 cases, the debtor will receive in the mail a written discharge of his or her debts. The discharge should arrive roughly sixty days after the debtor appears at the meeting of the creditors. A discharge will also be granted after the successful completion of a three- to five-year Chapter 13 plan, and a copy of the discharge order will be mailed to the debtor.

—Answer by Judge David S. Kennedy, U.S. Bankruptcy
Court, Western District of Tennessee

The Role of the Bankruptcy Trustees

The primary role of the bankruptcy trustee is to be impartial and liquidate the debtor's assets. The trustee manages the debtor's estate, which consists of all the debtor's property and interests. After determining your exemptions, the bankruptcy trustee will assemble, liquidate (sell), and distribute the value of your non-exempt assets (if there are any). The trustee might "abandon"—that is, return to you—property that would bring no value to your unsecured creditors. This will include nonexempt assets with minimal resale value.

The first creditors to be paid are the secured creditors. The trustee will first distribute to secured creditors the value of their collateral or the collateral itself if the collateral is worth no more than the debt. So the bank will get your house back if you have no equity; it could keep it (unlikely) or sell it, but in neither case will your unsecured creditors benefit.

Next, the trustee will pay unsecured priority claims, such as most taxes and past-due support, such as alimony and child support. If any funds are left, the trustee will distribute them to your general unsecured creditors, such as credit card companies and hospitals, on a pro rata (proportionate) basis. Say, for example, that after the payment of secured and priority claims, the proceeds from the sale by the trustee of your nonexempt assets equal 20 percent of your remaining debts. Then the trustee will pay each general creditor 20 percent of what you owe. In return, the court will discharge you from paying any remaining balance on your general unsecured debts.

The trustee will also pay the administrative claims, such as

SHOULD BOTH SPOUSES FILE FOR BANKRUPTCY?

Whether married couples in debt should both file for bankruptcy depends on the nature of the debt. A debt may be a **separate debt** if it is in your name only. If you have been married for a short time, your debts are more likely to be considered separate debts. A debt may be a **joint debt** if both spouses signed a contract for the debt, as in the case of a home loan or credit card agreement.

In most states, a bankruptcy filing by one spouse wipes out the bankrupt spouse's separate debts. The separate property of the nonbankrupt spouse will not be affected. However, if spouses have co-signed for a loan, the bankruptcy of one spouse does not relieve the other of the obligation to pay the debt. After a bankruptcy filing, the creditor may look to the nonbankrupt spouse for payment, unless the bankruptcy case was filed under Chapter 13 and the bankrupt spouse plans to pay back 100 percent of the debt.

If you live in a community property jurisdiction, then the situation is a little different. Arizona, California, Idaho, Louisiana, Nevada, New Mexico, Texas, Washington, and the Commonwealth for Puerto Rico are community property jurisdictions. Alaska and Wisconsin also have community property features in their law. In community property jurisdictions, the separate property of the nonfiling spouse—property owned before the marriage, for example—is not affected. However, in community property states, the general rule is that the income of both spouses is considered community property, as is any property they acquire during the marriage.

Since all of the community property is available to pay community creditors and any other creditors of the spouse who has filed for bankruptcy, the filing of one spouse could have a significant impact on the other.

Filing by one spouse may be noted on the nonbankrupt spouse's credit record.

If you and your spouse both file for bankruptcy, then the bankruptcy will eliminate each spouse's debts as well as all jointly held marital debts.

When two spouses file together on a joint petition, their bankruptcy estates remain separate, unless the court orders them to be consolidated.

You should be wary of a joint filing if you have marital problems that appear to be leading to divorce court. Your best bet is to seek the counsel of a bankruptcy lawyer well versed in the laws of your state.

If both you and your spouse file for bankruptcy at the same time, only one case-filing fee with required charges (in all, about $270) will have to be paid to the court in a Chapter 7 or 13 case. State law may, however, require separate homestead deeds.

his or her commission fees (ranging between 3 percent and 25 percent, depending on the value the trustee recovers), and the fees of professionals, such as lawyers and accountants.

REMEMBER THIS

• Chapter 7 bankruptcy allows you to discharge most of your debts. It is the most common form of bankruptcy used by individual consumers. In a Chapter 7 bankruptcy case, a trustee is appointed to investigate and supervise your case, which means the trustee liquidates many of the debtor's assets, if there are any.

• When you file a Chapter 7 bankruptcy, you must file schedules and a statement of financial affairs. Information you must list on these forms includes your financial history, income, debts, and assets; the forms are quite detailed. On your schedules, list all of your debts, including priority debts, debts to secured creditors, and debts to unsecured creditors.

• Remember that if you are seeking to file for bankruptcy, you must file a certificate showing that you have received credit counseling within 180 days of filing for bankruptcy. You must also state that you received a budget plan from an approved nonprofit credit-counseling service, if you received one.

• Chapter 7 debtors must pass a "means" test that determines whether they really have the means to pay back creditors. This was developed to prevent abusive filings by those seeking Chapter 7 discharges when they really could pay their creditors.

• Under either federal or state law, some of your assets may be exempt from creditors during bankruptcy. States have different exemptions. Exempt assets are beyond the reach of unsecured creditors and the bankruptcy trustee.

• The Bankruptcy Code requires that, under Chapter 7, you give all nonexempt, unencumbered assets to your trustee. If these assets have sufficient value to make a sale worthwhile, the trustee will liquidate them to pay creditors.

• You may be able to reaffirm some debts—that is, promise to pay them—in order to keep certain assets, subject to the approval of the affected creditor. Do not agree to reaffirm debt until you speak with an attorney.

• You cannot avoid the reach of creditors during bankruptcy simply by transferring title to property that you own. Generally, this restriction applies to transfers made within one year of a bankruptcy filing, but, depending on the circumstances and state law, transfers made even earlier than that may also be undone.

• Bankruptcy does not discharge all debts. You are still liable for some tax claims, alimony, child support, fraudulent debts, student loans, and criminal obligations.

• Husbands and wives, depending on state law and the status of joint debt, may want to file jointly for bankruptcy.

CHAPTER 18

Wage-Earner Bankruptcy: Chapter 13

A Form of Bankruptcy for People with Regular Incomes

Mr. and Mrs. Jones make an excellent combined salary. Unfortunately, they have underestimated the effect of the declining stock market, the cost of college for their children, extreme and unexpected medical costs, and other expenses. They have substantial nonexempt assets that they don't wish to see swallowed up by creditors. They want to discharge some of their debts, but can still afford to make some payments to creditors; they just need some relief in the form of reduced or restructured payment plans. The Joneses might find that they are ineligible for a Chapter 7 bankruptcy because their high income disqualifies them under the "means" test. A Chapter 13 bankruptcy might suit them better because it will enable them to preserve some assets.

Chapter 13 allows individuals with regular incomes to pay a portion of their debts under a court-approved payment plan and keep both their exempt and nonexempt assets. This chapter will explain the basic features of a Chapter 13 bankruptcy plan.

CHAPTER 13 IN ACTION

The Basics of Chapter 13

In certain ways, a Chapter 13 bankruptcy is similar to a Chapter 7 bankruptcy. For each type of bankruptcy, debtors must obtain credit counseling within 180 days before filing for bankruptcy and complete a personal-financial-management course in order to secure a discharge. In addition, with each type of bankruptcy, you must list with the court all of your assets and debts. In each, you obtain an automatic stay upon the filing of the case, limiting creditor action against you. And in each, you can obtain a discharge that will eliminate personal liability for most debts.

However, Chapter 13 bankruptcies also have many differences from Chapter 7 bankruptcies. A typical Chapter 7 bankruptcy usually lasts about four to six months before the discharge is granted, while a Chapter 13 case can last three to five years (by law it cannot last longer than five years) and the discharge is delayed until the end of the case. Under Chapter 7, you do not make payments to your creditors, though your nonexempt assets may be sold and the proceeds split among your creditors. Under Chapter 13, on the other hand, you make monthly payments under a repayment plan.

If you have a steady income, Chapter 13 allows you to pay all or a portion of your debts under the protection and supervision of the U.S. Bankruptcy Court, with which you file a bankruptcy petition and a proposed payment plan. The law requires that your payments to creditors be no less than they would have been if you had filed a Chapter 7 case. An important feature of Chapter 13 is that you will be permitted to keep all your assets (both exempt and nonexempt) while the plan is in effect and after you have successfully completed it.

Eligibility for Chapter 13

Chapter 13 is available to almost everyone who has a regular income. The only other requirement is that you have less than $336,900 in unsecured debts (such as credit card debts) and less than $1,010,650 in secured debts (such as home mortgages and car loans). These figures are not doubled when husband and wife file a joint case and are subject to periodic adjustments; the law provides that they will be modified every three years. Anyone with greater debts usually must declare bankruptcy under Chapter 7 or 11 of the Bankruptcy Code.

Differences from Chapter 7

The major difference between Chapters 7 and 13 is that in Chapter 7 you pay debts out of your nonexempt assets, while in Chapter 13 you pay debts out of your future income. As a result, a repayment plan under Chapter 13 normally allows you more time to pay your debts than does a Chapter 7 plan, involves you paying off more of those debts, and allows you to deal more easily with secured creditors (e.g., home mortgage lenders and companies providing financing for your purchase of a car or truck). The permitted repayment period is usually three years for people with a low income, and five years for those debtors whose disposable income is above the median in their state.

Remember that not everyone is eligible for relief under Chapter 7. Because of these eligibility limits, these days, a greater percentage of bankruptcy filings have been filed under Chapter 13. For example, bankruptcy statistics from the calendar year 2003 show more than 473,000 Chapter 13 filings and total bankruptcy filings of more than 1.6 million (before the "means" test). This means that 30 percent of all bankruptcy filings were Chapter 13. Contrast that with statistics from 2007 (after the "means" test was put in place), which show more than 324,000 Chapter 13 filings and a total of 850,912 filings—38 percent. (To view bankruptcy statistics, go to the U.S. courts website at www.uscourts.gov/bnkrpctystats/statistics.htm.)

Typically, the amount that you repay under a Chapter 13 plan is equal to the total of your planned monthly payments over three to five years, assuming a good-faith effort to repay your debts. Thus, your payments represent either (1) full satisfaction of your debts; or (2) all of your disposable income for a three- to five-year period. **Disposable income** consists of whatever is left over from your total income after you have paid for taxes and reasonable and necessary living expenses, as determined on a monthly basis. Note, however, that the bankruptcy law changes the definition of "reasonable and necessary living expenses" for some above-median-income debtors. For these debtors, allowable expenses are determined in large part by IRS regulations. It will be important for you to consult with your attorney to determine what expenses are permitted. Under a Chapter 13 plan, debtors must also pay secured creditors the values of their liens over time and cannot change the terms of their home mortgage loans. Debtors do not get to select the time period and take advantage of all options.

Mechanics of Filing Chapter 13

Chapter 13 is a very public process that requires the debtor to make many disclosures of information that is usually considered "private." If you file for Chapter 13, you will have to provide a statement of monthly net income itemized to show how the amount was calculated, copies of all payments received sixty days before the filing of the petition, copies of federal tax returns, and a photo ID. As noted above, you will also have to file a certificate showing that you received credit counseling within 180 days before your bankruptcy filing (just like those who file under Chapter 7).

You will also need to file a repayment plan within fifteen days of filing your petition. In your payment plan, you agree to pay a certain amount each month to your creditors. Your plan will indicate the amount of money you propose to pay each month, the total amount to be paid, the percentage return you propose to pay to your creditors, and the expected length of the plan. You

 COUNSELING IS MANDATORY

Before you can obtain a discharge under Chapter 13, you must submit a certification with your bankruptcy petition indicating that you have completed a financial-education course. One major purpose of this is to provide greater personal responsibility. The thinking behind this requirement is that it will engender greater responsibility and help ensure that debtors will not have to return to bankruptcy.

must make your first payment on this plan within thirty days after you file it. You must make this payment within this time period even if the court has not yet approved the plan. Your lawyer will explain this to you.

After you submit your plan to the court, a Chapter 13 trustee is appointed to handle your case. The trustee will verify the accuracy and reasonableness of your plan. The plan will then be distributed to your creditors, who will have the opportunity at a creditors' meeting to challenge your repayment proposal if they believe it doesn't meet the specific requirements of the Bankruptcy Code. You must attend the creditors' meeting and answer questions under oath from your creditors and the trustee regarding your financial affairs and the proposed terms of the plan.

The Chapter 13 trustee attends this meeting, but the bankruptcy judge does not. The trustee will want to be sure that your plan provides enough money for you to live on, but will also challenge living expenses that seem unreasonably high. One issue will be whether you are making a good-faith and sincere effort to repay your debts, even if that effort means reducing your living standards, such as by eliminating entertainment expenses. Since the trustee's recommendation will carry considerable weight with the court, it pays to be honest and open with the information that you provide.

 CHAPTER 13 TRUSTEES

The role of a Chapter 13 trustee varies depending on the area. Most trustees work with debtors to help them learn to manage their finances. Often a trustee will arrange for (or require) monthly payments to be automatically deducted from a debtor's paycheck and credited directly to the trustee's account for disbursement to the various creditors. Generally, a small part of the debtor's monthly payments goes to the trustee as compensation for these services.

There are several positive features of a Chapter 13 plan. For one thing, under some circumstances, you can propose to repay a creditor at a lower interest rate than the rate stipulated in your original contract with that creditor (except in the case of a home mortgage). Moreover, your proposed repayment plan needn't provide that you pay back the entire amount you owe. Instead, you can reorganize your debts and submit a reasonable payback plan proposing that debts to secured creditors be paid back on your own schedule, without exorbitant interest. This flexibility can be a great advantage for Chapter 13 debtors. For example, if a person is stuck in a particularly bad car contract and wants to keep his car, he may be allowed to pay only the fair market value of his car, rather than the entire (often much higher) amount stipulated in the original contract. However, it is important to note that this option is somewhat limited (see the section below on the value of secured collateral). Also, keep in mind that you still must put forth your best effort to repay your debts.

A creditor might file an objection to a Chapter 13 plan if it will receive less under the plan than it would have under Chapter 7. Unsecured creditors are entitled to receive at least as much as they would have received under a Chapter 7 bankruptcy. This is called the **"best interest of the creditors" rule**. Another common objection is that the plan, in essence, does not require you to commit enough of your projected disposable income to repayment.

After a meeting of your creditors is held, the bankruptcy judge will hold a confirmation hearing and either confirm your plan or deny it. The confirmation hearing must be held twenty to forty-five days after the creditors' meeting. If the judge rejects the plan, you can propose another plan. If you are eligible to file Chapter 7, you could also convert your Chapter 13 bankruptcy into a Chapter 7 filing.

Bear in mind that you must start making payments to the trustee, your landlord, and on your secured debts within thirty days of filing, regardless of whether the plan has been confirmed by a judge or not.

IF YOU'RE SELF-EMPLOYED

Chapter 13 can also be an effective tool for self-employed individuals. If you are self-employed and filing under Chapter 13, you should list your average monthly business expenses, business income, and business debts when filing your payment plan and schedules. You should also include incidental income, such as part-time wages for babysitting, alimony and support income, and rental income.

Value of Secured Collateral

The law limits the practice of stripping, or dramatically reducing the value of, certain secured loans. Before the 2005 bankruptcy law, a debtor could reduce or strip down the amount of auto loans and pay only the actual value of the vehicle. Under this scenario, the difference between the actual loan and the value of the vehicle would be treated as unsecured debt. For example, if the blue book value of your car was less than what you owed, you could propose to pay only the blue book value in satisfaction of your debt. These days, however, you are prohibited from stripping down security interests in motor vehicles acquired within 910 days of the petition filing and of other secured debts incurred within one year of the bankruptcy. You must repay the full amount of the loans on such property even if the loan amount is much higher than the actual value of the collateral. Thus, as a result of the 2005 law, debtors may no longer strip down, or reduce, auto loans within 910 days of their filing.

CHAPTER 13 PAYMENT PLANS

Preparing Your Plan

As has been discussed throughout this chapter, you have some flexibility in preparing a Chapter 13 bankruptcy plan, provided

that your creditors raise no objections. The plan that you prepare for review by your lawyer should take into account your income from all sources and your reasonable necessary expenses.
It should also anticipate any known future changes in your income or expenses, such as retirement or a rent increase. What is
left from your income after paying living expenses will be available for disbursement to your creditors. Note that some items,
like child support payments and money used to pay certain
debts, are excluded from "available income."

Your plan must provide for payment in full of all **priority
claims**—that is, certain taxes and family support obligations,
including overdue child support and alimony. The law makes
domestic-support (e.g. alimony, child support) obligations a top
priority. A debtor can lose the protections of a Chapter 13 plan
if he or she does not remain current with these support obligations.

Besides keeping up with such current obligations, you'll
have to "cure"—that is, make up for—payments you have missed
in the past. You can arrange to pay such overdue debts over the
life of your repayment plan. If your disposable income is above
the median in your state, your plan may have to run for five
years. As noted above, a creditor or the trustee might object to
your plan. If this happens and the court rejects the plan, you
must redraft your plan to address the objection.

After the Plan Is Approved

Once the court confirms your payment plan, you must continue
to make regular monthly plan payments to the trustee. Bear in
mind that these payments must begin within thirty days after filing the plan or the initial bankruptcy petition, whichever is earlier, and both dates might precede the confirmation of your plan.
The trustee usually distributes payments among your creditors
in accordance with your confirmed repayment plan. You will
continue, of course, to pay for your ongoing utility and grocery
bills and other everyday expenses. The court will grant you a

TALKING TO A LAWYER

Q. What percentage of my debts do I have to pay in a Chapter 13 case? Is it the same percentage for all debts, or do I have to pay a greater percentage of certain debts?

A. This is a matter of local practice. The law provides that under certain circumstances you can pay as little as zero percent to unsecured creditors; however, you must provide full payment to priority creditors. Priority debts are specified in Section 507 of the Bankruptcy Code and include, among other things, child support and some taxes.

—Answer by Marc S. Stern, Law Offices of
Marc S. Stern, Seattle, Washington

A. There is no fixed percentage amount of debts that have to be paid under Chapter 13 plans. Some plans may pay 100 percent to unsecured creditors while others may pay 70 percent, 40 percent, 20 percent, 10 percent, or even zero percent, depending on the particular facts and circumstances. Generally, all unsecured nonpriority creditors—for example, credit card companies—will be treated the same and receive the same percentage of repayment. If an unsecured creditor objects to confirmation of a Chapter 13 plan, the debtor must submit all of his or her disposable income for a period of at least thirty-six months to pay whatever percentage of the debt can be paid during that period. For cause, the court may allow some creditors to be treated differently. If the debtor's income exceeds the state's median income, the plan may have to last five years.

—Answer by Judge David S. Kennedy, U.S. Bankruptcy
Court, Western District of Tennessee

Q. This is not my first time being deep in debt. I had many debts discharged three years ago under Chapter 7, but now I've got new ones. Can I file a Chapter 13 bankruptcy?

A. No. The eight-year discharge bar in Chapter 7 cases does not apply in Chapter 13 cases. However, a discharge would not be granted in a

Chapter 13 case if the discharge in the Chapter 7 case was granted within four years of the filing of the subsequent Chapter 13 case. So-called serial filings are allowed in Chapter 13 cases; however, Chapter 13 plans must be filed in good faith. Good-faith requirements are often said to be the "gatekeepers" of Chapter 13.

—Answer by Judge David S. Kennedy, U.S. Bankruptcy Court, Western District of Tennessee

Chapter 13 discharge after you complete the payments specified in your plan, usually in three to five years.

If you do not complete the payments, you will not obtain a discharge of any of your debts unless you qualify for a hardship discharge. Such a discharge requires proof of special circumstances beyond your control that made it impossible for you to make further plan payments (see page 273 for more information).

Additional Filing Requirements

These days, there are numerous other filing requirements that individuals filing for Chapter 13 may have to fulfill. Upon request from the judge or a party in interest (e.g., a trustee or creditor), debtors must submit annual financial statements showing "the amount and sources of income" and expenditures.

Payments under Chapter 13 Plans

You must do all you can to make the payments required under a Chapter 13 bankruptcy plan. If you don't make the required payments, the ramifications can be severe. If you fail to take the initiative in dealing with defaults under your Chapter 13 plan—for example, by seeking a change in the plan or a hardship discharge (discussed below)—a creditor or the trustee may seek to have your case either converted to Chapter 7 or dismissed outright.

If the case is dismissed, the automatic stay that arose upon the filing of the Chapter 13 case is dissolved. This means that the collection calls will begin again, and your car could be repossessed or your home foreclosed upon as if there had been no bankruptcy.

If you are eligible for Chapter 7, conversion to Chapter 7 could be good or bad for you, depending on the circumstances. For some debtors, conversion to a Chapter 7 case might be a good result. If you have little or no equity, Chapter 7 isn't much of a threat, so you might seek to have your Chapter 13 case converted to Chapter 7 on your own if you are having problems making the Chapter 13 plan payments. However, if you have a lot of equity in your home or your car that you want to retain, Chapter 7 could be something you'd prefer to avoid, since it would give your creditors a chance to recover nonexempt assets that you wish to protect. In that case, you'd have every reason to keep up with your Chapter 13 plan. Be aware, however, that conversion to Chapter 7 does not necessarily mean that you are eligible for a Chapter 7 discharge; conversion and eligibility for discharge are different matters entirely.

Sometimes, special circumstances can qualify a debtor for temporary relief from the requirements of a Chapter 13 plan. For example, if you have an accident that prevents you from working temporarily, you may be able to arrange a moratorium, which means that you can miss a payment and catch up later. Furthermore, if there is a major permanent reduction in your income—for example, from lost hours due to a chronic illness—the trustee may support a modification in the plan if you meet certain legal requirements. Modification might entail stretching payments out over a longer period (not to exceed five years) and reducing the amount of each payment accordingly, or perhaps giving up some asset for which you had planned to make payments. If you complete performance of your modified plan, you are entitled to a full Chapter 13–type discharge, provided you have satisfied the other requirements as well (i.e., completed debtor counseling and stayed current on all post-petition domestic-support obligations).

Hardship Discharge

If there is no modification of your plan but you have defaulted on your plan payments as a result of circumstances for which you "should not justly be held accountable," and if your unsecured creditors have already received as much as they would have received under Chapter 7, you may qualify for a hardship discharge if you can show that a modification of the plan would be impractical. This is a Chapter 7–type discharge.

WHICH DEBTS ARE DISCHARGEABLE UNDER CHAPTER 13?

A Chapter 13 discharge granted upon completion of a plan covers more types of debt than the Chapter 7 discharge. However, the difference between the two types of bankruptcy discharges has narrowed since the 2005 law. Debts **not** discharged by Chapter 13 include:

- Taxes, where returns either were not filed or were fraudulent;
- Debts left off the bankruptcy schedules;
- Support debts;
- Student loans;
- Debts for personal injuries caused by drunk driving;
- Criminal fines;
- Some restitution orders;
- Debts for money obtained under false pretenses;
- Debts for luxury goods bought on credit within ninety days of filing;
- Cash advances over $750 obtained within seventy days of filing; and
- Funds obtained by embezzlement.

Note that debts for property settlement and willful property damage are still dischargeable under Chapter 13, even though they would not be discharged under Chapter 7. The Chapter 13

CONVERSION TO CHAPTER 7

Sometimes, Chapter 13 bankruptcies are converted to Chapter 7 bankruptcies—either voluntarily or involuntarily. If there is neither a modification nor a hardship discharge of your Chapter 13 obligations, and if your income is low enough that you are eligible for Chapter 7, you may choose to convert your case to Chapter 7. Sometimes the conversion to Chapter 7 is forced upon you because you simply cannot meet the obligations of the Chapter 13 payment plan or because your disposable income is deemed too high to qualify for Chapter 7.

hardship discharge, as discussed above, covers only debts that would be dischargeable under Chapter 7.

REMEMBER THIS

• Chapter 13 allows individuals with regular incomes to pay all or a portion of their debts under the protection and supervision of a court. Under Chapter 13, you file a bankruptcy petition and a proposed payment plan, which can extend from three to five years, with the U.S. Bankruptcy Court.

• The percentage of Chapter 13 filings vis-à-vis total bankruptcy filings has increased since 2005. This is likely because fewer people are eligible to file under Chapter 7, and some Chapter 7 bankruptcies are converted to Chapter 13.

• The bankruptcy trustee will typically distribute your proposed payment plan to your creditors. Creditors will have a chance to challenge your proposals. Once the payment plan is approved by the court, you make monthly payments to the trustee, who then disburses the money among your creditors in accordance with the plan.

• If you cannot make payments under a Chapter 13 plan, you may be able to convert to a Chapter 7 plan or seek a dismissal of the Chapter 13 case.

• Important limits and disadvantages to Chapter 13 exist: It severely limits the stripping down of auto liens, many plans last up to five years, plans will not be confirmed if domestic-support obligations are not met, and certain debts are not eligible for discharge.

CHAPTER 19

Chapter 7 or Chapter 13?

Which Should You Choose?
Advantages and Disadvantages

Laurel has significant credit card debts that she cannot pay and is considering filing for bankruptcy. She has $50,000 of equity in her home, is paying off a car, and would like to keep both. But she can't stand the idea of committing her hard-earned wages to creditors for up to five years through a Chapter 13 bankruptcy. On the other hand, she hates the thought of giving up her car or having to move out of her home. How can she decide what kind of bankruptcy is right for her?

Choosing the best form of bankruptcy for a particular situation is often difficult. The chart on pages 283–285 summarizes the differences between the two most common types of consumer bankruptcy—Chapter 7 and Chapter 13—and provides a quick overview of your options with respect to each. To assist you in making an informed decision, this chapter will explore more thoroughly the advantages and disadvantages of both types. Bear in mind, however, that the current bankruptcy law passed in 2005 may make you ineligible for Chapter 7 bankruptcy if you earn more than the median income in your state and have disposable income above the minimum level (see page 242 for a discussion on this test).

ADVANTAGES OF CHAPTER 7

There are several reasons that straight bankruptcy (i.e., bankruptcy filed under Chapter 7) may be preferable to Chapter 13. First, there are many debtors for whom the advantages of Chapter 13 (outlined below) do not matter: debtors with no nonexempt assets they particularly wish to keep, no debts excepted from discharge under Chapter 7, no prior discharge within the last eight years, and no cosigners on their consumer debt loans.

Second, in Chapter 7, the debtor can keep post-petition earnings free and clear from discharged pre-bankruptcy debts. Under Chapter 13, a debtor must commit his or her entire disposable income to his or her creditors for three to five years.

Third, some debtors are not eligible for Chapter 13 bankruptcy, either because their income is not sufficiently regular to fund payments under a plan or because the amount of their debt exceeds the limits discussed in chapter 18.

ADVANTAGES OF CHAPTER 13

Chapter 13 bankruptcy plans have several advantages over Chapter 7 plans. Perhaps the most important advantage is that Chapter 13 plans allow you to retain most of your assets, so long as you make payments to your trustee as agreed in your court-approved repayment plan.

Another distinction between Chapters 7 and 13 is that a few debts are dischargeable in a Chapter 13 case that are not dischargeable in a Chapter 7 case (such as property settlement debts and debts for willful property damage). However, divorce-related alimony and child support payments are not dischargeable in either chapter—you have to pay them. Whether a debt is for support or property settlement is a question of federal, not state, law. Chapter 18 of this book contains more information about the kinds of debts that are not dischargeable under either chapter.

Chapter 13 may also be preferable if you are a party to one or more co-signed loans. Under Chapter 13, if people co-signed any of your consumer loans or other credit representing consumer debts, and the collateral for such loans is in your possession, your creditors cannot collect from these cosigners until it is clear that the Chapter 13 plan will not pay the entire amount owed to the creditors. This is called a "co-debtor automatic stay." In contrast, if you file Chapter 7, your creditors will have the right to demand payment from your cosigners immediately.

Another advantage of Chapter 13 is that you can use it more often than Chapter 7. The law forbids you to receive a discharge under Chapter 7 more than once every eight years. However, Chapter 13 allows you to file repeatedly, and receive the benefits of the automatic stay, though each filing will appear on your credit record and will be reviewed by the trustee to prevent abuse. You should remember that, regardless of the frequency with which you file, all Chapter 13 plans must be filed in good faith.

Although you may be able to file repeatedly under Chapter 13, it may not necessarily be possible to complete the bankruptcy and be discharged from your debts. Under the bankruptcy law, a Chapter 13 debtor will be denied discharge if he or she received a discharge in a case filed under Chapter 7, 11, or 12 during the previous four years, or in a Chapter 13 case filed during the previous two years. The advantage of being able to refile under Chapter 13 (even if debtors are not permitted discharge) is that debtors are given the temporary protection of the automatic stay. For example, imagine a debtor files for Chapter 13 bankruptcy two years after filing for Chapter 7. Under the law, the debtor cannot receive a discharge under Chapter 13 because the bankruptcies are too close together. But she would receive the benefit of an automatic stay, which would stop debt collectors from calling. She would also be able to spread out her existing debts over five years. Of course, if she still had debts remaining after five years, they would not be discharged and she would still be liable for them. However, the benefits of having a period of time—up to five years—to deal with secured debt, a time in which unsecured creditors must suspend their collection efforts, may outweigh not being able to get a discharge at the end of that period.

It is important to note that there is a limit on this ability to file multiple times. The bankruptcy law says that, in a debtor's second bankruptcy case within the span of a year, the automatic stay will end thirty days after the filing. This prevents debtors from filing Chapter 13 cases immediately after Chapter 7 cases or repeatedly filing Chapter 13 cases without ever finishing payments under Chapter 13 plans. Historically, some debtors used to do this in order to use the automatic stay to stave off foreclosure on a home or other asset. In addition to the restrictions on a second bankruptcy, in a debtor's third bankruptcy case within the span of a year, there will be no automatic stay at all, except as to unsecured creditors.

7 OR 13:
IS IT ALWAYS THE DEBTOR'S CHOICE?

When filing for bankruptcy, the choice between chapters is generally left to any eligible debtor. However, the bankruptcy law does give the trustee or any creditor the ability to bring a motion in court to dismiss a Chapter 7 bankruptcy if the debtor's income is too high (that is, above the state median). In effect, this forces the debtor into Chapter 13 bankruptcy, if the debtor is to file bankruptcy at all.

Remember that the federal law creates a "means" test to determine whether a debtor's income is too high for a Chapter 7 case. (See chapter 17 for a discussion of the "means" test.) If the debtor's current monthly income is above the state's median income for his or her type of family (e.g., four-person family, three-person family, and so on), then there is a presumption that the person should file bankruptcy under Chapter 13, not Chapter 7. The test is fairly complex and takes into account presumed income, your state's median income, and a number of deductions. Under the means test, debtors must file a statement of their calculations. If a debtor's income is considered too high for Chapter 7, then creditors are notified within ten days of the filing of the petition and can bring a motion to dismiss the bankruptcy petition.

Median income varies by state. In Illinois, for example, the median income in February 2008 (adjusted for inflation) was approximately $44,673 for a one-person household, $56,545 for a two-person household, $66,607 for a three-person household, and $77,634 for a four-person household.

CRAMMING DOWN

Cramming down is a process important for debtors who owe more on an asset than the asset is currently worth (for example, for someone who owes $8,000 on a car that is now only worth $5,000). Cramming down occurs when a court allows the debtor to use a lower number in creating the balance on the monthly payment plans. However, these days, cramming down is limited—it is available only if you have bought or refinanced the car more than two and a half years before filing for bankruptcy, and the loan can only be crammed down to the current retail value of the car, though this still might be less than the amount you have left to pay.

The law does not allow a debtor to cram down a first mortgage loan on a home, though some courts may allow cramming down of second and third mortgage loans if the home in question is worth less than the amount of the first mortgage loan.

If your income is under your state's median, your petition for bankruptcy still might be dismissed, although it is less likely. Courts also have the option of dismissing a Chapter 7 bankruptcy on grounds of **simple** abuse, though the new law does not clarify the precise meaning of this term.

It is also important to note that your case could be converted to a Chapter 12 or 13 case. The federal bankruptcy law provides in 11 U.S.C. § 706(c) that the "court may not convert a case under this chapter [Chapter 7] to case under Chapter 12 or 13 of this title unless the debtor requests or consents to such con-

 TALKING TO A LAWYER

Q. I'm told that if I file for Chapter 7 but have a regular income, my case might get shifted to a Chapter 13 case. Is this true? If it is, what effect would that have on me?

A. Under the bankruptcy laws, the court may dismiss a bankruptcy case either because the debtor has enough income to flunk the "income test" or because the debtor is otherwise abusing Chapter 7. It is not clear what facts constitute "abuse" where the debtor's income is not so high as to flunk the means test.

If the case is dismissed due either to failure of the means test or some other abuse, the debtor may voluntarily convert the Chapter 7 case to a Chapter 13 case if he or she still wants to obtain relief under the bankruptcy laws.

—Answer by Marianne Culhane, Professor, Creighton University School of Law, Omaha, Nebraska

A. Every individual debtor is subject to the Chapter 7 "means" test, which determines eligibility for relief under Chapter 7. The "means" test is essentially a formula that takes into account monthly income and reasonable and necessary expenses and compares these factors to the median income in the state where you live. If you fall below the median income level in your state, you can file a Chapter 7 bankruptcy; if not, your case will be converted to Chapter 13. Be advised, though, that the formulas and numbers used in the "means" test can be complicated and that the median income level varies from state to state. Your lawyer can advise you whether you qualify to file under the Chapter 7 means test. The conversion to Chapter 13 is expressly stated in the bankruptcy law as an alternative to dismissal of a Chapter 7 case.

—Answer by Judge David S. Kennedy, U.S. Bankruptcy Court, Western District of Tennessee

A. If your Chapter 7 bankruptcy is dismissed, and you choose not to convert it to Chapter 13, it will be as though the bankruptcy never occurred—so your debt will still be outstanding, and debt collection efforts can begin again.

—Answer by David Greer, Williams Mullen Hofheimer Nusbaum, Norfolk, Virginia

MEANS TESTING

The choice of whether to file under Chapter 7 or Chapter 13 is pretty easy for some debtors. As noted throughout this book, there are more stringent restrictions on the use of Chapter 7 by individual debtors whose incomes (based on actual income less set expenses, calculated under IRS workout guidelines) would fund significant payments to creditors if the debtors used Chapter 13 instead. The law requires that some Chapter 7 cases be converted to Chapter 13 cases where a debtor's income is high (above the state's median) and his or her debts could be paid in significant part. The determination of whether a debtor meets these criteria is called the **means testing**. Your lawyer should be able to tell you whether you qualify for Chapter 7.

version." Thus, a debtor may be faced with the choice of dismissal of the Chapter 7 petition or conversion to Chapter 13.

REMEMBER THIS

• There may be several advantages to filing Chapter 13 instead of Chapter 7. The major advantage is that under Chapter 13 you will be able to retain and use all of your assets as long as you make the promised payments. Also, the discharge of debts is a bit broader under Chapter 13 than under Chapter 7.

• There may also be advantages to a Chapter 7 bankruptcy. For instance, Chapter 13 debtors may have to keep making payments for three to five years. In Chapter 7, a debtor can keep post-petition earnings free and clear from discharged pre-bankruptcy debts.

• Most debtors can choose whether to file for bankruptcy under Chapter 7 or Chapter 13. However, some debtors are eligible for discharge only in Chapter 13.

GENERAL COMPARISON OF CHAPTER 7 AND CHAPTER 13 BANKRUPTCY

Chapter 7	Chapter 13
Straight Bankruptcy Liquidation	**Payment Plan for People with Regular Income**

Basic operation

Obtain mandatory credit counseling within 180 days before filing bankruptcy petition. File bankruptcy petition with court. Trustee appointed to administer bankruptcy. All nonexempt assets surrendered for liquidation and distribution. Debtor retains only exempt assets and those assets reaffirmed or redeemed and, if creditor agrees, collateral for loans. Money from liquidation is split among creditors, according to the priority established by the Bankruptcy Code.

Obtain mandatory credit counseling within 180 days prior to bankruptcy. If a debt management plan is proposed, that should be filed as well. File bankruptcy petition and proposed payment plan with court. Payment plan provides payments over a period of three to five years. Payments are made from disposable income (i.e., whatever is left over after necessities [food, shelter, etc.] have been allowed for), while debtor retains assets. Individuals must complete "an instructional course concerning personal financial management" to assure their discharge.

Limitations

Debtor must pass the "means" test, which determines eligibility for Chapter 7. Some people with income higher than state median income will not be eligible for Chapter 7.

For debtors owing less than $336,900 in unsecured debts and less than $1,010,650 in secured debts.

Percentage of consumer filings

67.2%

32.8%

Frequency

Discharge will be denied if a debtor got a prior Chapter 7 discharge within eight years, or a Chapter 11, 12, or 13 discharge within six years.

Discharge will be denied if the debtor got Chapter 7, 11, or 12 discharge within four years, or a Chapter 13 discharge within two years.

Effect on debts

With exceptions noted in the text (e.g., student loans, support obligations, taxes), most pre-petition debts are discharged upon conclusion of bankruptcy unless the court denies the discharge. Personal liability to creditors ends when the court enters a discharge order.

All or a portion of debts paid off over a period of time under a specific plan. With exceptions noted in the text (e.g., student loans, support obligations, taxes), most pre-petition debts are discharged. Personal liability to creditors ends when the plan is

Chapter 7	Chapter 13
Straight Bankruptcy Liquidation	**Payment Plan for People with Regular Income**

Court may except one or more particular debts from the discharge, and creditors may retain liens on collateral, such as a home mortgage.

completed and the court enters a discharge order, but creditors may retain liens on collateral, such as a home mortgage.

Effect on home
Debtor may keep home under homestead exemption if there is little nonexempt equity, and if mortgage payments have been maintained. The mortgage holder may require the debtor to reaffirm the mortgage. Marital ownership law may also preserve the home. However, the homestead exemption is limited to $125,000 for homes acquired within 40 months of filing or if the debtor committed certain fraudulent acts.

Home may be preserved if plan is successfully completed and if there is not substantial nonexempt equity. A homestead exemption cannot be for more than $125,000 if the home was acquired 40 months before filing or if the debtor committed certain fraudulent acts.

Effect on car or truck
Vehicle might be taken by trustee or secured creditor (unless necessary for work) or arrangements are made to pay off lien by redemption or reaffirmation.

Vehicle will be preserved if plan is successfully competed and appropriate payments made. If not, it might be taken by creditors (unless arrangements are made to pay off the lien).

Effect on nonexempt assets
All nonexempt assets may be required to be surrendered for distribution to creditors.

Debtor retains all assets if the plan is confirmed and successfully completed. If the case is converted to Chapter 7, nonexempt assets must be surrendered for distribution to creditors.

Time to repay
Not applicable.

Usually three years, sometimes up to five years.

Payments
Most debts will be discharged, but some, such as taxes, student loans, and child support, will have to be paid by the debtor out of post-petition income.

All "disposable income" is available for payments; that is, whatever remains after necessities (food, shelter, etc.) are taken care of. Chapter 13 provides that for debtors with above-median income, what is reasonable to pay will be determined in large part by IRS regulation.

Chapter 7

Straight Bankruptcy Liquidation

Portion of debt repaid

Will depend on the value of nonexempt assets surrendered to pay off debts.

Result at conclusion of bankruptcy

Bankruptcy court enters a discharge order, ending personal liability on all dischargeable pre-petition debts. Creditors may retain liens, such as a home mortgage, and foreclosure is still a possibility if the debt secure is not paid as agreed.

Effect on credit

Record of bankruptcy remains on credit record for up to ten years from the date of filing.

Chapter 13

Payment Plan for People with Regular Income

May allow for payment of less than the full amount of debts.

When all payments have been made, the bankruptcy court enters a discharge order, ending personal liability on all dischargeable pre-petition debts. The holders of a home mortgage may retain that lien and foreclose if the mortgage debt is not paid as agreed.

The borrower must have made all payments in accordance with the court-approved plan, after which the court enters the discharge order.

The record of the bankruptcy filing may remain on your credit report for up to ten years from the date of filing, although some creditors will report a Chapter 13 bankruptcy for only seven years.

CHAPTER 20

Saving Your Home

What You Can Do to Protect Your Home Under Bankruptcy

Mr. and Mrs. Williams have accumulated substantial debts during their twenty-year marriage. Maintaining their standard of living while putting three daughters through college has created even greater financial strain. When Mr. Williams loses his job, their financial situation becomes untenable. They have a beautiful home that they wish to keep at any cost, but they also know realistically that they must file bankruptcy to prevent a foreclosure. What can they do to save their home?

What's the most important step you can take to preserve your home? First, under either Chapter 7 or Chapter 13, you will be able to keep your home only if you continue to make the required ongoing monthly payments on your mortgage. If you've fallen behind, under Chapter 7 you must make arrangements acceptable to your mortgage lender to catch up on any delinquent payments, and it's up to the mortgage company to decide whether to work with you. Bear in mind also, as discussed in previous chapters, that you must qualify income-wise in order to file Chapter 13 bankruptcy. Under Chapter 13, you may be able to include any delinquent payments in your payment plan and pay them off over a specified period of time—say, three years—while maintaining ongoing monthly mortgage payments. To accomplish this, you must have sufficient cash flow to cover your regular payments to the Chapter 13 bankruptcy trustee as well as your regular ongoing mortgage payments.

A sincere willingness to make monthly payments on your mortgage, however, will not necessarily ensure that you can keep your home from repossession by the mortgagee (the institution from which you received your home loan). Though making such payments is necessary, it still may not be sufficient.

Another factor determining whether you'll keep your home either from repossession by the mortgagee or rights of unsecured creditors to access your non-exempt equity in your home is whether you own the property with your spouse. Let's say you have plenty of debt, but your spouse has little or none. Many states will completely block or significantly limit the ability of unsecured creditors to reach property that you own together with your nonfiling spouse. (This is not true, however, in community property states.) Much may depend on how (i.e., in what form of joint ownership) you hold the home. You should consult with an attorney in your state about whether your home could be protected.

CHAPTER 7

Even if you're willing to continue making the required monthly payments, you could still lose your home if you file for a Chapter 7 bankruptcy.

With a Chapter 7 filing, if you have no equity in your home and you haven't made your payments (you are in **default**), the creditor can foreclose on your home (take it from you) during or after bankruptcy, even if your unsecured debts are discharged. The Chapter 7 discharge does not release the lien on your home. Of course, a lender can also foreclose on your home in these circumstances if you do not file for bankruptcy; filing for bankruptcy will only delay the inevitable by a couple of months.

If you do have equity in your home, your unsecured creditors may also have an interest in your home, especially if it is worth more than the total of your mortgage debt and any applicable homestead exemption. In that case, the bankruptcy trustee may take possession of your home and sell it for the benefit of your unsecured creditors—in other words, it may become part of the assets collected for distribution by the trustee.

Whether the trustee will actually take your home will depend on two factors: how much equity you have in the home, and how much of the home's value is sheltered by legal exemptions from creditors.

The **homestead exemption** is the amount of your home's value that the law puts out of the reach of your unsecured creditors. In general, the lower your exemption and the greater the equity you have in your home, the stronger the chance that the trustee will take your home.

For example, assume that the market value of your home is $125,000, and you have a mortgage of $75,000. Your equity is the difference between those two figures, or $50,000. If your homestead exemption were $45,000 (as is the case in Colorado) your creditors could in theory seek to claim the $5,000 left over after your exemption is subtracted from your equity. As a practical matter, however, the trustee would probably not go to the expense and trouble of taking over your property and selling it for the benefit of unsecured creditors, especially since the costs of the sale would eat up the $5,000.

The federal law does put a lid on homestead exemptions in states with generous limits or no dollar limits at all. Under the law, if you bought your home in the forty months before filing—specifically, within 1,216 days of filing—you can exempt no more than $125,000 of its value, unless you rolled over an interest from another house you owned in the same state. However, if you live in one of the many states in which the homestead exemption is less than $125,000, the lower state limit applies.

In general, the greater the difference between the market value of your home and your mortgage debt, the more likely it is that the Chapter 7 trustee will find it worthwhile to take over your home and sell it for the benefit of creditors. Take the example of the house in Colorado given above, but now assume that its market value is $190,000, not $125,000. If the house is taken over by the trustee and sold for the benefit of the bankruptcy estate, the funds available for unsecured creditors would amount to $70,000:

Selling Price	$190,000
Less: Mortgage Loan	$75,000
Value of Your Equity	$115,000
Less: Homestead Exemption	$45,000
Available for Unsecured Creditors	$70,000

 TALKING TO A LAWYER

Q. My lender has filed suit to foreclose my home. Will bankruptcy stop that suit?

A. Yes. A bankruptcy may stop the foreclosure, at least temporarily, and assuming this is not your third bankruptcy case within a year. Upon the filing of a bankruptcy petition, an automatic stay ordinarily comes into effect. However, in Chapter 7 cases the automatic stay may just prolong the eventual foreclosure unless you and the holder of the mortgage can work out a satisfactory arrangement. When the discharge is granted, it is likely that the holder of the mortgage will again try to foreclose, assuming that it hasn't done so already.

In Chapter 13 cases, the debtor-homeowner might be able to cure the defaults on the mortgage under the payment plan and maintain ongoing payments. If so, the Chapter 13 debtor may be able to save the home from foreclosure. For this reason, Chapter 13 has been referred to as a "save the home" chapter. Chapter 13 offers broader and more effective ways of dealing with the possibility of foreclosure than does Chapter 7.

—**Answer by Judge David S. Kennedy, U.S. Bankruptcy Court, Western District of Tennessee**

A. Yes, bankruptcy can stop the foreclosure process in the short term. In order to retain your home in the long term, however, you need to be able to cure the arrears due to your mortgage company over a three- to five-year period—that is, make up in full all missed payments. In a Chapter 13 case, you must be able to make your payments to the Chapter 13 trustee each month—a portion of which will be used to repay the lender for your missed payments—*and* be able to continue making regular ongoing, mortgage payments. Bankruptcy may also be an effective way to buy some time in which to sell your home before foreclosure takes place, though the price you receive for your home may be reduced on account of the pending bankruptcy case. If you have equity in your home above and beyond your state exemptions and any cost of sale, a Chapter 7 trustee may be interested in selling your home for you—but again, the price you fetch will likely be lower than it would be if you had not filed for bankruptcy.

—**Answer by Shayna M. Steinfeld, Steinfeld &
Steinfeld, P.C., Atlanta, Georgia**

Q. *What effect will bankruptcy have on my ability to get a mortgage in the future?*

A. In my experience, future credit depends more on the phase of the moon than anything else. I have had several clients refinance houses out of Chapter 13 when they were current on their Chapter 13 payments.

Mortgage brokers have told me that it is possible to get a mortgage within two years of a Chapter 7 discharge. On the other hand, I have had other clients who found it incredibly difficult to obtain new credit under any circumstances.

—**Answer by Marc S. Stern, Law Offices of
Marc S. Stern, Seattle, Washington**

A. The bankruptcy filing is a matter of public record. Most home mortgage lenders want to know why you had to file for bankruptcy. Was it due to a job loss, health issues, or a divorce? Do you now have a steady job? Are you now a good credit risk? It's a matter of your convincing the mortgage lender that you are a potentially good customer and credit risk. Watch out for unusually high interest rates or lots of points.

—**Answer by Judge David S. Kennedy, U.S. Bankruptcy
Court, Western District of Tennessee**

A. It is likely that the bankruptcy will not prevent you from getting a mortgage in the future, but it will greatly increase the cost of that mortgage once you get it (e.g., instead of a prime-plus-3-percent rate, you may be saddled with a prime-plus-8-percent rate). If you are proceeding in a Chapter 13 case, you may not incur debt during the bankruptcy process without court approval, including a mortgage.

—Answer by Shayna M. Steinfeld, Steinfeld & Steinfeld, P.C., Atlanta, Georgia

Of course, determining equity is not a precise science. It depends on the selling price of your home—and how can you know that before it is sold? In your bankruptcy filings, it may be in your best interest to estimate the lowest possible sale price for your home, thus making the sale of your home a less attractive option for the trustee. For example, to determine your equity in the home, you could deduct its sale costs, such as a typical realtor's fee, which could seemingly knock 6 to 8 percent off its value. Or you could determine the value of your home using foreclosure results (typically about 80 percent of retail value), which could make your home seem to be worth about 20 percent less. Or you might make reference to a tax-assessed value that is relatively low. A recent federal bankruptcy court in Alabama wrote: "Tax assessments are generally considered inaccurately low as evidence of the value of the real property assessed," *In Re Moulton*, 393 B.R. 752 (N.D. Ala. 2008). These can all be useful strategies for making your estimated equity in your home seem as low as possible, thus making it less likely that the home will be sold to satisfy creditors. In all cases, however, your estimates must be honest and in good faith or serious penalties await.

In a few states, such as Florida, there is no dollar limit on the homestead exemption, only a limit on the acreage that can be shielded from creditors. In Texas, unsecured creditors cannot seek payment from a homestead, so long as that homestead is not larger than one acre (in a city) or two hundred acres (anywhere else), regardless of the value of the property. These generous ex-

WHAT IF THE FORECLOSURE ISN'T ENOUGH?

A lender who recovers less from the sale of your house than the amount that you owe will have an unsecured claim for the difference between the two amounts. Thus, if your mortgage debt was $100,000 and the sale of your house garnered only $90,000, you could be on the hook for the additional $10,000, especially if you are not in bankruptcy. Such a deficiency judgment puts the person on the hook for the difference between the market value of the house and the amount of the loan. In the above example, there is a deficiency judgment for $10,000. Depending on what state you live in, the creditor could assert a claim for that amount and try to recover it from your other assets. In some states, a confirmation action in state court is required to verify the foreclosing mortgage company's entitlement to such a deficiency claim. In most states, there is a limited right to a deficiency depending on the method of foreclosure. The point is that even if a person files bankruptcy, a court may not discharge a deficiency judgment.

emptions are permitted, even in light of the federal lid, provided that you purchased your home more than 1,215 days prior to filing for bankruptcy. However, if you purchased the home less than 1,215 days before the bankruptcy, the maximum homestead exemption allowed under federal bankruptcy law is $125,000. However, a homestead owner must still make required monthly payments to the bank that is financing his home—even for a $2 million townhouse in downtown Dallas or a home in Palm Beach. Note that a few states, such as Delaware, don't allow for any homestead exemption.

CHAPTER 13

To preserve your home under a Chapter 13 plan, you ordinarily must agree to continue your lender's lien on your home and to make the required ongoing monthly payments. You must also

KEEP THOSE PAYMENTS UP

To avoid losing your home under Chapter 13, you must make your regular monthly payments to the Chapter 13 trustee *and* make all future monthly mortgage payments as they become due after the filing. If you've skipped some mortgage payments before you filed your Chapter 13 bankruptcy, you can put the delinquent mortgage payments under the Chapter 13 plan. If the loan was made after 1994, then you do not need to pay interest on the delinquency. In other words, you can spread the missed mortgage payments out and cure the default. However, to be sure of keeping your home, you must also make the *future* monthly payments on your home mortgage loan as they come due. If you don't, you may have to turn your home over to the lender.

agree to pay any skipped payments (defaults) through your payment plan. Otherwise, you'll have to turn the property over to the lender.

It is possible that if housing values are greatly depressed, a lender might be willing to lower your monthly payments in order to gain some income and keep the house occupied. But don't count on it.

REMEMBER THIS

• Under either Chapter 7 or Chapter 13, you will not be able to keep your home if you don't make the required monthly payments on your mortgage after the filing.

• Whether the trustee will actually take your home will depend upon two basic factors: how much equity is in the home and how much of the home's value is sheltered by law from creditors.

• Often, there is a homestead exemption with a dollar amount that is shielded from creditors, but don't assume that you will be able to keep your home simply because you file for bankruptcy.

• Remember that bankruptcy law caps the homestead exemption at $125,000 in all states for houses purchased up to 1,215 days before filing, unless you rolled over an interest from another house you owned in the same state. Of course, if the state exemption is less than $125,000, the lower exemption applies.

• With your home on the line, you're well advised to discuss your situation with a bankruptcy lawyer.

CHAPTER 21
Getting Help

Susan knows she needs help with her credit cards and debt load. She has stayed on top of her bills, but she is dangerously close to falling behind. Susan would like to get help, but she doesn't know where to start. Does she need to talk to an attorney? If she does, how does she find one? What happens if she ends up in bankruptcy, where can she turn then?

Throughout this book, we've provided you with information and resources to help you find additional information on a variety of topics associated with credit and bankruptcy. But there are still other resources for you to explore. Some may have been mentioned in previous chapters, but we think they're still the best places for you to start. Also included are some reminders and tips you can use to go about finding additional information.

This chapter first looks at how to find a lawyer and what to expect when you are working with a lawyer, both in regards to fees and what the lawyer will need from you. Then, we turn to both credit and bankruptcy, providing you some general resources and tips. For more specific resources on a topic-specific basis, turn to The World at Your Fingertips section immediately following.

ATTORNEYS: FINDING ONE, WORKING WITH ONE

Finding the right attorney can be half the battle during any legal situation. In the United States, "lawyer" is a specific term used to refer to a licensed professional who advises and represents people in legal matters. A lawyer has two main duties: to uphold the law and to protect a client's rights. In order to do this successfully, a lawyer needs not only to understand the law, but also to be an effective communicator.

Not just anyone can call him or herself a lawyer. To understand how laws and the legal system work, lawyers require special schooling. Each state has standards that a person must meet before obtaining a license to practice law there. Before being allowed to practice law in most states, a person must:

- have a bachelor's degree or its equivalent;
- complete three years at an ABA-accredited law school;
- pass a state bar examination, which usually lasts for two or three days and tests knowledge in selected areas of law;
- pass required tests on professional ethics and responsibility;
- be approved by a committee that investigates character and background;
- swear an oath, usually to uphold the state and federal law and constitutions; and
- obtain a license from the highest court in the state, usually the state supreme court.

Finding a Credit or Bankruptcy Attorney

Not every legal situation requires the help of an attorney. However, if you have decided that you do in fact need the assistance of an attorney, the best place to start is to ask for recommendations from a trusted friend, relative, or business associate. However, be aware that your case is likely different and that a lawyer who is right for someone else may not suit you or your legal problem.

Most communities also offer referral services to help people find lawyers. You might be able to find them under "Lawyer Referral Service" or some similar heading in your yellow pages. These services usually recommend a lawyer in the area to evaluate a situation.

Bar associations in most communities also make referrals for attorneys who focus their practice in credit or bankruptcy. Many referral services have competency requirements for lawyers who wish to receive such referrals. You can find your local bar association in the phone book's white pages either under your community's name ("Centerville Bar Association") or under your county's name ("Cass County Bar Association"). You can also find your bar's website through your favorite search engine or through the ABA's website (see The World at Your Fingertips section, page 309).

Be careful when it comes to advertising. You can't always believe what you read or see on television. Newspaper, telephone directory, radio, and television ads, along with direct mail, can familiarize you with lawyers in your area who frequently work in the area of credit and bankruptcy. But keep in mind that a specific attorney may not be right for your situation or may claim to be "specialized" in bankruptcy, even though such a specialization isn't available in your state.

The lawyer you decide to work with should be one that you are comfortable with. The lawyer will be helping you solve some very personal issues, so you should feel comfortable enough telling him or her honestly and completely all of the facts related to your finances and spending. When selecting the lawyer for you, don't rely on what you hear or read. Judge the lawyer for yourself—only you can determine which lawyer is best for your situation.

Before you hire an attorney, you should be able to meet with him or her briefly or talk over the phone so that the two of you can get acquainted. This meeting is a chance to talk with the lawyer

 WHEN DO I NEED AN ATTORNEY?

If your debts are mounting and you find yourself falling behind or if you receive many a creditor notice or threat, it likely is time to consult an attorney to consider the possibility of filing bankruptcy—either Chapter 7 or Chapter 13. Many people are intimidated by the legal system or lawyers, but you should not be. A good lawyer can be the best advocate for you to help you navigate through a most difficult time for you and your family.

before making a final hiring decision. In many cases, there is no fee charged for an initial consultation. However, to be on the safe side, ask about fees before setting up your first appointment.

Legal Fees

Many bankruptcy attorneys will charge a flat fee for Chapter 7 and Chapter 13 cases. A flat fee means that they charge a specific amount (as opposed to charging by the hour). The fee for Chapter 7 cases will be less than the fees for a Chapter 13 case, as Chapter 13 cases generally are more complicated and extensive. Most of the time, there are more assets in play during a Chapter 13 case, as most Chapter 7 filings are no-asset filings (as discussed in chapter 16).

Some lawyers may be flexible on the time period for payment of the flat fee. For example, they may allow clients to pay the fee in installments. Again, most attorneys offer a free initial consultation. Make sure you ask up front about the fee arrangements. Attorneys are required under rules of professional conduct to charge reasonable fees—not exorbitant or excessive fees. One factor relevant in determining whether an attorney's fees are reasonable is the local, customary rate for similar legal services in the area. You may want to call and ask several attorney offices what their standard rates are for a bankruptcy case.

STARTING POINTS: CREDIT

There's definitely no shortage of credit-related sites on the Internet, but finding good, credible sources can be tricky. So you owe it to yourself to check out the sources we've culled below. Some of these websites are housed within larger sites, but they do contain detailed sections on topics associated with credit and personal finance. You're bound to find what you're looking for at one of these sites, or from a link at one of these sites (please note that they are not arranged in order of preference):

Federal Citizen Information Center—www.pueblo.gsa.gov

Downloadable articles on topics ranging from disputing credit report errors to getting credit when you're over the age of sixty-two. Click on "Money," or do a search for "credit." In the credit section, there are links to seven different articles on the following topics: ID theft, credit scoring, building better credit reports, consumer protection laws, choosing credit cards, and a general article on credit.

Federal Trade Commission—www.ftc.gov/bcp/menu-credit.htm

The FTC's site may be the best for consumers given its incredible breadth and depth of information. The FTC also continually puts out new information. For example, in December 2008, the FTC released a report talking about the use of Social Security numbers in identity theft. See www.ftc.gov/opa/2008/12/ssnreport.shtm.

The FTC's credit section includes articles and information presented in a variety of ways, including downloadable .PDFs and audio files. On the left-hand side of the page under "Consumer Categories," click on "Credit and Loans," and there are six categories covering topics such as credit reporting, debt management, credit scoring, and credit cards. There are also publications on the site dealing with credit and divorce, credit for seniors, and much more. Readers and consumers can access the site in Spanish.

The 'Lectric Law Library Lawcopedia's Banking, Finance & Credit Topic Area—www.lectlaw.com/tban.htm

This area of the 'Lectric Law Library's website includes articles on debt, credit and credit cards, loans and lenders, and scams and schemes. Helpful articles such as "Using Credit," "Complaining about Credit," and "How to Dispute Credit Reporting Errors" are included. Links to other pertinent areas of the 'Lectric Law Library are also included for easy reference.

Bankrate.com—www.bankrate.com

Bankrate.com offers one-stop shopping for tools and information to help consumers make the best financial decisions. The site includes information on credit cards and mortgages, as well as investments, banking, and taxes. The section on credit cards can be accessed at www.bankrate.com/brm/rate/cc_home .asp. It allows you to look for the best credit cards by comparing rates and offers.

CNN/Money—money.cnn.com

This site from CNN and *Money* magazine features a large section on personal finance that includes articles and tips on salient topics, such as credit and debt and college. Also featured is "Money 101," an interactive course on managing all your finances. It also contains links to articles about breaking news on the economic front.

Consumer World—www.consumerworld.org

This site, run by consumer lawyer/advocate/educator Edgar Dworsky, features numerous links to agencies, articles, and other resources on all things consumer-related. See the "Money" section for information on credit and banking, but also check out the general "Consumer Resources" area for a plethora of other pertinent information.

National Consumer Law Center—www.consumerlaw.org

The NCLC works to protect consumers and promote marketplace justice; publications and information about initiatives (such as credit discrimination, predatory mortgage reform, and student loans) abound at this site. Look for the section on the left titled "Homeownership and Consumer Credit." If a reader clicks on that, she will find articles on predatory lending, payday loans, debt collection, and more.

Suze Orman's Resource Center—www.suzeorman.com

The website of renowned personal-finance expert Suze Orman, the Resource Center includes a nice selection of links organized by topic area and features "Suze's Dictionary," a glossary of terms.

SafeBorrowing.com—www.safeborrowing.com

Developed by the American Bar Association, this site is geared toward helping consumers borrow safely when shopping for mortgage loans and reducing unfair mortgage-lending practices through information and education. The section on credit cards—www.safeborrowing.com/creditcards/home.shtml—is particularly helpful.

Credit Info Center—www.creditinfocenter.com

This site was started by a software-engineer-turned-loan officer-turned-software-engineer-again, and contains many helpful articles and links on topics such as consumer information, credit cards, mortgages, and loans. There are sections on credit repair, credit reporting, credit cards, and ID theft that are easy to navigate.

Open Directory's Personal Finance Information—
www.dmoz.org/Home/Personal_Finance

The Open Directory Project's website features a vast number of links relating to personal finance. Topics include identity theft issues, mortgages, loans, and debt and bankruptcy.

About.com's Credit/Debt Management—www.credit.about.com

This site includes articles and resources on debt counseling, debt reduction, credit law, fraud, getting credit, and more.

A Novel Idea: Read More About It

While none of the books listed below is actually a novel, each one makes for informative and valuable reading. Here are a few picks with which to start—though there are many, many more—on a variety of topics having to do with credit. Don't forget to check out what your local library has to offer in addition to Amazon.com and other online bookstores.

How You Can Profit from Credit Cards: Using Credit to Improve Your Financial Life and Bottom Line (FT Press, 2008).

Credit Scores and Credit Reports 3rd ed: How The System Really Works, What You Can Do (Privacy Times, 2007).

Personal Bankruptcy Laws for Dummies, by James P. Caher and John M. Caher (2d. ed. 2006, Wiley Publishing).

Your Credit Score: How to Fix, Improve, and Protect the 3-Digit Number that Shapes Your Financial Future, by Liz Pulliam Weston (Prentice Hall, 2004).

Mortgages for Dummies, by Eric Tyson and Ray Brown (For Dummies, 1999).

The Budget Kit: The Common Cents Money Management Workbook (Fourth Edition), by Judy Lawrence (Dearborn Trade, A Kaplan Professional Company, 2004).

Pay It Down! From Debt to Wealth on $10 a Day, by Jean Sherman Chatzky (Portfolio, 2004).

Rich Dad's Advisors®: The ABC's of Getting Out of Debt: Turn Bad Debt into Good Debt and Bad Credit into Good Credit, by Garrett Sutton (Warner Business Books, 2004).

The Fragile Middle Class, by Teresa A. Sullivan, Elizabeth Warren, and Jay Lawrence Westbrook (Yale University Press, 2000). A revealing study of why consumers go bankrupt.

Taming the Sharks, by Christopher L. Peterson (University of Akron Press, 2004). A study of consumers and the high cost of credit.

STARTING POINTS: BANKRUPTCY

There is one caveat before we get to these resources: The best source for you could be a qualified bankruptcy attorney in your state who can provide individualized legal advice that is current on both applicable federal and state law.

Go For Broke: Eight Websites To Get You Started

While there's not exactly a dearth of bankruptcy- and debt-related sites on the Internet, finding good, credible sources can be somewhat challenging. Go for broke and check out the sources we've culled below. Some of these websites are housed within larger sites, but they do contain rather lengthy sections on topics associated with bankruptcy and debt. You're bound to find what you're looking for at one of these sites or from a link featured on one of these sites. (Please note that they are not arranged in order of preference.)

BankruptcyAction.com—www.bankruptcyaction.com: An extensive site featuring information in a question-and-answer format on a variety of topics associated with bankruptcy, such as: bankruptcy discharge, debt consolidation, secured credit cards, and rebuilding credit after bankruptcy. The site also includes a selection of audio clips (in the "Audio Answers" section), forms you can use with your bankruptcy lawyer, and more. The home page of this site contains a map of the United States and allows you to click on your individual state to find potential lawyers to assist you with your legal issues.

American Bankruptcy Institute—www.abiworld.org: Click on "Consumer Education Center" to access FAQs and a host of resources about bankruptcy. For example, one of the FAQs is titled "Should I file for bankruptcy?" It then lists a "Considering Bankruptcy Checklist," which is helpful. Other topic areas include Chapter 7, Chapter 13, and filing for bankruptcy. Suggestions for further reading are also featured. The ABI's website also contains several publications explaining the ramifications of the new bankruptcy law. They are accessible at abiworld.net/bankbill/index.html. Note that some of the materials from the American Bankruptcy Institute are not free.

Cornell's Legal Information Institute: Bankruptcy—www.law.cornell.edu/topics/bankruptcy.html: This LII site about bankruptcy law includes texts of federal and state statutes and federal and state judicial decisions. Be sure to visit the "Law About

Commerce" section (featuring such subsections as "Debtor" and "Creditor") to find other topics of interest.

I Hate Debt—www.ihatedebt.com: An extensive website run by Tom Allen, who also hosts the "I Hate Debt" radio show. This site contains information on everything from the history of debt to steps you can take to get out of debt, as well as a monthly newsletter for which you can sign up. Visit the "I Hate Debt Radio Show" section to listen to the live show, or check out past shows. These shows feature experts who cover a variety of topics, including debt negotiation, kids and money, dealing with creditor harassment, and more. The "I Hate Debt" site now also has a blog at blog.ihatedebt.com that provides even more information to consumers.

U.S. Bankruptcy Courts—www.uscourts.gov/bankruptcy-courts.html: This site of the Federal Judiciary features "Bankruptcy Basics," a downloadable seventy-seven-page booklet that covers discharge in bankruptcy, liquidation, individual debt adjustment, terminology, and more. The booklet comes in two versions—for bankruptcies filed before the new bankruptcy law (before October 17, 2005) and those filed after the passage of the new law. Most readers would need to make sure they click on the version "for cases filed on or after October 17, 2005." The site includes statistics and links to courts around the country.

Nolo.com—www.nolo.com: Click on "Property and Money" and then "Credit Repair and Debt" to access articles and information on a variety of topics, including overspending, strategies for repaying debts, student loans, and credit repair. Financial calculator tools are also available.

Commerce Clearing House—www.cch.com/bankruptcy/Bankruptcy_04-21.pdf: A very readable source of information about the bankruptcy law passed in October 2005, which as the preceding pages have emphasized, has changed bankruptcy law.

For those interested in obtaining more information and commentary about current bankruptcy law issues, consider a bankruptcy blog, such as "The Bankruptcy Lawyers Blog" at blog.startfreshtoday.com. For instance, it contains information about a recent study from the New York Federal Reserve Board titled "Seismic Effects of Bankruptcy Reform" that claims that the 2005 bankruptcy law helped lead to the current foreclosure crisis in the country.

DON'T FORGET. . .

It's To Your Credit, Don't Forget It . . .

While websites and books are great places to get information, you might also want to see if any local venues are offering courses, lectures, seminars, or expert panels relating to the topics of personal finance, credit, debt, and so forth. Check with your local library, bar association, colleges, and senior citizens' centers (to name just a few) to see if anything is in the works. Your local radio and TV stations might also provide some salient programming. And if you can, be sure to check out the plethora of informative programs on national TV; they can be found on such cable channels as CNBC and CNNfn and often feature finance television personalities such as Lou Dobbs and Suze Orman. If you're not a cable subscriber, many of these shows and channels also have websites.

And don't forget to look beyond libraries, TV, and radio. Countless message boards, user groups, mailing lists, and chat rooms exist on the Internet—many of these could help you in your quest for knowledge and provide a "been there, done that" perspective from others about the issues you're facing. Communicating with others who have been in your position is a great way to learn about other avenues to explore and what pitfalls to avoid. Some websites may also provide an area where you can send in your questions and get answers. And many of the sites associated with debt and bankruptcy include online tools (e.g., forms, calculators) you can use for free.

That's about all for now. You owe it to yourself to begin checking out the resources we've provided.

How to Resolve Credit Disputes

What if you believe that a credit grantor has treated you improperly? Resolving the problem involves a sequence of four possible steps, each one more aggressive than the other, though the first two steps are generally sufficient to solve most disputes.

1. Check to be sure that you have the correct information regarding your rights under the law and the credit grantor's obligations to you under the law. In addition to the information included in this book, this appendix provides information about other resources that you may wish to review.

2. Contact the creditor by phone. By talking to the creditor, you can get information about why the matter was handled in the way it was handled. Or you might just find that the creditor will take steps to satisfy you even if there hasn't been any violation of law. It's always a good idea to follow up by letter. Be sure to provide your name, address, account number, and a statement of your concern. If your initial contact is by telephone, get the name of the person with whom you talked. To compete effectively, most credit grantors wish to keep good customers by settling complaints fairly and quickly. Nonetheless, create a "paper trail" by keeping a written record or log of all of your contacts with the creditor. If you are not satisfied with the first response to your complaint or if you feel that the first person you talk to lacks authority to resolve your problem, ask to speak to a manager or write a letter to a senior executive, such as the creditor's president or a senior vice president.

3. If you are not satisfied with the resolution offered by the creditor, based on your study of your rights under the law, the next step is to contact any state or federal agency that regulates your creditor. It is best to write the appropriate agency and to supply a copy of the written record that you have maintained. By sending a copy of the letter to your creditor, you may focus attention on your complaint. While the regulatory agency may re-

quire some time to get to your problem, it will often be able to arrange a solution that will be satisfactory to you. Descriptions of the various regulatory agencies that might be involved, and their addresses, can be found in appendix B.

4. If the regulatory agency fails to satisfy you, you can hire your own attorney to pursue the matter. However, if you do not win, you might be liable for your attorney's fees. In some cases this may be true even if you do win. Most attorneys will offer an initial consultation free of charge and will tell you if you appear to have a good case that is worth pursuing.

Appendix B outlines various government agencies and other resources that can be useful to you in step three of the resolution procedure detailed above. If you are looking for more information or want to file a complaint, the best place to start is likely the appropriate state or federal agency. If a financial institution has violated the law, the regulatory agency that oversees that category of institutions might be able to help you.

APPENDIX B

The World At Your Fingertips

This resource aims to provide you with up-to-date, relevant information and resources to help you and your family understand your rights and responsibilities when it comes to credit and bankruptcy.

We start off by listing offices, agencies, and general resources as starting points. Then, we list some resources specifically chapter-by-chapter.

GENERAL RESOURCES

Federal courts—the main access points for the various levels of the federal court system, including district courts and bankruptcy courts: (202) 502-2600 or www.uscourts.gov.

Federal government—a comprehensive listing of U.S. government links: (800) FED-INFO or www.usa.gov.

Federal Trade Commission (FTC)—the federal agency charged with protecting consumers: 1-877-FTC-HELP or www.ftc.gov.

Local consumer protection agencies—You can find the addresses and telephone numbers for consumer protection offices in your local telephone directory. You also can find them online at www.consumeraction.gov/state.shtml.

Federal Reserve—the central bank of the United States: www.federalreserve.gov.

Internal Revenue Service (IRS)—the federal tax agency: (800) 829-1040 or www.irs.gov.

National Consumer Law Center—consumer protection advocacy group: (202) 452-6252 or www.consumerlaw.org.

Credit Reporting Bureaus—the three major nationwide credit reporting agencies (these are the people to call to see your credit report and report any problems):
- Equifax: (888) 766-0008 or www.equifax.com
- Experian: (888) 397-3742 or www.experian.com
- TransUnion: (800) 888-4213 www.transunion.com
    You can also order a copy of your credit report, for free, at www.annualcreditreport.com.

American Bar Association (ABA)—offers information on legal topics generally, on where to find a lawyer, and on where to find additional information and resources: www.abanet.org.

ABA Legal Services Referral—links to state and local lawyer referral services: www.findlegalhelp.org.

Federal Citizen Information Center—government office charged with housing an array of information and resources about the U.S. government, including information for consumers and on money: (888) 878-3256 or www.pueblo.gsa.gov.

Nolo.com—web-based resource for "do-it-yourself" books and guides for legal topics, including bankruptcy—(800) 728-3555 or www.nolo.com.

Chapter 1–Dealing with Debt
- The FTC has a publication titled "Knee Deep in Debt" that is available online at www.ftc.gov/bcp/edu/pubs/consumer/credit/cre19.shtm.
- Our Family Place provides information on developing a budget on its website at www.ourfamilyplace.com; click on "Budgets and Finances."
- Author Dave Ramsey, the head of Lampo Group, Inc., has a website that may be worth a look if you feel you need help in

developing a budget and getting out of debt, at www.daveramsey
.com.

• The Legal Information Institute gives a brief overview of
consumer credit and provides links to relevant legislation and
to other consumer credit sites, at www.law.cornell.edu/topics/
consumer_credit.html.

Chapter 2–Credit: What Is It and What Does It Cost?

• The Federal Citizen Information Center runs a website ded-
icated to consumer credit information at www.consumeraction
.gov. This site offers news and tips for consumers interested in
obtaining credit.

• The Federal Reserve has many publications related to credit
available on its website at www.federalreserve.gov/consumers
.htm. These guides include ones on understanding mortgages,
credit cards, and how the Federal Reserve can help consumers.

• The Federal Trade Commission has a consumer protection
website on credit with a long list of publications available online, from "Avoiding Credit and Charge Card Fraud" to "Understanding Vehicle Financing" to "Building a Better Credit
Report." This site also has links to important federal laws, and
is at www.ftc.gov/bcp/consumer.shtm.

• MsMoney.com has a section on credit, which provides
some good practical information: www.msmoney.com/mm/
banking/credit/crupdown_intro.htm.

Chapter 3–Your Right to Equal Credit

• The text of the Equal Credit Opportunity Act is available on
the U.S. Department of Justice's website at www.usdoj.gov/crt/
housing/documents/ecoafulltext_5-1-06.php.

• The U.S. Department of Justice's Civil Rights Division does
a great deal of work around the Equal Credit Opportunity Act.
Its website provides information and links regarding equal
credit rights: www.usdoj.gov/crt/housing/housing_ecoa.php.

• The Federal Trade Commission has an FTC Facts for Consumers publication titled "Equal Credit Opportunity" available
at www2.ftc.gov/bcp/edu/pubs/consumer/credit/cre15.pdf.

• myFico, a website run by FairIsaac's offers an overview of your credit rights at www.myfico.com/CreditEducation/Rights/CreditApplicationRights.aspx.

• The Federal Reserve Bank of Boston has an excellent publication titled "Closing the Gap" that discusses the Equal Credit Opportunity Act. It is accessible at www.bos.frb.org/commdev/commaff/closingt.pdf.

Chapter 4–Applying for Credit

• The Federal Trade Commission has a publication titled "Getting Credit," available online at www.ftc.gov/bcp/conline/edcams/gettingcredit.

• The Federal Trade Commission has a short report titled "Credit and Divorce" that is available online at www.ftc.gov/bcp/edu/pubs/consumer/credit/cre08.shtm.

• The Federal Trade Commission also has a publication on credit insurance titled "Credit Insurance: Is It For You?" available online at www.ftc.gov/bcp/edu/pubs/consumer/alerts/alt118.shtm.

Chapter 5–Applying for a Credit Card (and Choosing the Right Card)

• The Federal Reserve Board website contains useful information about choosing a credit card at www.federalreserve.gov/pubs/SHOP/default.htm.

• The Federal Trade Commission provides another useful publication warning consumers about paying close attention to the terms and conditions found in credit card solicitations. The publication is titled "Credit Cards: The Deal Is In the Disclosure" at www.ftc.gov/bcp/edu/pubs/consumer/credit/cre05.shtm.

• Cardtrak is a resource that provides information—APRs, annual fees, and so on—about different credit cards and is a useful tool when shopping for a credit card, at www.cardweb.com/cardtrak. Other websites like www.kiplinger.com provide similar information. In addition, many large banks offer information on their websites about the cards they offer.

• For a detailed overview of credit cards, from their history to the meaning of all types of charges, see www.money .howstuffworks.com/credit-card1.htm.

• For an excellent resource from Fair Isaac explaining credit scoring, see www.myfico.com/CreditEducation/CreditScores .aspx.

• The Federal Trade Commission has information on your financial privacy rights, available online at www.ftc.gov/privacy/ privacyinitiatives/glbact.html.

• There are server places online where consumers can get information that will help them choose a credit card including:
  • Cardweb: www.cardweb.com
  • Bankrate: www.bankrate.com
  • CreditCardSearchEngine: www.creditcardsearch engine.com

• The American Bankers Association offers a Credit Card Guide that explains credit card basics and how to choose a card at www.aba.com/ABAEF. Click on "Consumers" to find their resources.

Chapter 6–How to Correct Billing Mistakes

• The Federal Trade Commission provides information on the Fair Credit Billing Act. The text of the law is found at www .ftc.gov/os/statutes/fcb/fcb.pdf and a sample letter that could be copied and sent to a credit reporting agency, at www.ftc.gov/ bcp/edu/pubs/consumer/credit/cre21.shtm.

• The Federal Trade Commission also has a helpful publication for consumers that discusses the Fair Credit Billing Act, titled "Billed for Merchandise You Never Received? Here's What To Do," at www.ftc.gov/bcp/edu/pubs/consumer/credit/ cre28.shtm.

• The Colorado State University Cooperative Extension published a paper on credit cards that explains consumers' rights under the Fair Credit Billing Act, including when defective goods are purchased on credit cards. It is available at www.ext.colostate.edu/pubs/consumer/09144.pdf.

• 'Lectric Law Library provides a concise overview for consumers confronted with billing errors, available online at www.lectlaw.com/files/cos73.htm.

Chapter 7–Credit Records

• The text of the Fair Credit Reporting Act (FCRA) can be found online at www.ftc.gov/os/statutes/031224fcra.pdf.

• The Federal Trade Commission publishes a useful summary of your rights under the Fair Credit Reporting Act, which includes information on whom to contact in the event of a complaint, at www.ftc.gov/os/2004/07/040709fcraappxf.pdf.

• The Federal Reserve Board has a section on credit histories and records in its Consumer Handbook to Credit Protection Laws, at www.federalreserve.gov/pubs/consumerhdbk/histories.htm.

• The three credit reporting agencies, TransUnion, Equifax, and Experian (contact information is listed above), offer a great deal of information regarding your credit record, how to order a copy, how to dispute mistakes, and understanding what it means.

• A free copy of your credit report can be obtained once a year at www.annualcreditreport.com.

• The Fair and Accurate Credit Transactions Act of 2003 amended the FCRA in numerous ways. For an overview and summary of these amendments, see the National Consumer Law Center's summary of the law at www.nclc.org/initiatives/facta/contents/nclc_analysis_content.html.

• The Consumer Data Industry Association provides general information for consumers on credit reporting and the laws governing the credit reporting industry at www.cdiaonline.org; click on "Consumer Info."

• The Federal Trade Commission provides information on how to obtain free credit reports, as well as general information about consumers' rights under the Fair Credit Reporting Act at www.ftc.gov and by searching "free credit report" in the search field.

Chapter 8—**Electronic Payments and Credit**

• The Electronic Payments Association has a website that provides a great deal of helpful information to consumers, including a variety of tips for avoiding losses from electronic payments, at www.nacha.org.

• The Federal Trade Commission has a host of publications available online to help consumers understand e-commerce. These include:

• "Credit, ATM and Debit Cards: What to do if They're Lost or Stolen," available at www.ftc.gov/bcp/edu/pubs/consumer/credit/cre04.shtm.

• "A Consumer's Guide to E-Payments," available at www.ftc.gov/bcp/edu/pubs/consumer/tech/tec01.shtm.

• "FTC Facts for Consumers: E–Checks (Electronic Check Conversion)," available at www.ftc.gov/bcp/edu/pubs/consumer/credit/cre31.shtm.

Chapter 9—**Identity Theft**

• For a good article that compares and contrasts several identity theft statutes, see "Identity Theft Statutes: Which Will Protect Americans the Most?" by Catherine Pastrikos, 67 Albany Law Review 1137 (2004).

• For another excellent article on identity theft, see Holly K. Towle, "Identity Theft: Myths, Methods, and New Law," 30 Rutgers Computer & Tech. Law Journal 237 (2004).

• If you believe you have been the victim of identity theft, call the Federal Trade Commission's Identity Theft Hotline's toll-free number, 877-IDTHEFT (877-438-4338).

• For information about the President's Task Force on Identity Theft and its 2008 report, see www.idtheft.gov. For a copy of the Task Force's 70-page report, see www.idtheft.gov/reports/IDTReport2008.pdf.

• The Federal Trade Commission has published an informative booklet, "Identity Theft: What's It All About?," to warn consumers about the dangers of identity theft. This booklet is available online at www.ftc.gov/bcp/edu/pubs/consumer/idtheft/idt08.shtm.

• Another potential source for consumers worried about identity theft is the nonprofit organization the Identity Theft Assistance Center at www.identitytheftassistance.org.

• The Identity Theft Resource Center (www.idtheftcenter.org) offers information on ID theft statistics, as well as ways to protect yourself and what to do if you are a victim.

Chapter 10–**Unfair Lending**

• The Federal Trade Commission has a publication on payday loans titled "Payday Loans = Costly Cash" that is accessible online at www.ftc.gov/bcp/edu/pubs/consumer/alerts/alt060.shtm.

• The Federal Trade Commission also has congressional testimony from one of its officials regarding the dangers of predatory lending, available online at www.ftc.gov/os/2000/05/predatorytestimony.htm.

• The U.S. Department of Housing and Urban Development warns against predatory lending on its website, www.hud.gov. It specifically addresses the subject at www.hud.gov/offices/hsg/sfh/pred/predlend.cfm.

• The Joint Center for Housing Studies at Harvard University has an excellent white paper on the issue of whether federal regulation contributes to unfair lending, available online at www.jchs.harvard.edu/publications/finance/babc/babc_04-21.pdf.

• The Center for Responsible Lending has information on predatory lending available online at www.responsiblelending.org.

• The National Consumer Law Center has information available on its website about payday loans and mortgage reform; visit www.consumerlaw.org/initiatives/payday_loans/index.shtml.

• NeighborWorks has many resources on predatory lending at www.nw.org/network/comstrat/predatoryLending/nwresources.asp.

Chapter 11–**Mortgage/Home Equity Loans**

• The Federal Trade Commission has an excellent publication on mortgages titled "Looking for the Best Mortgage: Shop, Compare, Negotiate." See www.ftc.gov/bcp/edu/pubs/consumer/homes/rea09.shtm.

- The U.S. Department of Housing and Urban Development has an excellent resource page devoted to the Real Estate Settlement Procedures Act. See www.hud.gov and search "RESPA."
- The Federal Trade Commission has numerous publications regarding home equity loans. Go to www.ftc.gov and search for any of the following:
  - "Home Equity Credit Lines";
  - "Home Equity Loans: The Three-Day Cancel";
  - "Home Equity Loans: Borrowers Beware!";
  - "Shopping for a Home Equity Loan?";
  - "Need a Loan? Think Twice about Using Your Home as Collateral"; and
  - "Putting Your Home On the Loan Line."
- The Federal Reserve also has numerous publications on mortgages that can be accessed on its websites (www.federal reserve.gov) by clicking on "Consumer Information."

Chapter 12–Auto Financing and Leasing

- There are several informative websites available to consumers that provide information about car values and prices. These include: www.autosite.com, www.edmunds.com, and www.carprices.com.
- The Federal Trade Commission has published several booklets that help consumers learn more about the purchase of automobiles. Go to www.ftc.gov and search for any of the following:
  - "Buying a New Car";
  - "Understanding Vehicle Financing";
  - "Keys to Vehicle Leasing: Quick Consumer Guide"; and
  - "Vehicle Repossession."
- For information about the value of your trade-in vehicle and how much you can expect to get for it, consult the Kelley Blue Book value: www.kbb.com.
- The Consumer Justice Center provide information on leasing on the Consumer Leasing Act at www.consumerjusticecenter .com (click on "Legal Information").

Chapter 13–**Debt Collection and the Law**

• The Federal Trade Commission provides simple information on the Federal Debt Collection Practices Act and what debt collectors can and cannot do; go to www.ftc.gov and searching "fair debt collection."

• The FTC has a publication specifically devoted to the FDCPA (it provides the entire text of the law) at www.ftc.gov/bcp/edu/pubs/consumer/credit/cre27.pdf.

• Consumer Credit Counseling Services, nonprofit credit counseling services can be found online at www.cccsintl.org.

• If you have a complaint about a debt collector or a consumer credit reporting agency, contact your state department of consumer affairs or contact the FTC. The FTC has an online complaint form that can be accessed at its main site and clicking on "Consumer Complaint?"

Chapter 14–**Credit Counselors**

• The Federal Trade Commission's pamphlet "Fiscal Fitness," which informs consumers about credit counselors, is available online at www.ftc.gov/bcp/edu/pubs/consumer/credit/cre26.shtm.

• The Federal Trade Commission has a publication for consumers on credit repair, "Credit Repair: How To Help Yourself," available online at www.ftc.gov/bcp/edu/pubs/consumer/credit/cre13.shtm.

• Consumer Credit Counseling Services has resources on its website at www.cccsatl.org.

• To find credit counseling services that are approved by the U.S. Bankruptcy Trustee, visit www.usdoj.gov/ust, and click "Credit Counseling and Debtor Education."

Chapter 15–**Problem Debt**

• Myvesta.org, formerly known as Debt Counselors of America, offers an interactive website focusing on non-bankruptcy remedies such as debt consolidation; visit myvesta.org.

• Debt Advice is a major nonprofit site, affiliated with the National Foundation for Credit Counseling and offering much information for consumers; visit www.debtadvice.org. A Spanish site can also be accessed.

• Another nonprofit site is American Consumer Credit Counseling; visit www.consumercredit.com.

• DebtReliefUSA.net is a for-profit site that can help you reduce your debt; visit www.debtreliefusa.net.

• The National Foundation for Credit Counseling provides debt relief advice, credit counseling, and related services at www.nfcc.org.

Chapter 16–**Bankruptcy Defined**

• To find a certified bankruptcy lawyer, access the American Board of Certification website at www.abcworld.org/abchome.html.

• To understand more about bankruptcy, access the U.S. Bankruptcy Code and bankruptcy rules at www.thebankruptcysite.com/bankruptcy_law.htm.

• For bankruptcy basics and forms, access the site of the U.S. Bankruptcy Courts at www.uscourts.gov/bankruptcycourts.html.

• To find out what exemptions you are entitled to in your state, and whether you can choose between state or federal exemptions, click on "bankruptcy exemptions" at www.bankruptcyaction.com.

• Bankrate.com has an informative article titled "12 Myths about Bankruptcy." It is accessible online at www.bankrate.com/brm/news/debt/debt_manage_2004/bankruptcy-misconceptions.asp.

• The American Bankruptcy Institute runs a Consumer Bankruptcy Center (www.consumer.abiworld.org) that provides helpful tips when deciding whether to file bankruptcy and also how to find an attorney experienced in bankruptcy proceedings.

Chapter 17–**Straight Bankruptcy: Chapter 7**

• For a list of exemptions in different states, visit Bankruptcy Site.com at www.thebankruptcysite.com/what_do_i_keep.htm.

• The Nolo website features information on bankruptcy and automatic stays. Visit www.nolo.com/lawcenter/index.cfm and click on "Bankruptcy."

• For a Q & A on bankruptcy debts, access www.debtwipeout .com.

• A law firm from Arizona provides a detailed list of bankruptcy FAQs at www.doney.net/faq.htm.

• For a discussion of reaffirmation of debt in bankruptcy cases, visit www.mauilaw.com/article5.htm.

• You can download official bankruptcy forms for all types of bankruptcy from the U.S. courts website at www.uscourts.gov/bkforms.

• The U.S. courts website also has an excellent overview of Chapter 7 bankruptcy at www.uscourts.gov/bankruptcycourts/bankruptcybasics/chapter7.html.

• In addition, the U.S. Census bureau has information on the median state incomes. Visit www.census.gov and click on "State Median Income." (This is an important factor that can determine your eligibility for Chapter 7 bankruptcy.)

• Information on the "means test" can be found at the trustee's website (www.usdoj.gov/ust) by clicking on the link for the "Means Testing Information."

Chapter 18–Wage-Earner Bankruptcy: Chapter 13

• The required forms for filing a Chapter 13 bankruptcy are available online at www.uscourts.gov/bankruptcycourts.html. Each judicial district has its own form of Chapter 13 plan. You should use the Chapter 13 plan form that applies in your district.

• You can find more information and FAQs about Chapter 13 bankruptcy at the Nolo website (www.nolo.com). Just click on "Bankruptcy" and follow the links for more information on Chapter 13.

• The U.S. courts site has a section on Chapter 13 in its "Bankruptcy Basics" at www.uscourts.gov/bankruptcycourts/bankruptcybasics/chapter13.html.

Chapter 19–**Chapter 13 or Chapter 7?**

• A word of warning: When seeking legal information on the Internet, only consider information that reflects the changes imposed by the bankruptcy law passed in 2005. If you are seriously contemplating bankruptcy and you want to ensure that you receive accurate, up-to-date information, it may be worth talking to a bankruptcy lawyer.

• Good overall information on bankruptcy can be found on the American Bankruptcy Institute's website, which has particularly useful areas such as the Consumer's Corner, links to lists of lawyers who are certified bankruptcy specialists, and highlights of recent legislative developments; visit www.abiworld .org.

• Filing-Bankruptcy.com features a section on the advantages and disadvantages of both Chapter 7 and Chapter 13. Visit www.filing-bankruptcy-form.com/advantages-disadvantages.html.

• FreeAdvice.com has a section where it lists advantages and disadvantages of Chapter 7 and Chapter 13. Visit www.freeadvice .com, click on "Bankruptcy" and then on "Types of Bankrtupcy."

• The Galler Law Firm in Atlanta, Georgia, has posted a chart on its website showing comparisons between Chapter 7 and Chapter 13. Visit www.galleratkins.com, then click on the link for "Bankruptcy" and then the link for "Chapter 7 v. Chapter 13 bankruptcies."

Chapter 20–**Saving Your Home**

• Legalhelpers.com features a Q & A section on bankruptcy law, including information on using Chapter 13 to save your home, at www.legalhelpers.com/legal_helpers/chapter13.html.

GLOSSARY

account takeover—a type of identity theft that occurs when someone, posing as you, contacts your card issuer, bank, or other financial services company (including insurance companies) to notify it of a change of address.

adjusted-balance method—a method for determining credit card balances. The credit card company will compute your balance for finance charge calculation purposes by subtracting payments made or credits given during the billing period from the total amount you owed as of the start of the billing period.

amortization—the process that occurs as part of a traditional mortgage repayment schedule and involves applying some aspect of each loan payment toward the principal and the rest toward accrued interest. An *amortization schedule* is a table showing how much of each loan payment will be applied toward the principal and how much will go toward the interest over the life of the loan, including the gradual decrease of the principal until it reaches zero.

annual percentage rate (APR)—a measure of certain credit costs over the course of a year in terms of a percentage.

arbitration—dispute settlement conducted outside the courts by a neutral third party—may or may not be binding.

assignee—a person or institution that receives the rights or property of another party.

automatic stay—imposed when bankruptcy proceedings are filed. An automatic stay prevents creditors from attempting to collect from the debtor for debts incurred before the filing.

auto title loans—a type of short-term loan that is structured as a pawn transaction. Such loans often carry a high rate of interest. For one of these loans, a person turns over the title to his or her vehicle as collateral. When the loan is repaid in full, the lender returns the vehicle's title to the consumer. The term of an auto title loan is typically six months or less.

average daily balance–the most common method for determining credit card balances. When using this method, the card issuer determines your average daily balance owed for the monthly billing period and then applies the monthly periodic rate (corresponding to the APR divided by twelve) to that average figure to determine the amount of interest you owe for the monthly billing period.

balloon payment–a large payment at the end of some loans. The final payment is often so large because earlier payments on the loan consist primarily of interest and include only a very small amount to be applied to reduce principal. In other cases, the earlier loan payments might not even cover all accrued interest, so that unpaid accrued interest would be added to the unpaid loan balance.

bankruptcy–refers to statutes and judicial proceedings involving persons or businesses that cannot pay their debts and seek the assistance of the court in getting a fresh start. Under the protection of the bankruptcy court, debtors may *discharge* their debts (no longer be liable for them), in some cases by paying a portion of each debt, and in some cases, where the debtor has no assets, by paying no portion of them.

bankruptcy trustee–the individual who is appointed by the court to administer the estate of the person filing for bankruptcy.

billing error–a term used to describe a problem with a credit bill. Can include an error on a bill that represents a charge for something that you didn't buy, or for a purchase made by someone not authorized to use your account; a billing item that is not properly identified on your monthly statement, or that is for an amount different from the actual purchase price; or a billing item that is for something that you refused to accept on delivery because it was unsatisfactory or the supplier did not deliver according to your agreement.

broker–a party who serves as a bridge or intermediary of sorts between a buyer and a seller. Brokers usually receive a commission for their efforts in facilitating the exchange of property or commodities. There are many different types of brokers, including investment brokers, insurance brokers, and mortgage brokers.

charge account–a credit account whereby the balances owed are usually required to be paid within thirty days.

closed-end credit–see *installment credit*.

closed-end lease–the most common form of consumer lease, usually for automobiles. Under a closed-end lease, you may return the vehicle at the scheduled end of the lease term, pay any scheduled end-of-lease costs, and walk away. As compared to an *open-end lease*.

compensatory damages–damages that compensate people for any actual damages they sustain as a result of a violation. Also called *actual damages*.

consideration–something of value, includes a promise to do (or not do) something, given in return for another's performance or promise to perform. Consideration is one of the requirements of a contract.

consumer-reporting agencies–see *credit bureaus*.

contract–an agreement between two or more parties that will be upheld by the law, made either orally or in writing. To form a contract, the parties must be of the requisite age and mental capacity; there must be consideration; and the subject of the promise cannot be illegal.

credit–an individual's ability and willingness to make payments when they are due; also involves acquiring money for a certain price.

credit accident and health insurance–a type of credit insurance that makes minimum monthly payments on the covered debt for the period of time that you cannot work as a result of accident or illness. Such coverage may not become available until after you have been disabled for a specified number of days.

credit bureaus–organizations that maintain records of your financial-payment histories, public-record information, and personal-identifying data. There are three major competing credit-reporting agencies: Experian, Equifax, and TransUnion Credit Information Company. Also called *credit-reporting agencies* or *consumer-reporting agencies*.

credit counseling–individual or group counseling that outlines the opportunities and options available for people in debt, and assists such people in analyzing their budgets.

credit grantors–see *creditor*.

credit insurance–insurance that some consumers buy to repay their loan if they are or become disabled or involuntarily unemployed. There are various kinds of credit insurance, including *credit life insurance, credit accident and health insurance*, and *credit unemployment insurance*.

credit insurance packing–in this practice, the lender or broker adds in, or packs, credit insurance and other benefits into the terms of the loan, sometimes without fully explaining the benefits to the borrower. The borrower might not realize that adding the cost of insurance and other benefits to the loan amount will increase the fees and payments payable to the lender or broker. Lenders or brokers may also earn a commission when they sell insurance and other benefits to borrowers, further increasing the total fees they may earn in connection with the loan. Can be a predatory lending practice.

credit life insurance–credit insurance that will pay off the balance owed on covered debt in the event of your death.

credit-reporting agencies–see *credit bureaus*.

credit-scoring system–systems used by creditors to determine how likely it is that a consumer will pay his or her debts. Factors used by these systems include: your payment history, the amount of your outstanding debt, the length of your credit history, the number of recent credit applications you have filed, and the number of credit accounts you currently have.

credit unemployment insurance–credit insurance that provides for payments on covered debt during a period in which you were involuntarily unemployed.

creditor–the person/institution who extends a second party credit; also called *credit grantors*.

daily balance method–a way to calculate credit card balances whereby the credit card company takes each daily balance owed during the billing period and applies a daily periodic rate (corresponding to the APR divided by 365) to the daily balance, to come up with the finance charge owed for each day in the billing period. Then, all of these daily finance charges are totaled to come up with the finance charge owed for the billing period.

dealer-assisted lending–a type of automobile lending in which the dealership arranges for the buyer to obtain a loan directly from a finance company, bank, or credit union.

dealer sticker price–during an automobile sale, this is the regular sticker price plus the suggested retail price with the dealer-installed upgrades and options. As compared to the *"Monroney" sticker price*.

debt collector–someone, other than a creditor or its employees, who regularly collects consumer debts on behalf of creditors.

debtors–individuals/institutions who receive credit.

declaratory relief–a court's declaration, or pronouncement, that a certain practice violates the law.

depreciate–decrease in value.

direct lending–a type of automobile financing where the buyer obtains a loan from a finance company, bank, or credit union.

discharge–to release from an obligation; for example, when a bankruptcy is discharged, a person is relieved from the liability to pay debts.

disparate impact discrimination–an illegal form of discrimination that occurs when a practice that seems neutral on its face has a disproportionately negative impact on a certain protected category of people.

disparate treatment discrimination–an illegal form of discrimination that occurs when a creditor intentionally treats someone differently than otherwise similarly situated individuals who are not members of the same protected category (e.g., who are not members of the same race or sex).

disposable income–whatever income is left over from your total income after you have paid for taxes and reasonable and necessary living expenses, as determined on a monthly basis.

Dumpster diving–when identity thieves rummage through trash cans or Dumpsters to locate account numbers and other personal financial information.

electronic check conversion services–services that allow information from your paper check to be used to initiate an electronic fund transfer rather than submitting your paper check for processing and payment (and instead of processing your payment with a debit card).

encumbered assets–assets pledged as collateral on a loan. As compared to *unencumbered assets*.

exempt assets–during a bankruptcy proceeding, assets that may be protected from unsecured creditors.

equity–the current value of your home (assuming *home equity*) minus the amount of any existing mortgages, liens, and attachments on the home.

equity stripping–see *loan stripping*.

Fair Credit Billing Act–This federal law gives consumers an avenue to challenge incorrect information on credit accounts, such as an incorrect charge on a credit card.

finance charge–fees charged by creditors to debtors for the use of money extended on credit. Examples include interest, late fees, and annual fees.

injunctive relief–an injunction, or court order, prohibiting a party from engaging in certain unlawful conduct.

foreclosure–a legal action in which a lender takes ownership of the property used to secure the loan because the owner failed to make the required payments.

fraud alert–a recourse under federal law for individuals who think they have been the victim of identity theft. Fraud alerts are designed to help protect consumers who fear that they have been or are about to become victims of identity theft. They direct users of consumer report information to proceed with caution and to ensure that they are dealing with the right consumer, rather than with an identity thief.

garnishment–a legal proceeding in which a debtor's money, in the possession of another, is applied to the debts of the debtor.

homestead deed–a document that a bankruptcy filer must file in some states. It describes the filer's property and assigns an approximate value to it. Such a filing is intended to protect the filer's property from creditors.

homestead exemption–the amount of your home's value that the law puts out of the reach of your unsecured creditors during a bankruptcy proceeding.

identity theft (ID theft)–when one person take another person's personal information in order to commit fraud or theft.

Identity Theft and Assumption Deterrence Act of 1998–this federal law imposes criminal penalties for those who take another person's personal information and commit fraud.

income tax refund anticipation loans (RALs)–short-term loans intended to be repaid by the proceeds of a pending income tax refund. RALs are often offered through income tax preparation services. The amount owed in connection with a RAL is typically scheduled to be repaid at the time an income tax refund is scheduled to be deposited into the borrower's bank account.

installment credit–a credit account whereby the consumer agrees to repay the amount owed in two or more installments over a definite period of time. Also called *close-end credit*.

interest–the price charged for obtaining money on credit.

invoice price–the manufacturer's charge to the dealer for an automobile.

joint debt–when referring to the debt of a married couple, the debt that is in both spouses' names. As compared to *separate debt*.

judgment proof–when a debtor has so little money, income, and property that he or she would be unable to pay a court judgment entered against him or her.

lien–a creditor's right in a borrower's property. A lien does not convey ownership of the property, but gives the lienholder a right to have his or her debt satisfied out of the proceeds of the property if the debt is not otherwise paid. Can also be called a *security interest*.

liquidating–during bankruptcy, the process where the administrator sells the debtor's available assets.

loan flipping–when a creditor encourages a consumer to refinance a loan several times in a relatively short period of time, each time adding more points and fees to the outstanding unpaid principal. Can be a predatory lending practice.

loan packing–when a creditor adds fees to a new loan for optional loan-related services or products or adds the borrower's old debt into the new loan. Can be a predatory lending practice.

loan stripping–when a creditor bases the terms of a loan on a borrower's equity in his or her home, rather than on the borrower's ability to repay the debt. If the mortgage loan amount and the required periodic loan payments are too high for the borrower, eventually, foreclosure and sale of the property will occur, and money received from the foreclosure sale is rarely enough to cover the debt secured by the owner's property. Any equity the owner had in the mortgaged property is "stripped" through foreclosure and given to the lender for repayment. Can be a predatory lending practice. Also called *equity stripping*.

lessor–the person/institution who leases property to a second party.

means test–a test used to determine whether a consumer is eligible for Chapter 7 bankruptcy or has sufficient means that the case should be a Chapter 13 case.

"Monroney" sticker price–the price that federal law requires be attached to the car window. It includes the base price, manufacturer-installed options and their retail prices, trans-

portation (destination) charges, and the total manufacturer's suggested retail price. As compared to the *dealer sticker price*.

negative amortization—a schedule for loan repayment where no portion of a loan payment is applied toward the principal, and the loan payment is too low to cover all accrued interest, so the unpaid accrued interest is added to the unpaid principal balance of the loan, creating a larger amount owed, with interest being charged on the full amount owed (including the unpaid accrued interest). Negative amortization may in some cases require the borrower to pay close to the entire original principal amount of the loan at the end of the loan term, or even more than the original principal.

negative equity—describes the condition where you owe more on a contract or loan than the property securing the loan (for example, a home in a mortgage loan) is worth.

no-asset filings—bankruptcy filings for which there are no nonexempt assets with value left for unsecured creditors after the exempt assets have been claimed and the secured assets returned to the creditors.

open-end credit—see *revolving credit*.

open-end lease—an automobile lease agreement in which the amount you owe at the end of the scheduled lease term is based on the difference between the residual value of the vehicle (defined as the estimated value of the vehicle at the end of the lease) and its actual value at lease end. As compared to a *closed-end lease*.

oversecured—when a debt is secured by collateral that has a value exceeding the loan balance at the time of bankruptcy. As compared to *undersecured*.

payday loan—a loan granted to a borrower that is designed to cover the borrower's expenses until his or her next paycheck. Sometimes lenders who extend payday loans charge very high penalty fees and interest rates.

payroll card accounts—accounts that allow employers to directly deposit wages on a regularly recurring basis and from which employees may withdraw or transfer (pay out) their wages using their payroll cards.

points–fees paid to the lender and/or broker for the loan at or before loan closing, usually a percentage of the principal amount of the loan. For example, one "point" is 1 percent of the principal amount of the loan. Points are prepaid finance charges and can greatly increase the total cost of credit.

predatory lending–a type of lending that is considered discriminatory, deceptive, fraudulent, or unlawful. It is a term used in a pejorative fashion to describe unscrupulous lenders or lending that is very unfavorable to the borrower.

pre-petition debts–debts incurred before a debtor files for bankruptcy.

previous-balance method–a method for calculating credit card balances by which any payments you make during the billing period are not subtracted from the total amount that you owed at the start of the billing period for finance charge calculation purposes.

priority claims–certain financial responsibilities that take priority during a Chapter 13 bankruptcy, including overdue child support and alimony.

private right of action–the ability of an individual to bring a lawsuit against a person or company or the government.

punitive damages–damages designed to punish the wrongdoer and deter (or discourage) such unlawful conduct in the future; they are intended to penalize creditors for violating the law. Punitive damages are not designed to compensate the plaintiff for actual harm suffered as a result of the violation.

purchase money security interest–interest created when a buyer uses a lender's money to make a purchase and then gives the lender a security interest in the property that was purchased.

reaffirm–when a debtor, if the applicable creditor is willing to allow him or her, promises to pay the creditor (usually, but not always, in full), and the debtor keeps the property involved, so long as he or she keeps the promise to pay. But if the debtor later defaults, the creditor can repossess the property and the remaining balance will not be discharged.

rent-to-own purchases–short-term, renewable rentals of consumer appliances or similar items on a weekly, bi-weekly, or monthly basis.

repossess–to take back property or assets—as in a seizure or foreclosure—to satisfy the obligation to the seller, bank, or finance company after the debtor defaults on his or her payments.

reverse mortgage–a loan that lets you borrow against the equity in your home, without having to repay the loan right away. You can get the money in a lump sum, in monthly cash payments for life, or by drawing on a line of credit (a revolving loan account that a consumer can tap into for loan advances as needed). You can also choose a combination of these options (e.g., monthly payments plus a line of credit for emergencies).

revolving credit–a credit account whereby the consumer may draw on an open-end credit line from time to time, and then pay off the entire outstanding balance, pay only a specified minimum required payment, or pay some amount in between each month. Also called *open-end credit*.

right of redemption–a right under state law for an individual whose property is being repossessed to reclaim the property by paying the entire amount owed, plus additional costs incurred by the holder in repossessing the property.

right of rescission–a right included in some mortgages or other loan agreements that gives the borrower the right to release him or herself from the loan obligations within the first three business days after the mortgage loan closing.

secured credit card–a credit card issued by a bank or other financial institution that is secured by a savings account that you have deposited with that particular institution.

secured debt–is a debt that a creditor is entitled to collect by repossessing and selling certain assets of the debtor if payments are missed.

security interest–see *lien*.

separate debt–when referring to the debt of a married couple, the debt that is in one partner's name only. As compared to a *joint debt*.

subprime lending–the provision of credit to borrowers with past or recent credit problems. Subprime loans are often made at a higher cost or on other less favorable terms than "prime" loans available to borrowers in the "conventional" credit market.

subvented lease–a vehicle lease that is favorable to the consumer due to a special dealer-offered subsidy. These are frequently used when a car dealer really wants to move certain types of cars.

surplus–any extra money a forced sale during a repossession or foreclosure may bring in.

true identity theft–a type of identity theft that occurs when someone, posing as you, opens one or more accounts in your name. The thief often uses your personally identifiable information, such as your Social Security number and other confidential information, to open up new accounts in your name.

undersecured–used to describe a lender who has secured a loan with collateral that is now worth less than the amount of debt it secures. As compared to *oversecured*.

unencumbered assets–those assets on which there is no lien at all and the debtor's equity in assets that are collateral for oversecured claims. As compared to *encumbered assets*.

variable-rate provision–a provision in some credit card agreements that allows the credit card issuer to set an annual percentage rate that varies based on some interest rate index, such as the market rate on three-year U.S. Treasury bills (T-bills) or the prime rate charged by banks on short-term business loans.

yield spread premium–a fee paid by a lender to a mortgage broker if the interest rate on a mortgage loan referred by the broker is higher than a certain minimum interest rate set by the lender. The higher the loan's interest rate, the higher the yield spread premium the lender might pay to the mortgage broker.

INDEX

ABOUT THE AUTHOR

David L. Hudson, Jr. is an attorney and author residing in the Middle Tennessee area. He is a research attorney for the First Amendment Center at Vanderbilt University. He also teaches legal research and writing and constitutional law at Middle Tennessee State University in an adjunct position. He has authored or co-authored 10 books, including several on legal subjects. He writes regularly for the *ABA Journal* and the *ABA Journal E-Report*. He also is a First Amendment contributing editor for the ABA's *Preview of United States Supreme Court Cases*. He earned an A.B. from Duke University and a J.D. from Vanderbilt University Law School.